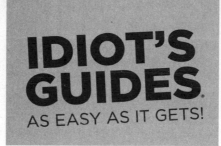

IDIOT'S
GUIDES.
AS EASY AS IT GETS!

Smoking Foods

by Chef Ted Reader

ALPHA

A member of Penguin Random House LLC

Pamela, Layla, and Jordan, you bring me everything I need in life: love, happiness, and buckets of smiles. I thank you for being the best and most important part of my life. You are my everything!

ALPHA BOOKS

Published by the Penguin Random House LLC

Penguin Random House LLC, 375 Hudson Street, New York, New York 10014, USA • Penguin Random House LLC (Canada), 90 Eglinton Avenue East, Suite 700, Toronto, Ontario M4P 2Y3, Canada (a division of Pearson Penguin Canada Inc.) • Penguin Books Ltd., 80 Strand, London WC2R 0RL, England • Penguin Ireland, 25 St. Stephen's Green, Dublin 2, Ireland (a division of Penguin Books Ltd.) • Penguin Random House LLC (Australia), 250 Camberwell Road, Camberwell, Victoria 3124, Australia (a division of Pearson Australia Group Pty. Ltd.) • Penguin Books India Pvt. Ltd., 11 Community Centre, Panchsheel Park, New Delhi—110 017, India • Penguin Random House LLC (NZ), 67 Apollo Drive, Rosedale, North Shore, Auckland 1311, New Zealand (a division of Pearson New Zealand Ltd.) • Penguin Books (South Africa) (Pty.) Ltd., 24 Sturdee Avenue, Rosebank, Johannesburg 2196, South Africa • Penguin Books Ltd., Registered Offices: 80 Strand, London WC2R 0RL, England

Copyright © 2012 by Chef Ted Reader

International Standard Book Number: 978-1-61564-155-0
Library of Congress Catalog Card Number: 2011938638

18   11 10

009-189970-April2012

Interpretation of the printing code: The rightmost number of the first series of numbers is the year of the book's printing; the rightmost number of the second series of numbers is the number of the book's printing. For example, a printing code of 12-1 shows that the first printing occurred in 2012.

Printed in the United States of America

Note: This publication contains the opinions and ideas of its author. It is intended to provide helpful and informative material on the subject matter covered. It is sold with the understanding that the author and publisher are not engaged in rendering professional services in the book. If the reader requires personal assistance or advice, a competent professional should be consulted.

The author and publisher specifically disclaim any responsibility for any liability, loss, or risk, personal or otherwise, which is incurred as a consequence, directly or indirectly, of the use and application of any of the contents of this book.

Most Alpha books are available at special quantity discounts for bulk purchases for sales promotions, premiums, fund-raising, or educational use. Special books, or book excerpts, can also be created to fit specific needs.

For details, write: Special Markets, Alpha Books, 375 Hudson Street, New York, NY 10014.

Publisher: *Marie Butler-Knight*
Associate Publisher: *Mike Sanders*
Executive Managing Editor: *Billy Fields*
Senior Acquisitions Editor: *Brook Farling*
Development Editor: *Lynn Northrup*
Senior Production Editor: *Kayla Dugger*

Copy Editor: *Monica Stone*
Cover Designer: *Rebecca Batchelor*
Book Designers: *William Thomas, Rebecca Batchelor*
Indexer: *Brad Herriman*
Layout: *Ayanna Lacey*
Proofreader: *John Etchison*

Contents

Part 1:   Where There's Fire, There's Smoke 1

1   For the Love of Smoked Foods 3
A Brief History of Smoking.................................. 4
The Current Smoking Craze............................... 8
Smoking vs. Grilling.. 9
The Different Types of Smoking........................ 10
    Cold Smoking Foods.................................... 10
    Hot Smoking Foods 11

2   Smokers and How They Work 13
Smokers for the Novice................................... 14
    Gas Grill... 14
    Charcoal Kettles 15
    Electric Smokers 16
Smokers Best Suited for Adventurous Amateurs 19
    Vertical Box Smokers................................. 19
    Water Smokers 21
    Offset Barrel Smokers 23
    Kamado-Style Smokers............................. 25
Smokers Best Suited for Experienced Smokers........... 28
    Homemade Smokers 28
    The Big Rigs.. 33
    Industrial Smokers 34

3   Fuel + Wood = Smoky Deliciousness 35
Propane and Natural Gases................................ 36
Electricity 37
Charcoal... 39
    Types of Charcoal 39
    Hardwood Charcoal Flavoring Guide................ 40
    Ted's Homemade Charcoal Blends 42
    General Tips for Buying and Working with Charcoal.......... 42
Hardwoods.. 43
    Hardwood vs. Softwood 43
    Sawdust, Chips, Chunks, Pellets, Pucks, and Logs...................... 43
    To Soak or Not to Soak?............................. 45

Bark vs. No Bark..*46*

A Wood Flavoring Guide..*46*

Trade-Secret Smoke Flavor Boosters........................*48*

Plank Smoking: All the Flavor in Less Time............48

Woods for Plank Smoking...*49*

When It Comes to Planks, Size Matters.....................*51*

Where to Find and Buy Planks....................................*51*

4   Smoking 101 ....**53**

All You Need to Know About Charcoal Smoking.....................54

Smoking on Gas and Propane Grills.............................56

Plank Smoking...58

How to Smoke Safely Indoors...60

Stove and Oven Roasting Pan–Style Smokers..............*61*

Stove-Top Kettle Smokers...*62*

Smoking Bags...*63*

Turning Your Oven into a Smoker..............................*63*

5   Buying a Smoker and Accessories **65**

How Much Do You Want to Spend? 65

Conservative Budget ($500 or Less).............................*66*

Midrange Budget ($500 to $1,500) *66*

Spending Some Bucks ($1,500 to $5,000)....................*66*

Big-Daddy Range ($5,000 and Up).............................*67*

Talk to Anyone Who Will Listen....................................67

Helpful Smoking Accessories and Tools......................68

Fire Starters..*68*

Thermometers *70*

Toolkit for the Frequent Smoker *72*

Gadgets for the More Advanced Smoker....................75

6   Ted's 10 Commandments for Smoking Foods.....**79**

Commandment #1: Be Prepared 79

Prepare the Food..*80*

Prepare the Fire...*81*

Prepare the Smoker *81*

Commandment #2: Be Patient.......................................81

Commandment #3: Don't Peek! 83

Commandment #4: Keep 'Er Steady 83

Commandment #5: Keep It Moist..................................85

Commandment #6: Keep It Safe and Clean 86

    Smoker Safety... 86

    Practicing Proper Food Safety 87

Commandment #7: Practice, Practice, Practice........................ 91

Commandment #8: Take Notes 92

Commandment #9: Make It Tasty 94

Commandment #10: Have Fun! 94

Part 2:   Layering the Flavor **97**

7   Brines, Marinades, and Cures **99**

Brines 100

Marinades 101

Cures 102

    Basic Brine *104*

    Apple-Honey Pig and Bird Brine *105*

    Juicy Citrus Brine *106*

    Maple Whiskey Brine *107*

    Dark Ale Marinade *108*

    Cubano Mojo Marinade *109*

    Dragon Marinade *110*

    Smoked Garlic Marinade... *111*

    Honey Riesling Wine Marinade................................. *112*

    Whiskey and Cola Marinade *113*

    Basic Cure *114*

    Fish Cure *115*

    Aromatic Cure... *116*

8   Rubs, Pastes, and Injections **117**

Rubs... 117

Pastes... 119

Injections.. 121

    Ted's World-Famous Bone Dust BBQ Seasoning Rub *121*

    Crazy Cajun Rub... *122*

    Garlic-Herb Fresh Rub *123*

    Jamaican Jerk Rub *124*

    Memphis Rib Rub *125*

    Tandoori Rub... *126*

    Mediterranean Spice Rub *127*

    Cinnamon Chipotle Rub... *128*

Smoked Sea Salt 129

Hot 'n' Spicy BBQ Paste 130

Margarita Paste 131

Java-Java Paste 132

Chive Butter Injection 133

Rum Runner's Maple Injection 134

9   Basting, Saucing, and Spritzing **135**

Basting with Caution 135

BBQ Sauces from Around the World 136

A Spritz Can Make All the Difference 137

Kansas City BBQ Sauce 138

Bourbon-Wasabi BBQ Sauce 139

Four-Ingredient Cherry Cola BBQ Sauce 140

Apple Butter BBQ Glaze 141

Memphis-Style BBQ Sauce 142

Carolina Sweet Mustard Sauce 143

Lemon-Ginger Wine Spritz 144

Cherry-Pom Spritz 144

Honey-Herb Spritz 145

Part 3:   Meat, Meat, and More Meat ... and Fish **147**

10   Blazing Beef **149**

Breaking Down the Different Cuts of Beef 150

Forequarter 151

Hindquarter 151

Beef Buying Basics with Your Buddy Ted 152

Shredded Beef Sandwiches with Chimichurri Mayonnaise 153

Korean Bulgogi Smoked Top Sirloin Roast 155

*Four-Pepper–Crusted Beef Tenderloin with Armagnac
    Butter Injection* 156

*Coffee-Porter N.Y. Strip Steaks with Blue Cheese–Pecan
    Butter* 157

*Prime Rib with Whiskey Mist and Hot Horseradish
    Mustard* 159

Cherry Whiskey–Smoked Eye-of-Round 160

*Smoked Beef Ribs with Chocolate Stout and Horseradish
    Baste* 161

*Smoked Prime Rib Demi-Glace Burgers with
Smoked Garlic and Onions*.. *163*

Santa Maria Tri-Tip with Cabernet Wine Mop.....................*165*

Texas Cowboy Beef Jerky.. *166*

11   Glorious Pork **169**

Assorted Pork Cuts... 169

All You Need to Know About Sausage 171

Let's Talk Bacon.. 173

Rockin' Ribs..174

*Pork T-Bones with Smoked Strawberry and Rhubarb
Compote* *177*

*Fire Ball Spritzed–Extra-Meaty Back Ribs with
Smoked Honey Glaze* *178*

Smoked BBQ Ribs with Redneck White Sauce......................... *180*

Maple Smoked Bacon *182*

Smoked Peameal with Bloody Mary Injection........................... *184*

Smoked Ozark Sirloin *185*

Smoked Spam *186*

Smoked Polish Sausage.. *187*

12   Delicious Lamb and Wild Game **189**

Domestic vs. Imported Lamb..................................... 190

Assorted Lamb Cuts.. 190

Lamb and Wild Game Basics..................................... 192

Smoky Rack o' Lamb with Goat Cheese................................. *194*

Owensboro Smoked Lamb Shoulder *195*

Smoked Lamb Ribs with Garlic-Ginger-Lemon Soy Baste....... *197*

Smoked Veal Chops with Blackberry Butter *198*

Smoked Bison Short Ribs with Black Currant–BBQ Sauce *200*

Venison Ribs with Cranberry-Orange Honey Glaze................. *201*

13   Smokin' Chicken and Other Poultry...................**203**

Chicken and Poultry Basics....................................... 203

Air-Chilled vs. Water-Chilled Birds........................... 205

Assorted Poultry Cuts... 206

Pork, Cheddar, and Apple–Stuffed Bacon-Wrapped Chicken.... *208*

*Georgia Peach–Dunked Smoked Chicken Thighs with
Potato Chip Crust* *210*

Smoky Chicken-Cheese Dogs.................................... *211*

Cinnamon Sugar–Smoked Chicken Halves............................. *213*

Smoked Buffalo Wings with Blue Cheese and Celery................ 214

Cozy Corner Smoked Cornish Game Hens........................... 215

Dry-Cured Smoked Turkey Breast.................................... 217

Cajun-Rubbed and Honey-Dipped Smoked Turkey
    Drumsticks 218

Maple-Cured Smoked Duck Breasts.................................. 219

Beer-Brine Smoked Pulled Duck...................................... 221

14   **Succulent Fish and Shellfish** **223**

Fish and Seafood Basics 223

Cold- and Hot-Smoked Fish... 225

The Right Fish for the Right Recipe 226

Irish Whiskey–Smoked Salmon 226

Plank Hot-Smoked Salmon... 227

Smoked Soy-Sesame Salmon 229

Smoked Mackerel with Maple and Dark Rum 230

Honey-Hoisin Smoked Oysters 231

Smoked Razor Clams.. 233

Smoked Halibut with Hot Curry Rub and Lime Butter........... 234

Whiskey Butter–Injected Smoked Scallops with Halibut
    and Crab Topping... 235

15   **The Big 5** **237**

What to Know Before Entering a BBQ Competition 237

Brisket 239

Pulled Pork 240

Ribs.. 240

Chicken and Turkey 241

Whole Hog 242

Big Beefy Texas-Style Smoked Brisket 243

Smoked BBQ Pulled Pork with Apple Jack Spritz.................. 245

Smoked St. Louis Ribs with BBQ Icing 246

Smoked Chicken with Buttery Love Injection 248

Thanksgiving Smoked Turkey... 249

Part 4:   Starters, Sides, and Sweets **251**

16   **Sides and Accompaniments** **253**

Smoked Eggplant Dip... 254

Smoked Vidalia Onion Relish 256

Smoked Beet and Pear–Blue Cheese Salad with Walnuts 257

Smoked Corn and Smoked Cream Corn....................................259

Planked Mashed Potatoes 261

Warm Potato Salad with Bacon, Green Apple, and Molten Brie...262

Smoked Risotto with Spinach, Prosciutto, and Smoked Mozzarella...264

Smoky Baked Macaroni and Cheese 265

17   Weird and Wonderful **267**

Pulled Pork and Cheese ABTs 268

Plank-Smoked Camembert...270

Smoked Bacon–Wrapped Meatballs..271

Smoked Frittata with Grape Tomatoes and Cheese..................273

Smoked Fois Gras Terrine 274

Smoked Honey 275

Smoked Ice Martini 276

Smoked Chocolate-Banana Ice Cream 278

PB&J Plank-Smoked Twinkies with Chocolate-Marshmallow Topping...279

Appendixes

A   Glossary **281**

B   Resources **289**

Index **293**

Introduction

As far as historians can tell, the art of smoking foods dates back to a period just shortly after the discovery of fire. No one can say how or when prehistoric man realized that if he smoked his meat it would last longer than the fresh stuff, but as they say: necessity is the mother of invention. I guess getting through a long, cold winter huddled in a cave required a certain amount of ingenuity.

Regardless of the when, where, or how smoked foods came to be, I live for this thrill ride of deliciousness. I am a barbecue guy—always have been. I have been obsessed with food, fire, and smoke almost my whole life. I have grilled and smoked my way through a crazy variety of foods, from chocolate to cheese to whole prime ribs. Almost nothing has gotten past my gaze—not even the Twinkie! What can I say?! As my passion developed, my curiosity grew.

My career as a chef has taken me around the world: I've been to Germany and am in awe of the incredible array of sausages there; to Italy to enjoy Speck Alto Adige, which is smoked prosciutto from the South Tyrol region. I've eaten smoked eel sushi in the Ginza district of Tokyo, and enjoyed smoked ocean king prawns in Sydney. I remember a trip to Riga, Latvia (my mother's homeland), and walking through its ancient market: I was just amazed at the variety of smoked foods—everything from pork and beef to chicken, turkey, and game birds. Then there were the smoked fish options, which seemed endless, so I ended up having a sampling feast in the park. I was so excited to be in my mother's homeland for the first time, seeing (and tasting) the stories I grew up on. What has struck me through my adventures is that the tradition of smoking foods exists, on some level, in every culture's cuisine. In India, they have the tandoor oven. In Alaska, native populations still drape long, thin strips of caribou meat, often accented with wild herbs and berries, on wooden racks over a smoky fire.

Some of my greatest relationships, apart from the one I have with my beloved wife, are with butchers. I grew up in a small town outside Toronto and going to the butcher shop as a kid was definitely a highlight of my youth. Staring through the glass at all the glistening cuts of meat and listening to my mother or father discuss the relative merits of a rib eye steak versus a strip loin steak was like music to me. My dad was definitely a barbecue guy; I guess that's where I got it from. He even built his own first grill. When my dad started stoking up the grill I was right there watching and getting the lowdown from him. Some of these conversations were great bonding moments for us. When it became obvious that the culinary world was where I was going, I don't think he was surprised.

Later, when I attended culinary school at George Brown College, I found myself in the heart of one of the oldest open-air markets in North America. It was at Kensington Market that my fellow students and I were free to roam through the spice shops, cheese shops, and, especially, butcher shops. There was even an old kosher shop where you could still choose a live bird and wait for it to be killed, blessed, and dressed to take home the freshest product possible. Then there were Spanish shops with serrano hams, sausages, and smoked meats hanging from the ceiling. The Ukrainian and Polish shops were filled with kielbasas, sausages, hams, hocks, chickens, and all sorts of oily fish. All these shops had one thing in common. They all had—and still have today—an old smoker out back pumping out rich, oily smoke.

Those butcher shops sent out subtle wisps of smoke into the air that got stronger as you approached the market; it's almost like an aromatic invitation. That smell of smoke has a familiarity, regardless of the seasonings that are particular to a country or region. I think it wakes up my inner caveman. Smoked food is a part of the history of mankind. It was our first method of food preservation; it even predates salt. I suspect it's actually a part of our genetic makeup.

What's more, I'm a meat guy. I just am. Which is why, as my culinary career progressed, I found myself drawn to the grill and then to the smoker. It started when I reached the lofty position of corporate chef for one of the largest grocery chains in Canada. I was sent all over the place to research suppliers and learn about various cooking and culinary events in numerous locations. While on the job, I ate brisket that was to die for at 4Rivers Smokehouse in Orlando—it was so moist your napkins needed napkins. I researched the most incredible smoked duck at R.U.B. BBQ, Paul Kirk's barbecue joint in New York City. I studied many a sausage in Texas. But the most satisfying work was analyzing the St. Louis ribs at Dinosaur Bar-B-Q founded by John Stage.

It was because of all these business trips that I began to look into this phenomenon further. It's been over 15 years and there's no stopping now. I'm known as the barbecue guy far and wide, but the smoking aspect of barbecue is my real passion. There is absolutely nothing I won't put in the smoker.

That's my story. It is my hope that this book will be the beginning of your own smoking story. It doesn't have to turn you into a pro or a fanatic, but it might. To me, smoking foods is about spending time in the great outdoors and preparing some outrageously delicious food. The thing I most want you to get from this book is that smoking foods *is not hard!* I'll take you through every step of smoking by offering you the basic principles. I'm not gonna lie: there will be times when you'll have to figure a few things out for yourself. Every smoker is different and every situation is different, so I can only predict and troubleshoot so much for you. But I believe this book will give you the tools to be prepared for most smoking obstacles that may come your way.

The biggest key to smoking foods with success is patience. If you don't think you're someone who can patiently tend to a fire and wait up to 3 days for the perfect meal, then this book may not be for you. All I can say is, give it a shot; I hope you'll not only like it, but genuinely fall in love with it. I know I did!

How This Book Is Organized

I've divided this book into four parts to make it easy to follow. Feel free to read the book cover to cover, or go directly to a part (or a recipe) that interests you.

Part 1, Where There's Fire, There's Smoke, separates facts from misconceptions when it comes to smoking foods. You learn that it really isn't difficult—and it doesn't take a lot of money or equipment—to get started on your smoking adventure. In these chapters you get all the details on choosing the right fuel, buying a smoker and accessories, and more. I finish with my 10 commandments to help make the experience successful—and fun!

Part 2, Layering the Flavor, shows you just how to use brines, marinades, rubs, cures, and more to make your meat more flavorful, tender, and moist. I share my favorite recipes for basic marinades, cures, rubs, spritzes, and more.

Part 3, Meat, Meat, and More Meat … and Fish, gives you information on different cuts of beef, pork, chicken, and other meats, as well as a rundown on fish and shellfish, so you know what to ask for when you head to your butcher or grocery store. The recipes in these chapters are some of my favorites—they're sure to make your mouth water!

Part 4, Starters, Sides, and Sweets, fills you in on some of the more unusual things you can smoke, such as side dishes, desserts, and even a cocktail. Expand your smoking repertoire and have fun trying these more unconventional recipes. You can truly smoke just about anything, as you see in these chapters!

I also include two helpful appendixes in this book that are geared toward the novice smoker: a glossary of terms I use throughout the book, and a list of recommended books and websites for those who wish to continue their smoking adventure.

Extras

As you read through the book, you will notice bonus sidebars that contain definitions, Ted's tips, safe smoking, and miscellaneous tasty tidbits of information to help in your understanding of the art of smoking food.

DEFINITION

Read these sidebars for definitions of important terms that will help you better understand the world of smoking foods.

TED'S TIP

Look here for information on how to accomplish a task more efficiently and to help you make your smoked foods taste better.

SAFE SMOKING

These sidebars contain cautions you should keep in mind when it comes to smoking food. These will help you avoid making mistakes that could ruin your food.

TASTY TIDBIT

These sidebars are full of practical nutritional information that might just surprise you. There are interesting tasty treats that I thought you would enjoy reading.

Acknowledgments

Pamela, you are my heart and soul, and the foundation of our beautiful family. You are the very best—I love you!

Layla and Jordan, my wickedly delicious little eaters, your smiles bring me sunshine and inspiration every day.

Greg Cosway and Les Murray, my partners in Ted's World Famous BBQ and Chef Events: you have worked very hard to rebuild Ted Reader and my world of barbecue—T2, as you like to say. I am proud to be in business with you and I love your focus and passion for my barbecue world. Thanks for taking care of business and allowing me to do what I do best. Cook! Cheers with many beers, my friends! (tedreader.com)

My angels, Marian, Caiti, and the entire Chef Events Canada team; you lovely ladies truly make my life delicious. Thank you for your dedication and passion that keep this barbecue train on the rails. You girls are the best! (www.chefevents.ca)

Sabrina Falone and Amy Snider-Whitson at The Test Kitchen—WOW! Thank you for all your hard work; this book would not have happened without your expertise and dedication. Thank you for the continued "pushes" to keep me on track. Gotta love The Test Kitchen! Thank you so much. (theTK.ca)

Chef Scott Bowser, you have been a true blessing. You fired up my many smokers, tended the fires, and made the smoke that powered the delicious foods we created. Losing you to the CIA (Culinary Institute of America) is bittersweet. I wish you good luck, Scotty, but I'm sad to see you go and I hope we will work together again. You kept my barbecue world running smoothly for two years and have definitely left your mark on Casa BBQ. Thank you, thank you, thank you!

My dearest friend, Wendy Baskerville, thank you for coming to my rescue to help me with this book. We have shared many great times together. You are a part of our family and my children love their Aunty Wendy. Your knowledge and talent with food is truly passionate. Thank you. I love ya!

Thank you to the entire team at Alpha Books for the opportunity to write *The Complete Idiot's Guide to Smoking Foods*. I look forward to future projects together.

Stephen Murdoch, what can I say? You are one amazing publicist. You're a movable feast in the promotional world. Thanks for all your support and for getting me some truly amazing press.

Thank you to Duff Dixon and Ontario Gas BBQ for all your support over the years. You are the world's biggest barbecue store and you definitely make things sizzle. (bbqs.com)

Ralph James, my wickedly amazing agent: you bring the sizzle to my rockin' barbecue world. Thanks for all your support and encouragement. May our fires continue to burn hot! (theagencygroup.com)

Brown-Forman, there can never be enough Jack! Thanks for your continued support. Jack lives here! (brown-forman.com)

Thanks to Chris Brown and the team at Yorkshire Valley Farms for all the delicious organic chicken. Truly spectacular. (yorkshirevalley.com)

Thank you to the world of barbecue, including all the barbecue chefs, fanatics, grill masters, and smoke masters. Thank you all for your continued support. Your passion for the world of smoke and barbecue fuels my fire. You are my inspiration. Keep it sticky and always make it delicious!

I would also like to thank the following companies for their kind help in providing me with smokers for the testing of this book. Thank you so much for your support.

> The Big Green Egg
> Onward Manufacturing's Big Steel Keg
> Bradley Smoker Inc.
> The Brinkmann Corporation
> Napoleon Gourmet Grills
> Primo Grills and Smokers
> ProQ cold smoke generator
> BBQ Innovations' Rib-O-Lator
> Whitetail BBQ Smokers, distributor of Horizon Smokers

Special Thanks to the Technical Reviewer

The recipes in *The Complete Idiot's Guide to Smoking Foods* were reviewed by an expert who double-checked their accuracy. Special thanks are extended to Rhonda Lerner.

Rhonda Lerner has spent over 12 years in the culinary field, first as a business owner of a gourmet coffeehouse and later as a culinary instructor. She holds a Culinary Certificate from the French Culinary Institute in New York City. Rhonda currently works full time as a freelance culinary consultant.

Trademarks

Where There's Fire, There's Smoke

Many people out there are under the impression that smoking is a lot harder than it actually is. And to the untrained eye, smoking food can seem daunting. There's all the equipment needed, the length of time it takes, and the countless fuel and wood combinations. But don't let the unknown deter you from taking up this great activity. (I didn't, but now I suffer from a serious illness—one that occasionally drives my wife a little crazy. It's called OCBD, or Obsessive Compulsive Barbecue Disorder.)

The fact is you don't need to buy a lot of equipment to smoke a great meal. I'll cover all the details on choosing the right fuel, buying a smoker and accessories, and more in these chapters so you know what you're in for when you finally decide to start smoking.

For the Love of Smoked Foods

In This Chapter

- A brief history of smoking
- The current smoking craze
- Smoking versus grilling
- The different types of smoking

Through the centuries our eating habits have gone through an amazing evolution as we've adapted to our surroundings and the ingredients and tools available to us. Different cultures have picked up their own unique culinary traditions. For example, at some point in history, some of us figured out how to use a fork while others invented chopsticks, and still others created a whole class of etiquette around eating with our hands. Depending on where in the world you live, you may eat yak, zebra, camel, or buffalo. To round out our meals, we learned to cultivate grains such as rice—which is a cornerstone of many cuisines today. And, fortunately, we also learned that the roots under those pretty potato flowers are delicious when boiled and mashed with butter and roasted garlic.

As much as we've adapted our culinary repertoires around the world and over the centuries, one thing remains true: everybody smokes food. There are examples everywhere: from smoked-tea eggs in northern China to glorious *churrasco*-style meats in Spain and Portugal; from cured and smoked meats in Eastern Europe and Italy to the quintessential oily smoked whitefish of Lake Baikal in Russia. And let's not forget that peat is burned to dry and smoke the barley malt used to make whiskey in Scotland.

Then there's the relatively new approach to smoking food, the world of American barbecue! This particular art of smoking really gets me excited. Firing up the smoker awakens my inner caveman; I am almost hypnotized by the fire. Give me a cool fall day, a few beers, and a big hunk of meat or maybe some nice slabs of ribs, and I am in the zone.

A Brief History of Smoking

Smoked food has been around nearly as long as man has been cooking over fire. *Smoking* was the first way to preserve meat. Archaeologists have discovered that Neanderthal man may have smoked strips of meat to make primitive jerky that was carried on long hunts and stored to feed them over cold and snowy winters. They didn't have salt yet and I don't suppose they knew about marinating, brining, and inventive seasoning rubs, but there is evidence that they may have used certain herbs and woods to make things taste better. Man has always had a yearning to play with his food and I'm quite sure, even back then, that there were good cooks and not-so-good cooks. I'll bet there was plenty of bragging going on around that big fire, just like today.

DEFINITION

Smoking is the process of flavoring, cooking, or preserving food by exposing it to smoke from burning or smoldering plant materials—most commonly wood.

Hot burning lump charcoal.

It was cavemen who first started cutting fish into nice, thin strips to hang over the fire. This early smoking process would draw all the moisture out of the flesh and stop bacterial growth. Our ancestors weren't concerned about bacteria; they just knew if they hung fish over a fire for a certain amount of time they would have food to sustain them over long distances. Smoking foods, no doubt much like the discovery of fire itself, guaranteed the survival of man.

TASTY TIDBIT

According to *Archaeology* magazine (September/October 2009), the world's oldest barbecue was found in 2009. Archaeological excavations, at a 31,000-year-old site in the Czech Republic, discovered a cooking pit with the remains of two mammoths along with other animal remains.

In the Middle Ages, all manner of foods were heavily smoked and salted to get people through the winter, until early spring when new crops came in and the hunt began again. One notable example, heavily salted red herring were smoked for up to 3 weeks in a kiln. Those herring never went bad. I'm not kidding. Smoked red herring has been found in archaeological digs in modern times and, when tested, still didn't show any bacterial activity. (Something tells me even though they may technically be safe to eat, they're probably not very tasty.) These smoked fish were perhaps one of the first exported food products as they were sent all over the world on trade and exploration ships.

Without refrigeration, meat and fish had to be cooked and eaten quickly after slaughter, or go through a spicing process or smoking period to preserve the meat. The spicing process used large amounts of salt to fully dehydrate the meat. The lack of water slows the growth of microorganisms and bacteria that cause food to spoil. Smoking was a popular preserving method during this time because it offered the same effect as salting but didn't require such huge amounts of salt. This meant that the meat didn't require soaking, to remove the extra salt, before it could be eaten. Another common technique to preserve meat was cold smoking, where the meat was dried by exposure to the sun and then preserved by the addition of smoke. (I discuss cold smoking later in this chapter.)

Smoking foods for preservation was not exclusive to meats and fish because fruits, especially berries, were often smoked as well. Cheeses were also smoked using the cold-smoking method. The original purpose was for preservation, but along the way people began to acquire a taste for the dusky flavor of smoked foods. Appearing on tables in castles everywhere, smoked foods were a mandatory part of a good old-fashioned banquet. Smoked hams and sausages became standard fare in every larder and maintained their popularity until the arrival of refrigeration.

When the first Spanish explorers arrived in the Caribbean, the native people preserved meats in the sun. To drive away bugs they built small, smoky fires and then placed the meat on wooden racks built over the fires. The smoke kept away the insects and though they weren't sure why it helped, it preserved the meat. The Spaniards and the natives called, and still call, this process *barbacoa*. Some believe this is the genesis of the word *barbecue*, but there is much debate on that topic.

As Europeans and Africans started to populate the southern United States, this style of smoking continued to evolve. The Europeans brought pigs and cattle, which became the primary meats consumed in the New World. Pork was the meat of choice in the South, mainly because pigs can thrive with little care. The racks they used to dry the meat were replaced with pits, and later smokehouses, as time went on. It's not certain how pits became a fixture throughout the Caribbean, although it is known that pit smoking was a technique used for hundreds of years by Polynesians. Another way pit smoking could have come to the Caribbean was with African slaves, whom the British began importing in the 1700s.

TASTY TIDBIT

The modern word *barbecue* could be derived from French-speaking pirates who referred to Caribbean roasted pork as "*de barbe à queue,*" which means "from beard to tail" or "snout to tail." The hog was the most versatile animal and could be eaten from the tip of the snout through the end of the tail.

The early American slave population brought with them many delicious cooking traditions. Slaves were typically left with all the worst cuts of the animals. Given the poor quality of the food, the low and slow gentle smoking of the pit was the only thing the slaves could do to make the toughest cuts on the animal not only edible, but enjoyable. Their method transformed "waste cuts," such as brisket, ribs, pork belly, and so on, into yearned-for delicacies. Sauces were created that further enhanced these meats, and women would fill bean pots and slowly bake them in the pit to pick up subtle smoky notes. These delicious smoked foods began to make a jump into the main house sometime in the late 1800s, as far as we can tell.

After the Civil War, many former slaves found that one of the quickest ways to begin making a living was to offer their delicious smoked food for sale. Soon, every small town had some sort of pit-style roadhouse. Legends grew around the various communities, and different regions began to be known for particular dishes or styles. Everyone knew that for beef you wanted to go to Texas, Kentucky became famous for lamb, and the Carolinas were the home of awesome succulent pork.

Barbecue sign in rural Tennessee.

In the late 1800s, the world began to industrialize an infrastructure for the rapid delivery of perishable foods like seafood and produce. The need for heavily preserved foods began to wane, but people still longed for the smoky flavors they were accustomed to. It's at this time that we begin to see the growth of smoking on a different plane; lightly smoking foods for added flavor, without the heavy salting of the past. The modern foods that we know so well, like smoked salmon and sliced bacon, were born.

For many years, the pit traditions were a local fixture in small towns of the southern United States, but with the upwardly mobile 1950s and 1960s, leisure time made barbecue a new phenomenon. Barbecue grills became a must-have for every backyard in America. We were simply fascinated with the whole grilling concept. As the profile for this hobby grew, diehards wanted to experience the true, smoke-filled tradition of barbecue and re-create it in their backyards. Small obscure companies became larger as they re-created equipment they had been supplying to the foodservice market for backyard application. As fun as it was to have a shiny barbecue grill, it became even cooler to have your own smoker.

Man has a relentless way of investigating a subject until it is completely exhausted, but smoking foods continues to open up new vistas. The number of ingredient combinations—not to mention wood mixes, flavoring agents, techniques, and more—is limitless. Every weekend somewhere in North America, someone with a great imagination is trying out some crazy combination of meat, flavoring, and wood under the dome of a smoker, maybe not even realizing how old an art it actually is.

The Current Smoking Craze

The current smoking craze owes a fair bit to the rising celebrity of chefs in general and to the world of competitive barbecue specifically. Television has been a major force in inspiring new interest in smoking foods. Programs like *Pit Masters* on TLC and documentaries on events such as the Memphis in May World Championship Barbecue Cooking Contest and Jack Daniel's World Championship Invitational Barbecue in Lynchburg, Tennessee, have made our mouths water and created a new generation of smokers.

Takin' a bite of a smoked-barbecue pulled-pork sandwich.

The number and diversity of attendees at some of the contests and shows I've done has grown by leaps and bounds in the last 10 to 15 years. For those who just want to eat, authors like Jane and Michael Stern have created travel guides that feature great pits as must-see destinations. Some travel agents will help you plan a trip around the legendary establishments you want to visit.

TASTY TIDBIT

Over 15 million grills and smokers are sold in the United States every year—now that's a craze!

Having visited the Dinosaur Bar-B-Que roadhouse in Syracuse, New York, one cannot deny that smoking has infiltrated every aspect of North American culture. There you may find yourself sitting beside a biker or a CEO. I think a good old-fashioned pit-smoked barbecue could hold the key to world peace!

Smoking vs. Grilling

Simply put, *grilling* is the act of cooking meat (or other foods) by setting it on a grate over a gas flame or hot coals. Tender cuts of meat, as well as seafood and vegetables, are best suited for this cooking method. Grilling is sometimes done covered, but it's always done at relatively high heats; anywhere from 350°F up to 800°F (in the case of some kamado-style grills or barbecues with infrared pads).

Smoking is generally done over charcoal or wood and, although it's not as common, gas can be used, too. It may or may not involve fully cooking the food because its main purpose is to infuse smoke flavor into the item being smoked. Smoking always happens in a closed, that is to say lid-down or doored, atmosphere. The phrase "low and slow" was coined to describe the relatively low temperatures used for smoking and the lengthy amount of time it takes to infuse and cook the food. The temperature for smoking typically sits between 180°F and 225°F.

I am not gonna be that guy who tells you that grilling is better than smoking, or that smoking is better than grilling. I will tell you that they both have a place in your cooking repertoire. I say, if you can afford it and have the space, get yourself a smoker and a grill. If you can only have one, look for the best unit available that will do both. Smoking and grilling can accomplish essentially the same thing, namely good and tasty food.

A grill provides you with a quick and convenient way to cook outdoors and it doesn't make a huge mess. It sits out there and all you have to do, in most cases, is trot out, turn on the gas, scrape the grate, and start cooking. Within 30 to 45 minutes you're eating something tasty. Even if you have a charcoal grill, you'll likely be eating in an hour or so. A smoker can't really be called convenient. With a smoker you have to plan ahead. Mind you, I don't necessarily feel that way in my own life. Then again, not everybody has six to nine grills and a half-dozen smokers set up in their backyard at any given time—it is my job!

There have been studies done on differences in taste reactions of food cooked on various grills. Studies show that, unless you have an amazing palate, you won't be able to tell the difference between burgers cooked over gas, charcoal, or electric grills. Even grilling over charcoal doesn't add a whole lot of smoke flavor. (Of course you do get some, and we all know how good a charbroiled steak can be.) However, when you take it up a notch and go to the smoker, you are literally forcing smoke into the food. The whole point of the process is to input that flavor.

Preparing a meal on a smoker requires some planning. Even if all you want to do is smoke a steak, you need to be sure you can afford a couple of hours to wait for your dinner. The average guy may not try smoking a steak because, let's face it, men love immediate gratification—but you're missing out on a really good thing if you don't try it. Low and slow can challenge those who are used to fast results on a grill but the end results will be worth the effort.

If you can learn the patience required to control the temperature, you'll find yourself eating undeniably great food. If one of your goals is to find that delicious smoky note in your meat, then the smoker is the way to go. All you need is a good chunk of time, some patience, a lot of beer (if you're like me!), and a large appetite!

The Different Types of Smoking

While there are countless types of smokers on the market with seemingly endless accessories and gadgets to accompany them, there are really only two ways to smoke food. Both ways add that sweet flavor we all yearn for, but each has a different purpose: one cooks the food with heat from fire and the other cures the food.

Curing can refer to various types of food preservation and flavoring processes. It may include the addition of a combination of salt, nitrates, nitrites, or sugar. Some curing processes also involve smoking because the added flavor is desirable. Either way, the purpose of curing is to prolong food's stability by drawing out as much moisture as possible so bacteria can't breed and spoil the food.

Cold Smoking Foods

Cold smoking is the process of applying smoke flavor to foods without necessarily cooking them. Cold smoking generally occurs at temperatures in the range of 80°F to 100°F, and certainly no higher than 120°F. At times it can be as low as 40°F (although getting your smoker into the 40s can be tricky and is not recommended for the average home smoker; leave that to the pros).

Examples of cold-smoked foods include bacon, sausage, country ham, fish, and cheese. The best-known cold-smoked food in the world is probably a toss-up between bacon and smoked salmon. Some food—like smoked salmon—can be eaten straight out of the cold smoker, but most—like bacon or sausage—will require further cooking at a higher temperature.

Cold smoking is a curing process more than it is a cooking process. Some cold-smoked foods can be exposed to the smoker for as long as a week, which is the case for some sausages and hams. Properly prepared cold-smoked foods never reach a temperature above 80°F to 100°F. In the case of fish, it would be unusual to go over 80°F.

TASTY TIDBIT

I've heard (but have yet to try it myself) that you can build a cold smoker out of a pile of snow or blocks of ice, which seems like a great way to keep the smoke cold. Why not? I think it's time I made one!

Technically, cold-smoked fish is raw but cured, so it's safe to eat. It's similar to the principals of *ceviche*, where the proteins in the fish are "cooked" by acid (usually from citrus juices). Smoked salmon gets a long soak in saturated salt brine, causing its proteins to denature (which means it modifies the structure of the flesh). In a real and safe sense, you've cooked it by way of a chemical process. Then the salmon goes into the cold smoker to infuse it with flavor at low temperatures.

Hot Smoking Foods

Hot smoking is smoking in an enclosed atmosphere in the presence of heat and smoke. Heat is used to cook the meat and smoke provides the flavor. Successful smoking requires food to be cooked slowly and at a constant temperature ranging from 180°F to 230°F. The flavor imparted to the food comes from the types of wood used to create the smoke. The smoking process not only cooks and flavors the meat, but it can also help preserve it.

The term "low and slow" is used often throughout this book because it is the basis for the entire concept of smoking food. Cooking this way could be equated to your mother cooking pot roast in a slow cooker for 8 or 9 hours. It transforms cuts of meat that would be barely edible with any other cooking method into delectable dishes.

With hot smoking, food is placed inside the smoker so it is entirely surrounded by smoke; there should be a thick stream of smoke around the meat at all times. The smoking process is intended to give the smoke enough time to sink in and naturally tenderize the meat. Slow cooking gives tough connective fibers in heavily exercised muscles time to break down and become tender by dissolving. This is an integral part of smoking. Collagen, which is the tough connective tissue in meat, breaks down into several types of sugars when cooked slowly. Some tougher cuts are actually made sweeter by the smoking process.

Smoking is not a science. I believe smoking food is an art. And like many good things, practice and patience are required in large doses. You will read the word *patience* over and over in this book. Heed it well, my friends, and you will become the artist you yearn to be.

The Least You Need to Know

- The act of smoking food is almost as old as time.
- Heavily salting and smoking food was the best way to preserve it until refrigeration was invented.
- Grilling is fast and easy but doesn't create the deep smoke flavor a smoker does.
- Cold smoking is used mainly to impart smoke flavor and to cure foods.
- Hot smoking not only imparts smoky flavor but it also fully cooks foods.

Smokers and How They Work

In This Chapter

- Smokers for beginning backyard enthusiasts
- Smokers for adventurous amateurs
- Smokers for experienced smokers

Depending on the type of smoker you're using, smoking foods can be a lot of hard work or it can be fairly easy. Although there are purists who feel that only hardwoods and charcoal can create a true smoke flavor, that kind of smoking can require a lot of effort for some people. At the end of the day, you're the one who has to do the work, so there's no shame in getting one of the newer-style smokers. If the authentic flavor and smoking experience is what you're really striving for, then going for a more advanced smoker is worth the extra effort.

Selecting your first smoker can be tricky; there are many things to consider. You need to know what your options are, and what each of those options is capable of. We'll go through all of this, one step at a time.

In this chapter, I outline the most popular smokers on the market, how each smoker works, and what needs to be done in order to operate it properly and safely. There are specific do's and don'ts for each smoker, although there are some rules that apply to every smoker:

- Always follow the manufacturer's recommendations for the initial setup and firing of the smoker.

- Select a wood fuel based on the manufacturer's recommendations.

- Before you start smoking, ensure that you have enough fuel (propane or charcoal) to complete the job.

- Never move a hot smoker.

- Thoroughly clean every part of the smoker after every use.

- For your first time, start with a forgiving and inexpensive cut of meat, such as a pork shoulder. (Because it smokes for a prolonged amount of time, it will allow you to figure out all the quirks of your new smoker.)

It's important to understand how each smoker works and just how much effort you'll have to put into operating it before you buy one. Even if it looks all sweet and shiny in the showroom, it might end up being more trouble than you bargained for.

Smokers for the Novice

For all those first-time smokers out there, I recommend starting out nice and easy. You can smoke foods without too much fuss in your backyard using a gas grill or an inexpensive charcoal kettle grill. Experimenting with smoking on these units is pretty simple. The upside is that it's just another application for your existing grill, so you don't have to find a home for multiple units in your backyard like I do—unless you want to!

If you've decided that a dedicated smoker is the way to go, manufacturers have designed many electric units that are easy to use. These smokers need less tending and monitoring than traditional models, because they are automated. You just have to set the temperature, add the wood, and get your food smoking.

Gas Grill

Any gas grill with a lid can be used to smoke food. The two keys to success are indirect heat and temperature control. If your gas grill does not have a temperature gauge on the lid, you can pick up gauge kits at most stores that sell grills. You can use an oven thermometer, but it isn't ideal because you'll have to open the lid to check the temperature, which will result in losing heat and smoke.

TED'S TIP

To keep your smoking grates in good shape, spray them liberally with nonstick cooking spray prior to firing your smoker or grill. This will keep foods from sticking to the grates and make cleanup a lot easier.

Smoking on a gas grill with a charcoal tray and charcoal briquettes.

To achieve a temperature low enough for smoking, you can use indirect heat. Just place the food item over a burner that isn't lit and the remaining lit burners will produce the heat that will smoke and cook the food. The actual smoke itself can be produced by using wood chips loosely wrapped in aluminum foil to make a pouch, a metal wood-chip box, or a prepackaged smoking can (a small metal can filled with hardwood chips). Other options for producing smoke include external smoke generators, such as the SmokePistol system. Most gas grills are not insulated, so the outdoor temperature and wind will have a significant impact on the internal temperature of the grill. You'll find more instructions for smoking on a gas grill in Chapter 4.

Charcoal Kettles

One of the most popular backyard grills is a charcoal kettle grill. Smoking in one of these units is also accomplished by using indirect heat; charcoal is placed on one side and food on the other side. You'll need to monitor the temperature carefully. If your kettle grill doesn't have a temperature gauge installed on the lid, install a gauge kit or use a metal pocket thermometer or electronic probe thermometer and rest it in one of the vent holes in the lid.

A water pan needs to be placed to one side of the lower grate (charcoal tray); disposable aluminum pans from the supermarket work well. The water pan serves two purposes: it catches meat drippings and adds humidity to the cooking chamber.

Hot charcoal is placed in the kettle next to the water pan and the temperature is controlled using the air vents on the kettle's base and lid. Opening and closing the air vents on the kettle's base will have the greatest impact on the internal temperature.

Charcoal kettle grill/smoker.

Smoke production is achieved by using good-quality hardwood lump or briquette charcoal. If more smoke is desired, use wood chips loosely wrapped in a foil pouch; rest it on the coals or place soaked wood chips directly on the coals. (See Chapter 3 for more about soaking wood.) Controlling the temperature, humidity, and airflow is the key to success, even when using a beginner smoker.

Electric Smokers

The methods I've just discussed are the best way to start smoking and not break the bank. Being a beginner may seem a little challenging and daunting, so not wanting to spend a ton of cash right off the bat makes sense. However, once you've had a little practice, you may want to move on to an electric smoker.

Electric smokers create smoke by burning wood with an electrically powered heat element. For the most part, the type of fuel is governed by the type of electric smoker being used and the manufacturer's recommendations. Basic electric smokers will require you to add wood chips manually during the cooking process. On higher-end models, the wood fuel is fed onto the heating element automatically. Different smokers do this in a variety of ways. Many pellet smokers use an auger system to feed pellets into the burn pot. Wood-puck smokers mechanically feed pucks onto the heating element at timed intervals. (See Chapter 3 for a discussion of wood chips, pellets, and other fuel options.)

TASTY TIDBIT

Finding that perfect balance of fire, wood and/or charcoal, and smoke is a dance that takes practice; more often than not, Mother Nature is the DJ. I have a lot of experience smoking foods (a lot!) and I can honestly say that every time I smoke something it is a bit difficult because Mother Nature can be wicked. She mixes things up with high winds, rain, sleet, snow; even a hot humid day will affect the smoker's results. This is when experience comes in handy and helps you make the adjustments you need to achieve your high-standard results.

Portable electric smokers are available in a wide array of shapes and sizes such as kettle, vertical box, and barrel shape. Electric smokers with insulated cooking chambers can maintain more stable temperatures in adverse weather conditions.

The type of electric smoker being used governs the type of heat created within it. Some heat the wood fuel only to smoldering point, then use a separate electric heating element within the cooking enclosure to achieve the desired temperature. Other models heat the wood fuel until it catches fire, and then control the fire (and therefore the cooking temperature) by using forced ventilation and a precision-controlled fuel feed.

Even if your smoker has an electronic-control unit, it's not as simple as loading the unit with the required wood fuel and setting it to the desired temperature. You'll need to consider the conditions outdoors, especially on a particularly hot, cold, or windy day. The smoker needs time to build up to the desired temperature, and if it doesn't make it there or overshoots it, you'll need to adjust as you smoke.

Top left: digital-electric vertical box smoker with smoking pucks; top right: electric-coil smoker; bottom: electric horizontal pellet smoker.

For electric smokers without an electronic-control unit, you can control the temperature by monitoring the thermostat and adjusting the vents and (to a lesser extent) the amount of wood fuel added.

Here are some things to keep in mind when using an electric smoker for the first time:

- Check the amperage of the plug you intend to use to ensure it can handle the power requirements of the smoker.

- Although some electric smokers have fully enclosed electronic elements, not all do. Water-resistant is not the same as waterproof, so be sure to check the weather forecast before starting.

- There's no such thing as "set it and forget it," so keep an eye on your smoker. Grease flares, short circuits, and temperature-control issues can happen with even the best electric smokers.

- Keep an eye out for thick gray or black smoke. This is an indicator that a grease fire is burning inside the smoker.

- If your electric smoker has a water pan, fill it to the required level. If it is not designed for a water pan, do not use one because the added humidity can damage sensitive electronic components.

- If your smoker has adjustable vents, use them to control both the internal temperature and smoke flow within the unit.

Smokers Best Suited for Adventurous Amateurs

You're probably asking yourself, what exactly is an adventurous amateur? To me, this is a person who says, "I think I can, I think I can, I think I can"—and does! And it's that attitude that sets an adventurous amateur apart from a beginner. An adventurous amateur is not afraid to experiment, and will happily try again even if the first attempt didn't have perfect results. They always want to improve upon what they smoked last time. It's also for the person who wants more of a challenge, who is ready to graduate from smoking on their gas or charcoal grill. This is not to say that smoking on an electric smoker isn't exciting, but it isn't as much work as smoking with charcoal and hardwood.

TED'S TIP

If your smoker's grates are cast iron and not coated with porcelain, be sure to clean the grates immediately after a smoking session, and then season with nonstick cooking spray to prevent rusting while not in use.

Moving on to new challenges means you'll want to get another piece of equipment. So now, I will guide you through the smoking world of vertical box smokers, water smokers, offset barrel smokers, and kamado-style grills. These smokers work primarily off hardwood charcoal or hardwoods. I'll review the basics of what these smokers entail and which smoker might be best for your needs. In addition, I'll share my tips and tricks on how to operate each smoker, so you get the best results.

Vertical Box Smokers

A vertical box smoker is a box-shape cooking chamber with a heat source in the bottom. Higher-quality box smokers will have a separate firebox, either underneath or on the side of the box, which allows heat and smoke to flow into the cooking chamber. Separating the firebox from the cooking chamber allows for better temperature and smoke control. Box smokers can be charcoal, electric, or propane fired. Some use hardwood chips to create smoke, while others have wood pellet- or puck-feed systems to create smoke and generate heat.

Box smokers on the market today range from simple charcoal-fired, thinly walled cabinets with a couple of vents, up to fully insulated, microprocessor-controlled, gas-fired cabinets with ultraprecise temperature and smoke controls. Insulated cabinets provide a more consistent temperature than uninsulated boxes, particularly in wet or cold weather. Each type of box smoker has distinct advantages and disadvantages. Electric box smokers, as I already mentioned, are convenient but need a power outlet. Basic models use a simple thermostat, but more advanced models use onboard computers to control the temperature. Propane box smokers are more portable (no outlet is required, unless your smoker has an electrically powered pellet- or puck-feed system). Charcoal-fired box smokers are generally the least expensive and most portable type, but they require careful attention to maintain the fire and smoke temperatures.

Vertical charcoal box smoker.

For basic propane-fired and electrically fired box smokers, controlling the temperature is as simple as adjusting the thermostat (electric) or flow of propane until the desired internal temperature is reached. There may not be an adjustable lower vent on these smokers, since the heat source does not rely on a variable supply of oxygen to control the temperature. On advanced models, the internal temperature and fire are controlled by an onboard microprocessor.

In charcoal-fired box smokers, adjustable vents primarily control the temperature, but the type of charcoal and how it is arranged also play a part. Once the charcoal is lit and the desired internal temperature has been reached, adjust the vents toward the closed position. Keep an eye on the temperature gauge and make final adjustments to the vents until you've achieved a steady smoking temperature for 20 minutes.

If using wood chips, always soak them before putting them in the chip box, chip bowl, or directly onto the charcoal; where you put them depends on the model of the smoker. The wood chips should not have a large impact on the internal temperature because the goal is to keep them at a slow smolder (not flaming) during the smoking process. Box smokers with automatic pellet- or puck-feed systems remove the need to replenish wood chips. Depending on the model of smoker, these pellets and pucks may be burned at higher temperatures to create both heat and smoke, or simply heated to smoldering point to create smoke. Pellets and pucks are never presoaked with these box smokers because they will absorb moisture, disintegrate, and not work with your smoker.

The weather will have an impact on the internal temperature of all box smokers, though well-insulated boxes will be affected to a lesser degree. Adjust the controls as needed to reach and maintain the desired temperature, and always use a thermometer to check the internal temperature of your smoker. If you attempt to "set it and forget it," you may not get to the temperature you need on a cold day, or you may overshoot the temperature on a hot day.

Water Smokers

Water smokers are primarily constructed in two shapes: box and upright drum (or bullet-style). They can be fired by charcoal, electric, or propane and, like other smokers, they use soaked hardwood chips or charcoal to create smoke. The key difference is that a pan of water is placed directly over the chip box and heat source, underneath the food being smoked.

TED'S TIP

If the coals in your water smoker are getting too hot or you need to smoke at a lower temperature, just add some ice cubes or blocks of ice to the water pan to cool things down.

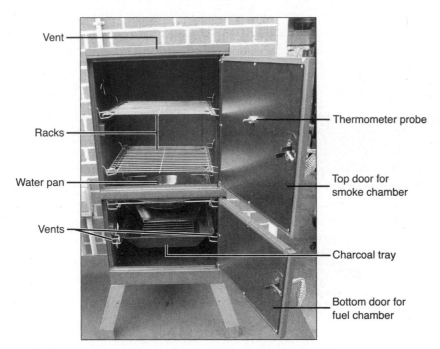

Vent

Racks

Water pan

Vents

Thermometer probe

Top door for smoke chamber

Charcoal tray

Bottom door for fuel chamber

Vertical water smoker.

Adding water to the smoking process has a couple key advantages. One, the steam created within the cooking chamber keeps the food moist. And two, any drippings from the food fall into the water pan instead of on the fuel, reducing the chance of flare-ups or snuffing out the fire. Perhaps, more importantly, the temperature within a smoker is much more stable and easier to maintain with a water pan in place. Be sure not to overfill the water pan but also keep an eye on the water level and replenish it as necessary. The weather will also have an impact on the internal temperature of water smokers. On cold days, it's a good idea to start with hot water in the water pan. Temperature control for water smokers is achieved using the same techniques as vertical box smokers.

Offset Barrel Smokers

The offset barrel smoker is a relatively recent invention. Its origins are in Oklahoma and West Texas, where inventive and industrious oilmen decided to use materials on hand to replicate the brick-and-mortar pit smokers from back home. Using heavy-gauge oil pipe and the skills of local welders, these men put together the very first offset barrel smokers, and the basic design hasn't really changed since. While they may vary widely in size and quality, every offset barrel smoker has three primary components: an offset firebox, a cooking chamber, and an exhaust flue.

The temperature in the cooking chamber is controlled using adjustable intake- and exhaust-vent dampers located on the firebox and atop the exhaust flue. Minor improvements over the years have included baffle and tuning plates to improve heat flow and distribution, as well as vertical smoking chambers on the end opposite the firebox. The traditional fuel used in an offset smoker is dried hardwood logs, although lump hardwood charcoal can be used either as an alternative to, or in combination with, the logs. Humidity can be introduced to the offset barrel smoker by placing a pan of water directly over the firebox's baffle plate, inside the cooking chamber. Offset barrel smokers are among the most labor intensive of the bunch, requiring frequent tending of the fire and careful control of the vent dampers to maintain a steady temperature in their smoking zone. But done right, the results are beyond comparison.

Airflow in and out of your offset barrel smoker is the primary method used to control the cooking temperature. Environmental factors will also heavily influence the cooking chamber temperature. Managing the fire on a beautiful, warm, and sunny day will be a different challenge than maintaining the temperature on a cold, wet, and windy day.

Adding a water pan in the cooking chamber has a benefit beyond adding moisture to the cooking process. It acts as a secondary heat baffle for the firebox and helps regulate the temperature. Keep in mind, however, that it will take longer for the smoker to initially reach cooking temperature when a water pan is in place.

The best offset barrel smokers are precision welded, with excellent fit and finish, high-quality gaskets, and carefully designed heat baffles and tuning plates. If you fire up your smoker and notice smoke escaping from around the chimney or through the closed cooking-chamber door, purchase heat-resistant gasket material and putty to seal things up. A properly sealed cooking chamber and exhaust flue make a huge difference in the ease of maintaining a steady temperature.

Chimney with vent control

Thermometer probe

Heavy-duty lids

Door with vents

Smoking chamber with racks

Firebox

Offset barrel smoker.

TED'S TIP

Keep in mind that there will be a variation of temperature within the cooking chamber(s): hotter near the firebox, cooler near the exhaust chimney. The temperature can vary by as much as 50°F. I recommend that you spend a few hours getting to know the peculiarities of your offset barrel smoker to become comfortable with it before trying to cook a piece of meat.

Here are some things to keep in mind when using an offset barrel smoker for the first time:

- Most barrel smokers need a good burn-in to get rid of chemical residue left from the factory before the first use. Heat the smoker according to manufacturer's instructions.

- Lower-priced models often are better suited to using charcoal instead of hardwood logs.

- If your smoker has a drain valve, either make sure it's closed (if you plan to drain after cooking) or set a heatproof bucket or bowl directly underneath to catch drippings.

- Most cuts of meat will benefit from added humidity, so use a water pan near the firebox baffle in the cooking chamber, and check the water level at regular intervals.

- Airflow through the firebox vent damper has more of an effect on the internal temperature of the cooking chamber than the exhaust flue-vent damper.

- These smokers need TLC to get the job done right. Check both the cooking chamber temperature and the fire regularly, and add logs or charcoal as needed.

- After cooking, completely close the vent dampers to snuff out the fire. Or open the firebox and exhaust flue vent dampers to let the remaining wood or coal burn off at a high temperature (this method will also "season" the inside of the cooking chamber).

Kamado-Style Smokers

The kamado-style smoker originated in Japan, where domed, circular clay ovens have been used for centuries. In fact, the word *kamado* is Japanese for "stove." Modern kamado-style smokers have the same design elements as those clay ovens. They include: thick walls with excellent thermal properties, a domed lid (usually hinged) resting on a round- or oval-shaped pot, an internal grilling surface, and vent dampers on top and bottom to control the airflow in and out of the cooking chamber.

While kamado-style smokers constructed of clay or cement are still available, most modern kamado-style smokers are constructed of high-fire ceramic, terra cotta, insulated steel, or other more suitable materials. Traditional clay kamados are more prone to developing cracks, particularly when exposed to the elements and high temperature fluctuations.

Kamado-style smokers are capable of reaching and maintaining internal temperatures of up to 750°F, which is excellent for quickly searing a steak but much too hot for smoking food. With the right fuel (i.e., lump charcoal) and careful control of airflow, they are also one of the best smokers available. Maintaining temperatures in the smoking zone can be done with ease when using these smokers.

The airflow in and out of your kamado-style smoker is what will determine the internal temperature. Airflow is controlled by adjusting the vent dampers at the top and bottom of the grill. The wider the damper is opened, the more air will reach your coal and cause it to burn hotter. For smoking, we want to allow just enough air into the kamado-style smoker to maintain a low steady temperature, and to keep the coal burning slowly and evenly.

Kamado-style grills/smokers.

If using a temperature-control device, attach it to the lower vent damper according to the manufacturer's instructions before lighting the coal. Put a couple of pounds of lump charcoal onto the fire grate in your kamado-style smoker and form it into a mound. Be careful not to block the airway from the lower damper with little pieces of coal, and then completely open up the lower-vent damper. Only light a few pieces of coal in the center of the pile. If your smoker comes with a heat diffuser, put it in place. Once the coal in the center of the pile has ignited, put the grill in place, close the domed lid, and fully open the upper-vent damper. If you are adding wood chips, add them around the perimeter of the coal pile before you close the lid. Let the coals burn until the internal temperature has reached 350°F, then close both vent dampers nearly completely—leaving only a ¼-inch opening at top and bottom. While this temperature is too hot for smoking, reaching 350°F will help ensure your fire burns throughout the entire smoking process.

After opening the domed lid and placing your food inside the kamado for smoking, the internal temperature will drop considerably. Within a few minutes of the lid being closed the temperature will rise and then settle. If it's too hot, close the dampers completely for a few minutes. Once the kamado reaches the ideal temperature, open the top- and bottom-vent dampers ⅛ inch and keep an eye on the gauge. These small adjustments to the dampers can have a dramatic effect on the internal temperature.

SAFE SMOKING

When smoking with a kamado-style smoker, it is important to "burp" the smoker from time to time. Burping is when you open the lid of the kamado to allow excess heat to escape. Be sure to do this slowly and carefully because opening the lid quickly may allow too much heat to escape and you could get a face full of burning hot air.

Here are some things to keep in mind when using a kamado-style smoker for the first time:

- A kamado-style smoker is designed to retain moisture in the food being cooked, but even a splash of water inside a hot ceramic unit can crack and ruin your grill. Don't use a water pan or water to put out the coals.

- Airflow through the bottom-vent damper has more of an effect on the internal temperature than the top-vent damper.

- Always open a kamado lid slowly. The gust of hot moist air from a quickly opened lid can be a painful learning experience.

- When the kamado has cooled completely, clean out the cold ash and any remaining charcoal; be sure to pay particular attention to the inside opening of the lower-vent damper.

As I'm sure you've realized these kamado-style smokers require a bit of work, a lot of patience, as well as a small amount of good luck and instinct. Try to figure out which will work best for you. Keep in mind who you are cooking for, how much are you cooking, how hard you want to work, and how much fun you could have. Because that's what this is about, making some good food to enjoy with others and having a good time while you do it.

It'll take a while to get the hang of your new smoker and there are going to be frustrating moments. Remember, you're an adventurous amateur, you can do this—I know you can, I know you can, I know you can!

Smokers Best Suited for Experienced Smokers

Most experienced smokers want to show off a little bit, so they enter barbecue-smoking competitions, and whether it's regional or national, this puts them into the professional category. They're also always on the hunt for a new smoker or they might even build one on their own. I suggest starting with a trash-can smoker, which I'll describe in a moment. It's not fancy or hard to put together, but it'll get your feet wet and give you some serious bragging rights. The other must-have for a pro is the infamous big rig. Whether it's for smoking in a barbecue competition or catering a party, the problem with most small smokers is they don't hold enough meat. Hence the big rig.

Homemade Smokers

A quick internet search for "homemade smoker" will turn up thousands of articles, plans, videos, and discussion forums—some with well-made smokers and others with downright dangerous contraptions. One person's idea of a homemade smoker might involve copious amounts of welded heavy steel while another might decide outfitting an old refrigerator with electric hotplates will do the trick. From trash-can smokers to full-size outdoor smokehouses, your ability, budget, and experience will determine which type is the right (and safe) one to build.

There are many reasons to build a smoker at home. Whether you are doing it to save money, impress your friends, or you just want to "kick it old school," a properly constructed homemade smoker can sometimes outperform commercial smokers. Homemade smokers must operate using the same principles as store-bought smokers with reliable heat and smoke, stable temperatures, and controlled airflow.

Barbecue chefs Dr. Brownstone (Tim Grandinetti, left), Dr. BBQ (Ray Lampe, right), and me (middle), standing beside the homemade smoker we built in the Bahamas. It was made from an old wire rack, fired by charcoal on the bottom, and wrapped with many layers of heavy-duty plastic wrap. It worked wonderfully for smoking pork shoulders, brisket, and duck legs.

SAFE SMOKING

A clean smoker is a healthy smoker! Excessive grease buildup in a smoker can ignite if your smoker reaches too high a temperature. This is why it's important to clean your smoker thoroughly after each use. This includes the firebox, smoking chamber, racks, water pan, and other internal accessories, as well as removing used charcoal and excess grease. Grease also attracts bugs, rodents, and other critters. Your smoker can even grow mold if in the proper environment, so keep it clean. It's so much easier to clean after you're finished smoking, rather than having to do it the next time you want to fire up your smoker.

Some homemade smokers can be unique, like this roadside barbecue stand outside of Harrisburg, Pennsylvania, called Road Hawg BBQ. It's made from an old hot rod.

The easiest homemade smoker to build is the trash-can smoker. While some people make these smokers using electric hot plates as the heat source, this one is designed to use lump hardwood charcoal. Your local hardware store should have everything you need to get started. You'll need the following tools and materials:

- A power drill with $^3/_{16}$-inch, $^5/_{16}$-inch, $^7/_{16}$-inch, and 1-inch metal drill bits

- A set of small adjustable wrenches

- A sharp knife

- A small metal file

- 1 felt-tip permanent marker

- A 30-gallon galvanized steel trash can with lid

- 16 fully threaded $^3/_8$-inch×3-inch galvanized steel bolts with flat washers, lock washers, and nuts

- 1 generic replacement barbecue-lid thermometer with a $^1/_4$-inch diameter probe, with nut and lock washer

- 1 round cooking grate with handles (such as Weber model #7433)

- A stove-gasket replacement kit (such as Rutland Inc. Kit 96N-6)

- 2 cinder blocks

- A 1-quart metal bowl

- A 5-quart stainless-steel colander

- 1 steel pizza pan (without perforations) that is larger than the top of the colander

- 8 tapered corks or silicone bottle stoppers, $1\frac{1}{4}$-inch diameter at the wide end

After you've assembled your materials, it's time to get building! The first thing to do is to mark and drill all of the required holes in the trash can and lid. The cooking grate will rest on the six steel bolts; so make six evenly spaced, level marks around the perimeter of the can about 8 inches below the lip, and drill $\frac{7}{16}$-inch holes. Flip the can over (bottom-side up), mark, and drill a single $\frac{7}{16}$-inch hole in the bottom, 2 inches from the edge of the can. This is the drain hole.

Next, drill the lower air vents. These are four 1-inch holes, drilled horizontally along the bottom of the can with 1-inch spaces between the holes. The holes need to be 1 to 2 inches above the metal floor of the can, so that air can flow from outside to inside.

Drill upper air vents in the lid as close to the center as possible, but not under the handle—two holes on each side of the handle spaced about 1-inch part works well. The final hole to be drilled is for the thermometer. This will also be drilled in the lid, using the $\frac{5}{16}$-inch bit. Using the metal file, remove rough or sharp edges from around the 1-inch ventilation holes. Install the 6 bolts using flat washers on the outside and locking washers on the inside of the can and install the thermometer through the $\frac{5}{16}$-inch hole in the lid.

The next step is making a lid gasket with the stove-gasket kit. Set the lid in place on top of the can. Take the rope gasket and wrap it snugly around the can just underneath the lid, without stretching the rope. The goal is to have a gently snug—not tight—fit between the lid and the gasket during smoking. Cut the rope a few inches longer than the circumference of the can (wrapping the rope with a piece of scotch tape will keep it from unraveling when you cut it). Mark the can just above and below the rope gasket in a couple of spots. Now, run a bead of adhesive around the circumference of the can and press the gasket in place. As you finish, cut the gasket to the exact size so that it touches end to end. Let the gasket sealant dry for 24 hours before using your new smoker.

SAFE SMOKING

Using the right materials to build your smoker is crucial, from both fire- and food-safety perspectives. A poorly constructed homemade smoker, or one made with questionable materials, can pose serious risks to your home and health. For example, galvanized steel (most trash cans are dip galvanized) can be dangerous if heated near or beyond the melting point of zinc, 787.1°F. At or above that temperature, zinc oxide fumes could be released from the can. While this is typically far beyond anything resembling food-smoking temperatures, it is worth keeping in mind.

Controlling the airflow (by plugging and unplugging the vent holes with the wine corks) controls the temperature. However, the type of charcoal and how it is arranged also play a part. Once the charcoal is lit and the desired internal temperature has been reached, plug two vent holes on the top and bottom, and keep an eye on the temperature gauge. Plug or unplug the vent holes as needed until you've achieved a steady smoking temperature for 20 minutes. Soaked wood chips are placed directly on the chip tray (pizza pan) in a single layer. The weather will have a direct impact on the internal temperature since the trash-can smoker is not insulated around the cooking chamber.

Here are some things to keep in mind when using your homemade smoker for the first time:

- Put your trash-can smoker on top of the cinder blocks, and place the bowl on the ground directly under the drain hole.

- Leave all vent holes unplugged, top and bottom.

- Fill the steel colander with charcoal halfway, place it inside the smoker, and light the charcoal.

- Soak your wood chips before putting them on the chip tray (steel pizza pan).

- Once the charcoal is burning, put the chip tray on top of the coal colander, drop in the cooking grate, and put the lid on the smoker.

- When the internal temperature reaches 250°F or higher, plug two of the bottom vent holes and two of the top holes using the tapered corks (or bottle stoppers).

- Safety is paramount. Use heatproof gloves and tongs to lift out the chip tray and colander from a hot smoker.

- Plan to fire up your smoker without food the first time to season it, check for smoke leaks or temperature fluctuations, and just learn about your smoker.

- To season the smoker for the first time, add charcoal as needed until the smoker has run for 12 hours at steady smoking temperatures. The smoker is now ready for regular use.

The Big Rigs

I remember getting my first rig; I still have it 10 years later. It's not the biggest of the big rigs and it's not the smallest, but for me it's just right. It's a 10-foot-long offset-barrel-smoker trailer, fired by hardwood and charcoal. It can smoke 60 racks of ribs or 150 pounds of brisket and pork butts. It has three charcoal/propane grills on the side and a rocket burner on the front. Weighing in at a cool 3,500 pounds, it goes anywhere—including the lake!

Big rigs are the smokers used by many professional barbecue teams who need to cook up large amounts of food day after day on the road. They can be used anywhere, anytime. Manufacturers such as Ole Hickory, Backwoods, and Southern Pride build full-size, commercial-grade smoker trailers, designed to deliver excellent electronic temperature and smoke and moisture control in a road-worthy, extreme-duty design.

This is my barbecue rig—tasty and sweet.

Each manufacturer recommends a fuel type to achieve best results, but most of the top-quality big rigs are fired with a combination of hardwood logs and gas (propane or natural). The internal cooking chamber and the manner in which the result is achieved differ among manufacturers. Some have rotating racks, while others use a sophisticated airflow management system to achieve an even smoke. These rigs are built for frequent and rugged use and are priced accordingly.

Industrial Smokers

Modern industrial smokers are highly automated, efficient, high-capacity units that can be permanently installed or are semiportable. These smokers will outperform residential-type smokers in virtually every aspect and most are designed with simplicity of use for the end-user in mind. Available in a wide range of sizes (both physical size and internal capacity); the manufacturer determines the type of fuel. Some use hardwood logs fired with natural gas, while others might be electrically powered and use proprietary hardwood-sawdust compounds to create smoke. Many offer precise control of the humidity within the cooking chamber. Industrial smokers have specific requirements and maintenance costs, so they may not be the best option for the hobbyist.

> **TASTY TIDBIT**
>
> Food service or industrial smokers can vary in size and price. Some are attached to trailers and others are so large they are permanent installations. The price can go from the low thousand-dollar range to hundreds of thousands of dollars. I work in the meat industry and with smokers that hold 10,000 pounds of meat at one time. Our plant has five of them—mega-bucks!

The Least You Need to Know

- Beginners can start smoking with their regular gas or propane grills.
- To be considered an "adventurous amateur," you just need the right attitude.
- There are a variety of smokers that will challenge the adventurous amateur on his journey to smoky deliciousness.
- Making your own smoker can be a lot of work, but the end results are the tastiest.
- There are do's and don'ts for every smoker, so learn as much as you can to safely operate your smoker.

Fuel + Wood = Smoky Deliciousness

In This Chapter

- Fuel options for your smoker
- All about charcoal
- Different types of hardwoods
- When to soak your wood and when not to
- How bark impacts the smoke
- Plank smoking 101

Now you know more about smokers and the different types and styles available, but there's one more thing you should consider before going out to buy one: what type of fuel source you want to use. Many varieties of fuel options are available for smokers. Much of your decision should be based on how often you plan on using your smoker and how much food you are going to smoke at one time.

Why all the fuss about fuel? Because fuel is just as important as the smoker itself. The fuel you choose can affect the overall flavor of the food you smoke.

Electricity and gas versus charcoal and hardwood can be a very heated (ha, get it?!) debate among enthusiasts. Electricity and gas offer wonderful convenience, and they're very easy to use. Charcoal and hardwoods do a great job of heating your smoker and add a ton of flavor to the food, but they're more work to maintain.

What's right for you? Let's find out.

Propane and Natural Gases

Propane or natural gases are convenient ways of heating your fire. Natural gas burns just as hot as propane gas and both maintain a constant temperature, so they are equally capable to fuel your smoker. All in all, gas is an easy and efficient way to run your smoker. The only downside is that gas doesn't offer any flavor to the food you are smoking.

Many barbecue enthusiasts will say you're not truly barbecuing if you are using gas, which isn't at all true. It's the perfect option when you're short on time and you have a lot of food to smoke.

Pros to using propane and natural gas:

- Gas is economical and readily available.

- Propane is portable, allowing you to travel with your smoker.

- Gas burns efficiently.

- Gas is easily controlled with the temperature adjustments found on the grill's burners.

Cons to using propane and natural gas:

- Fuel explosions can occur but normally don't when proper storage and handling procedures are followed.

- Rising fuel prices could affect affordability.

- Hoses and valves need to be maintained regularly.

- If a tank runs out and you're not prepared with a backup, it could be "game over."

Always keep a full backup tank on hand so you don't run out of fuel halfway through your recipe. The best fuel tanks have gauges that indicate the level of gas remaining in the tank. This way you won't waste your fuel by returning what you think are empty tanks but are really half-full tanks.

Vertical-box propane-fuelled water smoker.

TED'S TIP

Over time, hoses can develop cracks and leaks due to wear and tear. Make sure you check your equipment often and ensure everything is in good running order based on the manufacturer's instructions.

Electricity

Many styles of smokers are powered with electricity. Electricity is efficient and relatively easy to use—except when you're in the outback without an electrical outlet or in the middle of a power outage.

Electricity offers a constant heat source to keep your smoker running smoothly. Most electric smokers use electricity to heat a burner, which slowly heats wooden smoke pellets or wood-style pucks that, in turn, create the smoke. An electric smoker needs to be close to an electrical outlet because using an extension cord will cause a drop in voltage that will result in a lower output of heat, resulting in longer smoking times and less efficiency.

Pros to using electricity:

- Electricity is an affordable resource.

- It is super convenient—just plug it in and turn it on.

- Electricity is pure and free of the by-products sometimes found in combustible fuels.

- Electricity is good for the production of supplementary heat, as well as for producing smoke.

Cons to using electricity:

- Need to have close access to an electrical outlet.

- Electric smokers cannot be used in the wilderness.

- Electricity does not work during a power outage.

- Electric smokers can be dangerous. The external generator must be kept out of the rain to prevent water damage or short circuits that could cause shock or even a fire.

Pig and steer pellet smokers.

Electric smokers make great cold smokers. And because of the heat and smoke controls, electricity allows you to control your heat more efficiently, which saves money and time.

Charcoal

When it comes to barbecue and smoked foods, charcoal rules as king of all fuels because low and slow is the way to go. Nothing else is more primal, more adventurous, or produces more delicious food. Most folks think working with charcoal is too hard and frustrating, but in reality it doesn't need to be difficult and it adds wonderful flavor to your food even without the addition of wood.

Selecting the right charcoal is as important as the food you're smoking, and not all charcoal is created equally, so choose wisely. Look for charcoal made from 100 percent, all-natural hardwoods—no softwoods should be in there. Hardwood charcoal burns more efficiently, lasts longer, and has no added chemicals. Let me say it again, you want to purchase *100 percent pure hardwood charcoal.*

Types of Charcoal

You're probably already familiar with some charcoal, but let's take a closer look at some you might not know about.

First up is *lump charcoal.* This charcoal is made of random-size pieces of hardwood charcoal. It is just wood that has been turned into charcoal—nothing more. Lump charcoal will burn at a higher temperature—approximately 800°F—but it doesn't burn for long. That's why it's normally used for grilling foods rather than smoking foods. But for some die-hard barbecue cooks, using lump charcoal gives a better, more natural flavor than briquettes. Look for 100 percent hardwood lump charcoal.

Briquette charcoal is typically pillow-shaped and usually made from leftover pieces of lump charcoal. Processors take the leftover pieces; grind them to a consistent size; and use corn, wheat, or potato starch as a binding agent. Briquettes burn at a lower temperature, approximately 600°F to 1,000°F, for a longer period of time, which makes them ideal for smoking foods. Look for 100 percent all natural briquettes.

Left: charcoal briquettes; right: lump charcoal.

Now for *hardwood charcoal:* Many varieties of hardwoods are available, and therefore many varieties of hardwood charcoals. Some charcoals are made from one type of wood, such as 100 percent maple hardwood charcoal. Others are made from a blend of woods to create a unique smoke flavor. Blends may combine hickory and maple or oak and mesquite, for example. Talk to your local barbecue retailer or supplier to ask what types of charcoal they carry.

Fast-light charcoal is a briquette that has fire-starting fuel mixed directly in or on it. This makes for speedy lighting of your coals, but the overall flavor isn't desirable for smoking foods. I suggest saving these fuel-infused coals for simple, quick grilling.

Hardwood Charcoal Flavoring Guide

All types of charcoal are available. I like to mix and match different types of charcoal to create new flavors. Creating a blend sometimes gives you the ultimate fuel that produces an even heat and lasts a good, long time—those are the things you want from your charcoal, maximum efficiency. Create your own unique recipes and blends to find out what flavors you like best. Just keep in mind that some charcoal smokers work better with a certain type of charcoal. The key is to have fun, experiment, and make some tasty food.

SAFE SMOKING

Do not use charcoal for preparing food indoors unless you have proper ventilation for exhausting *all* fumes outdoors. Charcoal produces deadly toxic fumes that can accumulate and cause death if not properly ventilated. No, really—*you could die!*

Here are some of the charcoals that are available.

Coconut: For thousands of years people have been using coconut shells to fuel their fires. It burns hot and offers a sweet, nutty, and robust flavor to food. Coconut charcoal is not made from the coconut tree but from the shells. It's a medium-flavored charcoal and is best used with poultry, pork, fish, and shellfish. It is produced in Indonesia.

Hickory: Hickory is the most common wood used for smoking foods. This hardwood burns hot, lasts a long time, and offers a rich, sweet, and strong flavor to foods. It's best used with pork shoulder, ribs, bacon, and ham, as well as with turkey and chicken. It is produced in the United States.

Kiawe: Kiawe charcoal is a Hawaiian-style charcoal made from the *Prosopis pallida* or kiawe tree, which is a relative of mesquite. This charcoal burns very hot due to its density and lasts a very long time. It has a very sweet aromatic smoky flavor with a spicy finish and is wonderful with just about any meat—beef, pork, poultry, lamb, game, and seafood. It is produced in Mexico.

Maple: Maple trees are a great source for hard wood charcoals. They burn hot and offer a sweet, buttery, and nutty flavor to foods. Great used on poultry, ribs, steak, lamb, and game meats. It is produced in the United States and Canada.

Mesquite: Mesquite is a very hard wood with a full flavor. This charcoal burns very hot due to it density and lasts a very long time. It has a sweet, aromatic smoky flavor with a spicy finish. It can be used to smoke virtually any meat—beef, pork, poultry, lamb, game, and seafood. It is produced in the United States and Mexico.

Oak: Oak is a very hard wood that is best used on red meats. Brisket smoked with oak is a Texan's delight. It burns hot and lasts a good, long time. Oak smoke has a medium-to-heavy flavor that is not too overpowering, and has a buttery and nutty smooth finish. It's great with beef, lamb, and bison. It is produced in the United States and Canada.

Orange: Orange wood charcoal is made from 100 percent citrus orange trees. This charcoal offers a tangy citrus note to foods with a mild-to-medium flavor. It is great for smoking seafood, fish, and chicken. It is produced in Mexico.

Ted's Homemade Charcoal Blends

I'm not kidding when I say secrets are huge in the barbecue world; no one ever lets their secrets slip. I thought I'd be a pal and get you started with a few of my own secrets—but don't tell anyone!

Brisket Lump Blend: I like to use a mixture of 2 parts oak charcoal with 1 part mesquite charcoal. I find oak produces a nice, smooth smoke but lacks sweetness. That's where the mesquite comes in, lending its sweet smoke to the mix. Because it's an extremely hard wood, mesquite works well with oak to make a great combination for burn length and overall flavor.

Ribber's Secret Recipe: If you ever have the pleasure of going to a smoking competition, you will soon find out that many things are kept a big secret. The rub, the sauce, even the wood is a secret. Well I'm here to blow the top off this secret and give you the winning blend for ribs: try 2 parts hickory charcoal, 1 part maple-hardwood charcoal, and 1 part fruitwood-based charcoal. Hickory provides heat and the body of flavor, maple gives you length of flavor (to give balance throughout eating), and fruit adds a bit of sweetness.

General Tips for Buying and Working with Charcoal

The sheer number and varieties of charcoals available can be overwhelming. Just keep it simple in the beginning and buy whatever sounds good.

TASTY TIDBIT

Bet you didn't know that the charcoal chimney started out as a coffee tin. Generations of boy scouts and cowboys knew that if you punched holes around the bottom of the coffee can, filled it with charcoal, and lit it, you would have red-hot glowing coals in no time.

Here are a few other tips to keep in mind when shopping for charcoal:

- Look for briquette charcoal that has been infused with hardwood smoking chips (hickory, mesquite, maple, oak, or apple). This saves you the step of adding smoking woods.

- When buying lump charcoal, avoid the little pieces. These burn up too quickly and will leave you frustrated and out of fuel. Look for charcoal with larger chunks that will burn longer and offer the most flavor.

- Always buy more charcoal than you need because as long as you have charcoal, you have a fuel source.

- Remember that less is more. You don't need a lot of charcoal to create enough heat for your smoker. Start out with a little and add more as you need it. It's easier to build your fire than to take it away.

- Never add cold charcoal to hot charcoal. Always add hot coals to your smoker, because it keeps the temperature constant rather than losing valuable heat by adding cold coals. (See Chapter 4 for information on how to preheat charcoal.)

- Keep in mind that the more oxygen you allow into your smoker the hotter the fire—and the more heat that will be produced.

Hardwoods

Hardwoods are the most traditional way to create fire, whether it's in a fire pit, grill, or smoker. At times, there's nothing better to flavor your food than creating heat from 100 percent natural hardwood. You start a fire with hardwood and burn the wood down to homemade charcoal. Fueling your smoker with these hot coals creates the ultimate 100 percent pure wood flavor. It's a lot more work to keep your fire hot and it needs constant attention, but the result is 100 percent authentic barbecue.

Look for hardwoods that are clean and dry. Wet woods don't burn hot enough and tend to go out. You can leave the bark on or strip it off (see the section "Bark vs. No Bark" later in this chapter).

Hardwood vs. Softwood

Hardwoods produce a better smoke flavor than softwoods. They burn longer and cleaner, and they have less resin. The resin from softwoods burns quickly and produces a bitter smoke flavor. The smoke from some softwoods can be toxic—horse chestnut, for example. So when shopping for woods, remember: if the wood comes from some kind of hardwood tree, it's good to go. Soft is a no!

Sawdust, Chips, Chunks, Pellets, Pucks, and Logs

The key to smoking is not the form in which the wood comes but the smoke that's created from the wood used. The type of smoking equipment usually determines the form of wood needed.

Sawdust is a relatively inexpensive raw material to use for smoking. It produces a nice, even smoke and burns efficiently. You will find, however, that it needs to be replenished fairly often. Always work with dry sawdust because it won't burn if it's soaked.

Wood chips are approximately 1 to 3 inches long and 1 to 2 inches wide. They come in a variety of flavors and are readily available in most barbecue-supply stores and specialty grocers. The key with wood chips is to starve the wood of oxygen so it smolders and smokes. You don't want your wood chips to burn because it produces a bitter smoke.

TASTY TIDBIT

Traditionally, the best burning woods for creating your own charcoal are hickory, mesquite, maple, and oak.

I recommend soaking wood chips, as they will smoke longer and make the flavor of the smoke a little more pungent. Soaking also keeps them from burning up too quickly. Wood chips are traditionally used for adding smoke to your gas grills by using a smoker box or foil pouch. They can also be directly applied to hot coals for charcoal smokers.

Wood chunks are larger pieces of wood ranging in size from 2 to 5 inches, which eliminates having to replenish the wood as often. Chunks are too large for smoker boxes or foil pouches. They're best for longer periods of smoking. You can use wood chunks dry or they can be soaked. Both methods work well with this size of wood.

Wood pellets are made of ground wood or sawdust that is pressed into small pellets and are held together by some kind of food starch (corn, rice, or tapioca). They're available in a wide range of flavors, such as alder, apple, black walnut, cherry, hickory, whiskey barrel, mesquite, oak, orange, pecan, savory herb, garlic, sassafras, sugar maple, and many more.

Wood pellets are very easy to use and best when used in smokers designed for them, but they're great to use in charcoal smokers as well. There's no need to soak them, just add a handful of pellets to the hot coals.

Smoking *pucks* are compressed wood shavings that are held together with some kind of good starch (corn, rice, or tapiocca). They are available in a wide range of flavors.

Logs pull double duty when it comes to smoking: they're the fuel source for creating heat and providing smoke. Logs are normally used for longer smoking periods. When smoking with logs, wait until the smoke takes on a blue tinge before putting meat in the smoker. Logs come in a variety of sizes, which typically depends on the size of the tree the wood came from. Logs from fruit trees are smaller in size compared to logs cut from maple, oak, and hickory.

Whatever option you choose, be sure to store your smoking woods—sawdust, chips, pucks, pellets, and logs—in a cool, dry place.

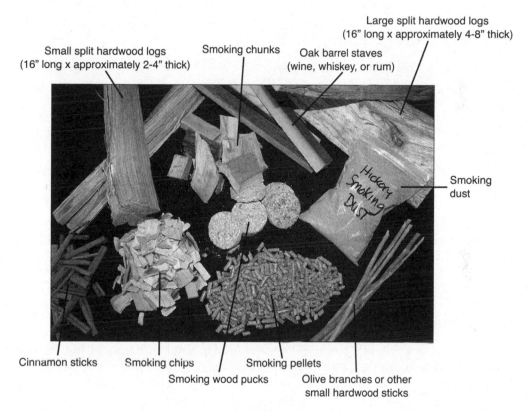

A variety of smoking woods.

To Soak or Not to Soak?

When it comes to using natural hardwoods for smoking, some folks like to soak their wood and others don't. You can buy green wood, which is naturally wet, or you can soak dried wood in water before smoking. Wet wood is going to produce more smoke than dry wood, which isn't necessarily a good thing. Certain foods do not perform well when smoked with wet wood. For example, when cold smoking cheese, you want the smoke to be dry and not carry any humidity.

I typically don't soak logs because water doesn't really penetrate into larger pieces of wood. But if you prefer to soak logs it should be overnight, at least. I do, however, soak chips and chunks; 1 to 2 hours usually does the trick.

Bark vs. No Bark

Some people claim the bark on smoking woods gives a bitter taste to smoked foods, so they remove all bark from their logs beforehand. Others believe bark adds good flavor to smoked foods, so they keep the bark on.

I've found that bark does affect the flavor of foods. It produces a stronger smoke flavor, not necessarily a bitter smoke (although I have found it to be bitter on occasion). It's just more pronounced, and I find it too intense.

SAFE SMOKING

Allow any leftover soaked woods to dry out completely before storing them or they will produce mold and other bacteria.

Most chips and chunks come without a lot of bark, but logs tend to have bark. So I order clean wood—bark removed—or I find myself peeling the bark from fire logs. It comes down to personal preference, so experiment and determine what works best for you.

A Wood Flavoring Guide

Most people can't identify the type of wood used to smoke their food, but the choice does affect the flavor. Smoking is an art, not a science, so choose whatever wood speaks to you.

Alder: Fragrant and delicate with a sweet yet musky smoke that is the perfect complement for fish, especially salmon.

Almond: Imparts a nutty, sweet flavor that is good for beef, pork (ribs or ham), poultry, and game.

Apple: The most pungent and fragrant of all fruitwoods and an excellent choice for poultry, ribs, pork, sausage, and ham.

Apricot: A mild and sweet fruitwood; good with seafood, pork, and poultry.

Ash: Fast burning with a light smoke flavor that's good for beef, pork, and poultry.

Beech: Mild wood with a delicate smoke flavor that is good for beef, pork, ribs, ham, seafood, and poultry.

Birch: Similar in flavor to maple but a little softer and burns much faster. Good for pork, poultry, seafood, and cheese.

Black walnut: An intense smoke that has a slightly bitter flavor; pair it with stronger flavored meats such as beef, ham, lamb, game, and turkey.

Cedar: Great for plank smoking but not for low-and-slow smoking; best with salmon and other seafood, but also works well with cheese and vegetables.

Cherry: Distinctive and flavorful with a sweet smoke that's great with beef, lamb, game, poultry, and hams.

Chestnut: Slightly sweet, nutty smoke flavor that compliments beef, pork, and game.

Citrus (orange, lemon, lime, grapefruit): These fruitwoods have a sweet and fruity smoke that isn't overpowering and works well with more delicate foods, such as seafood and poultry.

Grapevine: An aromatic and tart fruitwood that burns quickly and is wonderful with chicken, turkey, seafood, and pork.

Hickory: Hickory is the most popular hardwood. It has a rich and full-bodied, sweet flavor, especially when used for smoking bacon—my favorite. It's also great with beef, ribs, pork, ham, sausage, game, poultry, seafood, and cheese.

Maple: A wood that burns hot, with a spicy and earthy smoke; great with poultry, pork, ham, bacon, and cheese.

Mesquite: An extremely hard wood that's milder and sweeter than hickory and is best used with beef, ribs, pork, lamb, poultry, and game. Mesquite is a southwest smoker's delight.

Oak: A great wood for all types of meat and for smoking larger cuts for longer periods of time. It imparts a medium-to-heavy flavor, which is why it's the brisket smoker's wood of choice.

Olive: Smoky flavor similar to mesquite but much lighter and best used in Mediterranean-flavored dishes with lamb, poultry, and seafood.

Peach: Slightly sweet fruitwood; delicate in flavor and complements seafood and poultry.

Pear: Sweet and woodsy flavor that is similar to apple and great with poultry, game birds, and pork.

Pecan: Similar to hickory with a sweet, buttery flavor and great with brisket as well as other cuts of beef, pork ribs, ham, bacon, and poultry; works beautifully with cheese, too.

Trade-Secret Smoke Flavor Boosters

In addition to wood flavor-makers, let me share a few other trade secrets for adding more flavor.

Cinnamon sticks: Unsoaked sticks produce a nutty, sweet rich flavor that adds a warm and complex layer of flavor when added to other woods. It really complements oak, hickory, maple, apple, and whiskey barrels.

Dried spices: Star anise, fennel seeds, and peppercorns add a hint of flavor when added to the fire.

Fresh herbs: Rosemary, thyme, or lavender are great ways to enhance your smoke flavors. Rosemary added to hickory or oak wood when cooking a beef brisket brings out a sweet, aromatic smoke.

Licorice wood: Similar to grapevines, licorice wood produces a mild, nutty flavor that is great with lamb and game, as well as beef and poultry.

Whiskey barrels: Leftover or used whiskey barrels from distilleries are infused with the bold, sweet flavor of whiskey. Tennessee or Kentucky bourbon-whiskey barrels are prized for the sweet smoke they produce and are often the secret ingredient in competition smoke cooking. They're great with all meats, poultry, seafood, cheese, and vegetables.

At the end of the day, it's all about your own barbecue harmony. Whether you decide to use electricity or gas with added wood to create smoke flavor, or layer the smoke flavor with charcoal or hardwoods, it will all be worth it because you will definitely create smoky deliciousness.

Plank Smoking: All the Flavor in Less Time

Plank smoking is a hot, fast way of smoking foods on your gas or charcoal grill. It's not the real art of smoked foods but it adds a true, natural smoke flavor to your foods in a short period of time.

The key to good plank smoking is presoaking the wooden planks. Before placing the plank on your grill, soak it for at least 1 hour—or up to 24 hours—to reduce the chances of it catching fire. You can soak planks in a variety of liquids: water (of course), juice, soda, wine, or even beer. Just place the plank in a large container with your choice of liquid and weigh it down with something heavy so that it stays submerged. Soak the plank for at least 4 hours to allow the flavor to penetrate the wood. Never brush planks with any type of oil; this is literally adding fuel to a piece of wood that can potentially ignite.

TED'S TIP

Bark can impart a bitter flavor to food, so be sure to remove all bark before soaking planks. Bark also tends to ignite more easily than clean wood.

Woods for Plank Smoking

Much like woods used to fuel a fire, the type of wood used when plank smoking affects the flavor of foods. Semi-hardwood or hardwood (western red cedar, maple, and oak) are most suitable for planks, as they have less sap and do not burn as quickly as softwoods. Avoid using softwoods, such as pine, as they tend to produce a bitter smoke.

Alder: Soak in water, chardonnay, sauvignon blanc, Riesling, pinot noir, apple juice, lager, or ale. Alder is great for cooking vegetables, salmon, halibut, arctic char, pork, chicken, and fruit.

Apple: Soak in water, apple juice, apple ale, apple wine, apple cider, chardonnay, pinot noir, or pineapple juice. Use apple planks for planking poultry, fish, shellfish, pork chops and pork tenderloin, veal, and assorted vegetables and fruits.

Cherry: Soak in water, pinot noir, Shiraz, sauvignon blanc, chardonnay, cherry whiskey, cherry cola, or cherry juice. Cherry planks are perfect for venison, beef, turkey, pork chops, pork tenderloin, cheese, and fruits.

Hickory: A hardwood with a bold flavor from the southern United States. It's very much a "good ole boys" kind of wood. Hickory can be difficult to find, so when you do find it buy a ton and hold on to it. It works really well when slowly plank grilling a large cut of meat over low heat. For soaking, use water, beer, bourbon, ginger ale, cola, apple juice, pineapple juice, or cabernet sauvignon. These planks are ideal for pork (ribs, chops, and bacon), turkey, ham, steaks, game (venison, ostrich, buffalo, pheasant), and portobello mushrooms.

Maple: Soak in water, apple juice, chardonnay, cabernet sauvignon, honey brown lager, or even maple-flavored lager. Use for plank grilling poultry (chicken, turkey, duck, and quail), trout, salmon, arctic char, pizza, and steaks.

Mesquite: Mesquite is great for long cooking times due to its thickness. Soak in water, cider, pineapple juice, lemonade, or ginger ale. Mesquite is a strong flavor so it works best with beef, pork, and poultry.

Pecan: Soak in water, strong dark beer (like Guinness stout), cabernet sauvignon, merlot, chardonnay, apple juice, or ginger ale. Pecan is awesome for plank baking desserts, fruits, vegetables, mushrooms, quail, chicken, turkey, and pork.

Red oak: Soak with water, cabernet sauvignon, merlot, India pale ale, grape juice, cranberry juice, or orange juice. Grill beef, game, poultry, cheese, and desserts on this plank.

Western red cedar: Soak in water, chardonnay, hard cider, pilsner, Dr. Pepper, or cherry juice. This plank complements salmon, seafood, cheese, poultry, game meats, beef, pork, veal, and lamb. Cedar is even great for fruits, vegetables, and desserts.

TASTY TIDBIT

Western red cedar is the most commonly used wood to make planks. It imparts a big, sweet smoke that's especially aromatic and is the most versatile for plank grilling.

Assorted wooden planks.

When It Comes to Planks, Size Matters

Planks are available in different sizes and thickness. Thickness is the most important thing to consider when buying planks. The thinner the plank the less amount of time it can stay on the grill.

Use small planks for small portions, wider planks for roasts, and longer planks for longer items like whole sides of salmon. Recipes with a quick cooking time can get by with a thin plank, but a longer cooking time will need either a regular or thick plank.

Every recipe in this book will specify what thickness of plank to use, but the following table gives you an idea of what thickness plank to use with what food.

Types of Planks

Thickness	Maximum Cooking Time	Best Used For
Thin ($\frac{1}{4}$–$\frac{1}{2}$")	15–20 minutes	Mashed potatoes, risotto, vegetables, garlic
Regular ($\frac{3}{4}$")	20–60 minutes	Salmon fillets, fish fillets, steaks, pork loin, ribs, tuna, roast chicken, game
Thick (1+")	60+ minutes	Turkey, prime rib, veal roast, pork loin roast, whole fish

Thin planks tend to warp when heated—and that could lead to your food rolling off the plank and into the grill. To avoid this, place the plank over high heat (without food) for a couple of minutes, turn the plank over, and place the food on the lightly heated side. Hardwoods are less likely to warp than semi-hardwoods, but take this easy precaution just to be safe. Soaking the plank for a longer amount of time also helps prevent the plank from warping.

Where to Find and Buy Planks

When I first started planking nearly 15 years ago, the only place I could get planks was the lumberyard. I would go in, buy a great big piece of wood, and ask the guys to cut it into 10-inch-long planks. All these years later, the lumberyard is still the best place to get planks, but you do have other options.

SAFE SMOKING

Never use treated wood in your smoker—not even if you have a heap of scrap wood left over from a building project or find railway ties on the side of the tracks. The toxins in treated woods are released when heated and will get absorbed into your food, so only use untreated, 100 percent pure, natural wood.

Many grocery stores and gourmet shops carry planks, as well as many home improvement stores. However, they usually only have untreated western red cedar. While cedar is a great wood to plank with, there are so many other wonderful flavors of wood, as you now know! Other varieties might be harder to find, but they're worth it because of the wonderfully different flavors they bring your smoked food. I suggest speaking with your local lumberyard or searching online.

The Least You Need to Know

- Electric and gas-fueled smokers are convenient but don't add any flavor benefits.
- Charcoal is the most flavorful fuel option.
- Hardwood is the best option to create a fire with good smoke.
- Personal preference is the main factor when deciding whether you should soak your wood or remove the bark.
- Plank smoking foods is a tasty and fast way to get a smoky flavor.

Smoking 101

In This Chapter

- Charcoal smoking
- Smoking on gas and propane grills
- Plank smoking
- Safe indoor smoking

Learning the basics of how your smoker works is very important. Most smokers, other than electric and propane, use charcoal as the fuel source. Controlling the fire properly is essential to creating delicious foods because fire is what produces the heat and therefore the smoke, which cooks and flavors your food. It can be tricky, so in this chapter I give you all the inside tricks to help you nail it over time. Before smoking any actual food, I recommend you fire up your smoker and practice controlling the temperature. It's definitely a trial and error kind of situation. If you practice before adding the meat, you won't waste anything.

If you're not up for all the work associated with charcoal smokers, you still have plenty of other options. You can turn your backyard grill into a smoker very easily and inexpensively. And there's plank smoking, which is relatively simple and offers great flavor. You can even smoke in your house on your stove top or in the oven.

No matter what your goals, there is a type of smoking that will suit your budget and your lifestyle. In order to figure that out, you need to know what each type of smoking is, so let's get started!

All You Need to Know About Charcoal Smoking

Smoking with charcoal creates an abundant amount of smoke that deeply penetrates food simply and thoroughly. Using charcoal also provides excellent value when compared to some of the other fuels used to smoke foods. Because it directly impacts your end result, I recommend that you use the best-quality natural hardwood charcoal you can afford, whether lump or briquette. (Flip back to Chapter 3 for more about the different charcoal options.)

How your charcoal is arranged in the smoker plays a large role in temperature control, which as you know, can be the biggest challenge when smoking foods. You want to minimize the number of times you need to open the smoker to refresh the charcoal. To start, fully open the air vents on your smoker or grill, and make a low pile of cold charcoal on the charcoal tray or bowl. The charcoal can be lit in a number of ways: use a chimney starter, a fire starter cube, or an electric starter. We're aiming for a low temperature, so it's important to only light a few pieces of coal in the center of the pile. Doing this will give you a longer overall burn time and better temperature control right from the start.

Charcoal chimney starter with briquette charcoal.

A tried-and-true method for checking the temperature of your charcoal is the "hand test." Hold your hand 1 or 2 inches above the cooking grate and count how many seconds ("Mississippi-style") you can leave your hand there. If you can reach 4 or 5 seconds before it becomes too painful, the coals are ready for smoking. If the coals are so hot that you pull away before you reach 3 seconds, then they're too hot for smoking. If you can comfortably make it to 6 seconds, they're not hot enough yet. There are also visual cues to look for. The hot coals in the center of the charcoal pile should have a nice even coat of gray ash, with a gentle orange glow, before you put meat in the smoker.

It's best to replenish the smoker with hot coals instead of cold charcoal so the smoker can maintain its temperature. Preheat charcoal by placing it in a charcoal chimney, lighting it, and letting it burn until the coals develop a solid coat of gray ash. Add the hot coals to the center of the charcoal tray. Start preheating additional coals—about 10 briquettes or a 1-pound lump—as soon as you notice any decline in the smoker's temperature.

Before you even light the first coal, have a plan in place for putting out the fire when you're done smoking, or in case of emergency. You also need a plan for disposing of the ash and used coals. Ash and charcoal debris can seem to be totally cool but when you remove it from the smoker, there may still be a couple of live bits.

SAFE SMOKING

Always show respect for your fire and be a little afraid of what it could do. A little fear is a useful tool to prevent accidents. Before you start, make sure you have a bucket of water, a heavy-duty galvanized-metal bucket or other heat-proof container, heavy-duty foil, welder's gloves, and a small coal shovel.

If there is no chance that children or pets will come in contact with the smoker, you can use one of these methods to put out the coals:

- Slowly snuff out the charcoal by denying it oxygen. Simply close all the doors and air vents and, within a few hours, the charcoal will extinguish itself.

- Allow the coals to burn down to ash by fully opening all vents and doors. This method has the added benefit of burning off grease and drippings inside the smoker, making cleanup easier.

- Transfer the hot coals to a metal bucket and either douse the coal with water or smother the coals with sand. Keep in mind that soaking hot coals with water will create a plume of steam and fine ash, which might not be appreciated by anyone in its path—or with nearby clean windows.

Disposing of used charcoal is straightforward and simple, but you need to be careful. In a perfect world, you'd be able to leave the charcoal right where it is for 48 hours. But you might have to move them hot, like in a competition setting. If that's the case, start by stirring the coals to spread them out. Pour your bucket of water over the coals as you stir them. Once the coals are cool enough to safely handle, scoop the wood, ash, and debris and place in a metal bucket. When the ash is cool enough to handle, place it on a large sheet of heavy foil and wrap it. If necessary, make two or three of these packages in order to dispose of them easily once the packages have cooled for several hours.

Cold hardwood-charcoal ash is a natural, "green" substance and can be disposed of in the same manner as any other natural material, using proper safety precautions. The ash and small pieces of natural coal can be added to fertilizer or a compost container, or wrapped in foil and disposed of in a noncombustible trash can.

Smoking on Gas and Propane Grills

To effectively smoke on your gas grill, you need to learn how to use its lowest temperature. For single-burner models, start your fire, set the burner to low, close the lid, and wait an hour before checking the temperature. For grills with multiple burners, use an indirect heat method by using only one burner set to low. If your grill has a back burner for rotisserie cooking, don't use this burner. If after 60 minutes your grill is cruising along in a range of 200°F to 225°F, you're looking good. If the grill has reached 250°F or higher within an hour (too hot for most, but not all, smoking), you will have to wedge the lid slightly open to lower the heat. Wind and outdoor temperature could have a significant impact on the temperature inside your grill since most models do not have any insulation. Keep experimenting and tweaking by adjusting the heat until you can maintain a temperature in the smoking zone of 200°F to 225°F.

Cooking over indirect heat means not having the heat source directly under the food being smoked. For gas grills with multiple burners, it's as simple as putting the food over the unlit burners. For single-burner grills, this can be more challenging, depending on the configuration of the burner tube (whether it is a straight pipe or U-shaped). A way to solve this issue is by using a metal heat shield, such as a diffuser, between the grill surface and the heat source.

Smoking ribs on a gas grill with charcoal.

Once you've mastered the temperature control of your grill, it's time to decide how you want to produce smoke. A tried-and-true method is to use a wood-chip pouch. To make an aluminum foil smoking pouch for your grill, just fold a large rectangular piece of foil in half. Open the foil like a book and place wood pellets or presoaked wood chips in the center of one half. Fold over the other side of the foil, creating a pillow-shaped pouch, and crimp the edges together to create a tight seal. Poke several small holes on top.

Place the pouch under the cooking grate and directly over the hot burner. Metal wood-chip boxes and prepackaged smoking cans (small metal cans filled with hardwood chips) are also available. It's important to have your chips in a metal bag, box, or can with only one or two very small vent holes. This will ensure that the chips have enough oxygen to smolder, but not so much oxygen that they ignite and add heat to the grill.

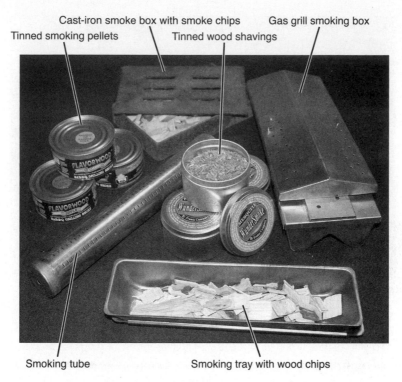

Cast-iron smoke box with smoke chips   Gas grill smoking box
Tinned smoking pellets   Tinned wood shavings

Smoking tube   Smoking tray with wood chips

Assorted gas and charcoal smoking accessories.

Plank Smoking

Plank smoking is another easy way to infuse smoke into your foods without the use of a conventional smoker. You can use a variety of woods for your plank depending on the flavor experience you're going for (see Chapter 3). Plank smoking can be done on a gas grill, charcoal grill, or over an open fire to produce delicious, moist, and juicy smoked foods. Just make sure your unit has a tight-fitting lid to keep the smoke in.

> **TASTY TIDBIT**
>
> Native Americans of the Pacific Northwest have practiced plank smoking for thousands of years.

Compared to conventional smoking, plank smoking uses higher heat to create a very hot smoke to quickly infuse and cook the food. Some may argue that planking is grilling rather than smoking, but I would disagree. True, you could use a grill as the heat source, but the fire heats the soaked wooden plank and creates smoke, which flavors the food as it cooks.

Plank-smoked chicken thighs.

The actual process of plank smoking is very simple. Preheat the grill to the desired temperature. I typically recommend medium heat, about 350°F to 450°F. Place the soaked plank on the grill and close the lid. Preheat the plank for 2 to 3 minutes or until it begins to crackle and smoke, then flip the plank. Carefully open the lid and place the meat onto the plank. Close the lid and let the cooking begin. Check every 4 to 5 minutes to ensure that the plank hasn't caught fire. Should a section of it ignite, use a spray bottle filled with water to put out the flames and reduce the heat to medium-low. Placing a foil pan that is larger than the plank under the grate to catch drippings will reduce the number of flare-ups.

It is important to use caution when plank smoking. Even properly soaked planks can catch fire. Plank smoking is a lot of fun but not if you burn the place down. Smoke is good; fire is bad. Here are a few tips to keep everyone safe:

- Keep a spray bottle filled with water handy to put out small flames.

- Keep a garden hose handy to put out large flames.

- Have a large, metal container filled with water, to throw the plank into if a fire breaks out.

- Have a fire extinguisher nearby, just in case.

- Keep a phone nearby to dial 911—better safe than sorry.

- Wear protective eyewear (swimming goggles, snow goggles, safety goggles, or even sunglasses) to protect your eyes from the smoke when opening the lid or removing the plank.

- Use a sturdy pair of long, well-made grilling tongs that can hold the weight of the plank with food on it.

- Wear thick, heat-resistant barbecue gloves to keep your hands safe.

- Always let the plank cool thoroughly before throwing it out.

TED'S TIP

Not all recipes specify the exact temperature your grill should be heated to because not all grills are the same, but just saying medium-high isn't enough information. Generally when instructed to set the grill to high, it means 550°F or higher. Medium-high is 450°F to 550°F, medium is 350°F to 450°F, medium-low is 250°F to 350°F, and low is 250°F or less.

There's no turning or flipping required, just leave the food on the plank. The heat and the smoke will do all the work so you don't have to fuss. When the food is smoked, carefully remove the plank from the grill and transfer the hot plank to a heatproof platter, baking sheet, or unused soaked plank. This will prevent damage to tabletops or counters, as the underside of the plank will be very hot. I usually use my planks a second time—in the fireplace! I have also cut planks into funky and interesting shapes to use solely for impressive table presentation.

How to Smoke Safely Indoors

With the right equipment and proper safety precautions, smoking food indoors is a great way to prepare healthy, flavorful food all year. It is a fantastic introduction to the world of smoking foods, with a minimal initial cost to get started. There are several different techniques available to infuse smoke into your food. Whether you're looking for an all-in-one solution to quickly smoke fish and vegetables, or equipment that'll let you infuse a deep smoky flavor into a rack or two of baby-back ribs, it's out there.

Stove-top smoking is normally used to achieve a quick infusion of smoke flavor into delicate, fast-cooking foods like fish and vegetables. A properly constructed stove-top smoker will contain the smoke within the cooking chamber. Oven smoking is ideal for foods requiring a longer cooking time and, because the smoke is produced in a completely sealed environment, more of the smoke is absorbed by foods over a shorter period of time.

SAFE SMOKING

Never use charcoal indoors. It produces toxic fumes that can be fatal.

Stove and Oven Roasting Pan–Style Smokers

Smoking foods on the stove or in the oven can be done using purchased indoor-smoking equipment or by making your own using a roasting pan with a small wire rack. Smoke is produced by using a small amount of wood chips arranged in a thin layer in the pan. The wood chips are heated to smoldering point on the stove and the cooking can be completed on the stove or in a preheated oven.

You can buy roasting pan–style smokers that come with everything you need to get started, including wood chips and detailed instructions. The wood chips used for stove-top smoking are usually ground finer than wood chips intended for outdoor use. This is because the goal is to produce smoke quickly using a minimal amount of wood.

To smoke indoors, set a burner at medium to preheat. If you are going to use the oven as well, preheat it to 250°F and set the rack on the lowest position. Arrange a handful of wood chips in a single layer on one side of the roasting pan. Place the wire rack in the pan and top with the food to be smoked. Cover the pan tightly with aluminum foil, but leave one corner slightly open.

Place the side of the pan with the wood chips over the burner. Once the wood starts to smoke, tightly seal the open corner. If you are doing a quick smoke infusion, reduce the heat to medium-low and continue cooking for 20 to 30 minutes. If you are using the oven for a longer smoke, transfer the roasting pan to the oven. Replenish the wood chips every 30 minutes until the food is done to your liking.

Stove-Top Kettle Smokers

Kettle smokers for indoor use (such as those made by Nordic Ware) are all-in-one solutions for stove-top smoking. They give you the ability to smoke larger cuts of meat for hours. Most models on the market have an internal water pan, which can be filled with other liquids (like beer, apple juice, or wine) for an additional infusion of flavor. The temperature inside the kettle is monitored with the installed lid thermometer and is adjusted by simply raising or lowering the heat on the stove burner being used.

Stove-top kettle smoker.

Kettle smokers have an adjustable vent on the lid so that the airflow within the cooking chamber (and around the food) can impart additional flavor compared to other stove-top smoking methods. Just remember that the air vent also lets out smoke, so don't overfill the kettle with wood chips—always follow the manufacturer's recommendations. Make sure your hood fan is turned on and working before putting the kettle smoker on your stove.

Smoking Bags

Ready-made smoking bags are great when all you want is a touch of smoke flavor and easy cleanup. Manufacturers coat one half of the inside of an aluminum pouch with a mixture of wood particles and natural syrup. A perforated ply of aluminum is placed over this coating. When you're ready to cook, the food goes on top of the perforated sheet and the bag is sealed up. It can then be heated in a pan or in the oven. There is very little air in the bag after being sealed, so this method is more like steaming than smoking. It is wonderful for lightly flavoring and steaming fish or vegetables, but it's not going to get the job done if you're looking for deep, smoky flavor.

Turning Your Oven into a Smoker

Using a stove-top kettle smoker or a roasting pan–style smoker are the safest ways to smoke indoors. It is possible to use your oven's cooking chamber as a smoker by smoldering wood chips on a baking tray directly in the oven. Some, including restaurant chefs, use wood chips in a perforated aluminum pouch or external smoke generators plumbed directly into the oven. Keep in mind that oven ventilation and fire-safety systems in restaurants are vastly superior to an average home kitchen. For this reason, I recommend that you leave this method of smoking to the chefs.

The Least You Need to Know

- Charcoal smoking has many steps but they're all easy to master.
- With a few simple adjustments and some know-how, smoking on a gas or charcoal grill can be done with ease.
- Plank smoking is a fast and easy way to achieve smoke flavor.
- There are several options for smoking foods indoors but one must be very careful and have a good-quality, highly functioning hood fan.

Buying a Smoker and Accessories

In This Chapter

- How much money is this adventure worth to you?
- Ask around before you buy a smoker
- Smoking accessories and tools
- Gadgets for the serious smoker

So you want to start smoking some food. Maybe some ribs, a brisket, or maybe some cold-smoked cheese or salmon. Every day, smoked foods are enjoyed around the world. Every day, someone, somewhere, is firing up a smoker to smoke something delicious. Before you start shopping around for a smoker, you should ask yourself a few questions and set some ground rules. This could be a big investment, so you want to make sure you know your stuff before slapping down a pile of cash for something that could end up bringing you more trouble than joy.

How Much Do You Want to Spend?

I'm sure you don't have a money tree in your backyard—I know I don't—which means there is only so much you're willing to spend on a smoker and the accessories to go with it. (It's important you don't forget about the accessories because they help to enhance your food-smoking experience.) I suggest allocating three quarters of your budget on the smoker itself and the remaining one quarter of the budget on the accessories.

Like anything, you can get cheap stuff, pretty good stuff, not-so-cheap stuff, and seriously pricey stuff. When creating your budget, look what you can get in the following price ranges to help you determine how much you should spend. (See Chapter 2 for details on the different kinds of smokers.)

Conservative Budget ($500 or Less)

Don't think that because you aren't spending a ton of money you won't be able to smoke as well as the professionals. Not true. Some of the best smokers are inexpensive. Many electric smokers, water smokers, charcoal kettles, and offset barrel smokers can be purchased for under $500—including some accessories. These types of smokers can be found on the internet and in most big-box stores, hardware or home-improvement stores, and specialty barbecue-supply stores, as well as restaurant supply stores.

Midrange Budget ($500 to $1,500)

Spending a little more will offer you a greater variety of smokers, including commercial units. Kamado-style grills tend to fall into this price range, as well as heavy-duty offset barrel smokers. Besides price, the main difference between the conservative- and midrange-priced smokers is the materials used to make them.

Typically, lower-priced smokers are made from thinner metals. The thicker the metal the more heat will be held inside the smoker. This is great for winter or cold-weather smoking. For example, the thickness of metal on an offset barrel smoker priced at $300 would be quite different from one priced at $1,300. This price range will also offer a larger variety of accessories that go with the smoker to enhance your smoking experience.

Spending Some Bucks ($1,500 to $5,000)

This is for those who want to spend some serious cash on a smoker with some bells and whistles. This range usually means a large smoker with lots of stainless steel that may take up quite a bit of real estate in the backyard. You could even get a small big rig for this kind of money (see Chapter 2). The smokers you get at this price are definitely heavy-duty and have a huge variety of accessories to complement them, but accessories usually cost extra.

Big-Daddy Range ($5,000 and Up)

This price range is for serious heavy-duty smokers. They either come on their own trailer (for competitive-barbecuing folk who want to have it all) or are for use in restaurants or catering kitchens. Smokers above the five-grand mark are not for the amateur.

Whether you spend $150 or $5,000, we're still talking about your hard-earned cash, so make it count. Get the best smoker you can afford that will help you achieve your goals. Don't forget to make sure it suits your lifestyle and the kind of smoking you want to do. Just avoid temptation and don't go into the red when buying a smoker, because then there won't be any money left to buy the meat!

Talk to Anyone Who Will Listen

We all need advice from time to time and if there's anything I've learned, it's that people like to show off how much they know. That's especially true of barbecue enthusiasts. If you're lucky enough to have a friend with a smoker, ask him or her a few questions before you spend your cash. This way you can ask anything you might be embarrassed to ask a stranger in a showroom. Sometimes a good friend can help point you in the right direction.

Talk to anyone who knows food: foodies, smoked-food enthusiasts, chefs, barbecue chefs, barbecue competitors, and food bloggers. Even if they're not experts on smoking foods, they might offer tidbits of information that you'll find useful—whether it's during the shopping process or the cooking stages. It never hurts to ask because it could help you find exactly what kind of smoker you're looking for.

The internet is often the best place to start your search. You can research specific types of smokers or search for info and reviews about a particular brand you're interested in. Also search barbecue or smoking-food forums, because those are the people who do this all the time and can offer you solid advice.

There are numerous reputable websites that can help you find what you're looking for (see Appendix B for a few to get you started). The web is also great for finding recipes, just type in what you want to make and in no time, you'll have found some solid instructions. You might even get inspired to create your own recipes by combining a couple that you found online.

> **TED'S TIP**
>
> One of my favorite places to start my online search is the Naked Whiz (nakedwhiz. com/nwindex.htm). It's a great resource for getting reviews and ratings on about all kinds of products from smokers, to fuels, to wood chips. Another one of the store sites you'll find me visiting often is Ontario Gas BBQ (bbqs.com). They even have a "room" dedicated to charcoal and wood smoking!

Social media websites are another great resource. I can't tell you how many interesting people I've encountered online, how much I've learned, and how much inspiration I've drawn from those avenues. I'm not sure what we did before all this connectivity, but it sure makes figuring stuff out a whole lot easier (and even more eco-friendly). It's a great way to find what you're looking for without ever leaving your home!

Finally, the most obvious way to learn what you need to know before buying a smoker, go to the store and talk to the guys who sell them. A professional smoker-and-barbecue retailer can answer most of your questions. I like going to the specialty stores because this is what they do best. The staff is trained to know what they're talking about, so they can really shine some light on all the varieties out there. Plus, you get to see the merchandise in person. To me, these places are more fun than a toy store is to a kid.

Helpful Smoking Accessories and Tools

Anyone who's been in the barbecue section of a box or specialty store knows just how many accessories there are to go with a grill or smoker. It's easy to go crazy, but we all know you don't *need* a battery-operated grill brush. My must-have list includes: a newspaper, a lighter, a chimney (I can't live without it), a couple of knives, a cutting board, tongs, a thermometer, a spatula, a spray bottle, foil, a few rags for cleaning up spills, and heatproof gloves. That will get you through quite nicely. That said, there are many extras that aren't silly and can really help make the smoking journey a bit easier and more enjoyable. I'll run through some examples of essential fire-starting and temperature-gauging tools. Then I'll get into a longer list of some of the must-have and optional tools and accessories you need to start smoking.

Fire Starters

There are a variety of products on the market to help you get your fire going, and obviously, some are better than others. Here's the 411 on some of the options out there.

Charcoal chimney: Most pros use this tool because it just needs a little newsprint and a lighter to give you the cleanest, longest-lasting fire for the least amount of money.

Electric-coil starter: Build your charcoal starter fire over the coil. When you're ready to start, simply plug it in and eventually the fire is slowly revved up to white hot coals. It's great if you don't like to handle fire and are not in a hurry.

Fire-starter sticks: Wood splints formed into a matchlike starter, these are paraffin-soaked to start the fire easily. I don't recommend them or use them myself, but they aren't the worst of the bunch.

Flamethrower: It's exactly what it sounds like. Some guys like to see sky-high flames when lighting a fire. It's not necessary but, hey, if you love flames, go for it—just use caution!

Liquid fire starters: There's nothing worse than a steak that tastes of nothing but lighter fluid and soot. It is not necessary to use an entire bottle of fluid to start a fire! In fact, don't use it—learn to light a proper fire.

Looftlighter: The latest in high-tech gadgetry, it's a patented device that blows highly heated air to ignite the fire.

Sugar cane–based fuel gel: An all-natural product made from sugar cane with no flavor. If you have to use something other than a few crumpled pieces of paper, this is the starter to use.

SAFE SMOKING

Moving hot coals from a charcoal chimney can be dangerous, so use caution by wearing long sleeves and heavy-duty heatproof gloves to help keep you from getting burnt. Pour the coal slowly into the smoker from a close proximity to the base of the smoker. This will keep sparks to a minimum.

Anyone playing with fire needs to have a hose nearby (or a bucket of water) and a fire extinguisher. Accelerants and electrical fires need different forms of extinguishers, and some fires can't be put out with water because it will actually make the flames increase. If you are going to be playing with accelerants or electrical tools, make sure you have the tools recommended by the product manufacturer for putting out the fire!

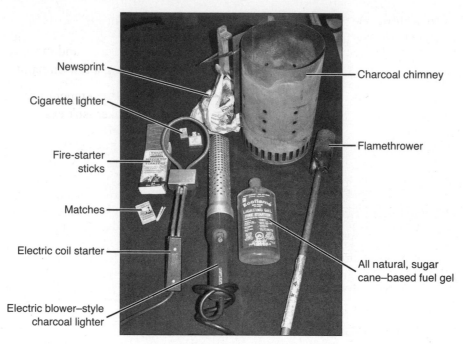

Newsprint

Cigarette lighter

Fire-starter
sticks

Matches

Electric coil starter

Electric blower–style
charcoal lighter

Charcoal chimney

Flamethrower

All natural, sugar
cane–based fuel gel

A variety of different fire starters.

Thermometers

All cooks—beginner, amateur, and pro alike—need to use thermometers when smoking foods. I recommend owning at least three or four different thermometers, and sometimes more than one of each. You'll need at least three different styles for smoking meat.

Digital internal-probe thermometer: These come in a variety of price points. Some are just like a regular probe and give you an instant digital reading. Others you can insert the probe into the meat and leave it there, and attach the readout portion to the smoker. There are also wireless versions that can be carried with you, giving you a constant reading throughout the smoking process. I confess I have a few of these as well.

High-heat thermometer: This is used to test the heat of the fire in your smoker, especially with charcoal or hardwood fires. Tracking your smoking times and temperatures is important because that is information you can use to make changes or repeat successful recipes. It can give you a more accurate cooking time for your meats, too.

Instant-read probe thermometer: These probes come with a sensitive thermometer. They are inserted into the meat at the thickest part, being careful not to come in contact with the bone. Use this probe to double-check your meat and make sure it's done safely and just the way you want it. I recommend having a few on hand.

Oven thermometer: This is another accurate way to take the temperature inside the smoker when the thermometer in the lid or door of the smoker isn't exact. I prefer to have one set inside at the grate level (or even on every shelf of a big rig) because temperature precision is key.

Smoker thermometer: This one stays in the smoker at all times to allow you to monitor the internal temperature of your smoker. Most smokers come with a thermometer built into the lid or door, but remember that it isn't always accurate. It will often give you the temperature in the air space above where the food is.

TED'S TIP

Check the accuracy of your thermometers regularly, at least once or twice a month if frequently used. You can also calibrate your thermometers by setting them in a bowl of ice water for 10 minutes. The thermometer should read 32°F. If it doesn't, it needs to adjusted, if possible; otherwise it's garbage and you need a new one. It pays to spend a bit more on thermometers that are adjustable. Inexpensive instant-read thermometers can get expensive if you replace them often.

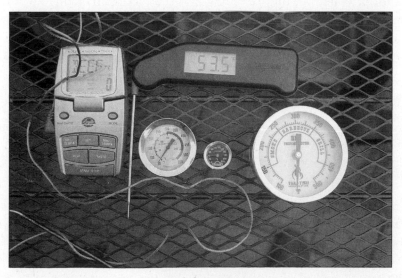

Assorted thermometers.

If you don't want to invest in all these thermometers, you *must*, at the very least, have an instant-read thermometer for checking the doneness of your meats. Nothing ruins a party like giving your guests food poisoning. Although I really do recommend having at least one each of the thermometers listed—if not a few extra thermometers on hand, in case one should stop working. You should have back-up batteries for your thermometers in case they run out of juice while you're smoking, too.

Toolkit for the Frequent Smoker

This may seem like an extensive list, but many of these are things you could (or should) already have in your home—you just didn't know they're part of the smoker's toolkit.

Aluminum foil: A great use for foil is to crumble it up and scrape it on your dirty grates to clean them if you don't have a brush. That's one use and there are too many uses to count, so make sure you always have it on hand. It's a good idea to have a regular 11-inch-wide roll and a heavy-duty 17- to 19-inch-wide roll, too.

Bamboo skewers: Look for long and thick sturdy skewers; they will hold larger amounts of food and require less soaking than flimsy ones you buy at the supermarket.

Basting brush: I like the new silicone basting brushes because you can clean them more easily than classic pastry brushes.

Basting mop: Wherever they're selling barbecue accessories, there will likely be a little mop and bucket kit. (They really do look exactly like an old-fashioned string mop in miniature.) Sometimes you may even find them in the cleaning aisle. This low-tech tool allows for the transfer of lots of mop liquid to the meat.

Blender/hand blender: If you only had one electronic gadget in your kitchen it should be one of these. A good one with a chopper attachment, a whip, and a blender attachment will give you virtually every tool you need to do multiple jobs: chop garlic, mix sauces, blend rub pastes, and—lest we forget—mix cocktails.

Butcher's twine: You never know when you might need to tie up a piece of meat, so a big roll of butcher's twine should always be hanging close at hand.

Cookbooks and magazines: Yes, even a chef looks to other chefs for tips and inspiration, and so should you. (Check out Appendix B for some of my favorite cookbooks.) I also watch for the summer issues of *Popular Plates, Bon Appétit, Food & Wine, Fine Cooking* magazine, *Saveur*, and others that have annual barbecue editions. These periodicals offer reviews of new equipment and recipes that range from beginner to expert.

Cutting boards: Please, please, please: no goofy little, cute color-coded slicing boards. Get yourself at least one nice big board—an 18-inch square is good. Wood or polypropylene, I don't care which (though I prefer wood). Learn to bleach it (and oil it if it's wood). Keep it clean and use it. And you should always put a damp cloth under it so it won't slide when you're using it.

Galvanized-metal bucket: Keep this on hand for holding hot coals removed from your smoker.

Grill brush: You need a sturdy, long-handled wire brush with a built-in scraper. Long, drawn-out smoking means a heavy buildup of ash; it should be cleaned away to prevent fires and gas buildup.

Heatproof gloves: I already mentioned that you need heat-resistant gloves. In fact, I recommend that you get welder's gloves. They're rawhide, which will never burn you even if they get wet. They have a nice long cuff so you can reach into a smoker without burning your arms. A good-quality pair will never wear out.

Heavy-duty, heat-tolerant plastic wrap: You want to use a heat-tolerant variety when you're wrapping meat—like a brisket or casing-less sausage—that is going into a smoker.

Injector: Most injectors look like large hypodermic syringes. Some have reservoirs that will hold as much as 2 cups of liquid for injecting into various meats.

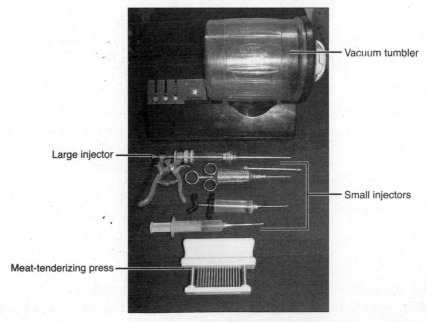

Assorted injectors and other tools.

Knives: You need good-quality knives, at least one of each of the following types: boning, french, paring, fillet, slicing, bread, and a cleaver. You also need a sharpening steel to keep the knives sharp. Learn to use your steel properly and take them somewhere every 6 to 12 months to get the blades ground.

Large bowls: Always use nonreactive materials (metal or glass) because of the high acid content in marinades and brines.

Large pails or bins: Large cuts of meat need to be contained during marinating and brining. Plastic storage bins are great for larger cuts like turkeys and briskets because they have tight-fitting lids. Make sure they'll fit in your fridge before you buy them, though. Reserve these bins for food use only, and always clean them well with hot soapy water before and after each use.

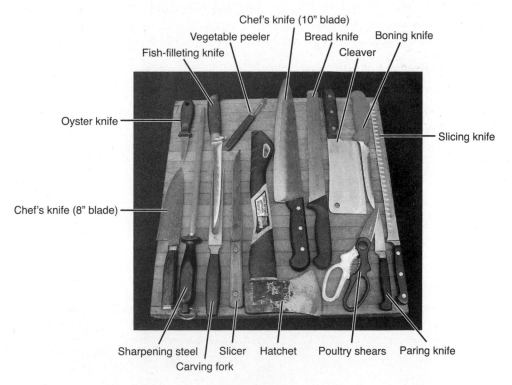

Assorted knives.

Long barbecuing tongs: This is where you need to learn from a chef. Don't go out and buy one of those cute, shiny sets of tools that look best hanging from hooks. You need some long (16-inch) stainless-steel locking tongs. There's nothing sadder than a steak on the ground because the tongs were useless.

Needle-nose pliers: Have a set reserved for cooking only; use them to pull pin bones out of fish fillets.

Nonstick cooking spray: Speaks for itself. It's one of those things I always like to have at hand.

Parchment paper: We smokers use it to make packages (*en papillote*), as well as to line trays or set directly on the grill to cook something fragile, like seafood or other small pieces. Parchment paper is safe up to 400°F before it will begin to smolder.

Rubber gloves: We smokers stick our hands in a lot of stuff, so these will make sure you're keeping clean. Rubber gloves are great for handling raw meat, but make sure you wash them, as you would your actual hands, with hot soapy water.

Smoking bags: These bags are not a must-have but are a great option for a beginning smoker. These bags give a light smoke flavor to foods. You just season the food as desired, place in the bag, then heat on the oven rack, barbecue grate, or directly on the coals.

Spatulas: Look for utensils with long, sturdy handles and a nice big lifting surface. You may actually need two or three spatulas of different sizes and shapes to handle anything from fish to cheese.

Spoons, ladles, measuring spoons, and vegetable peeler: All of these kitchen utensils are necessary to prepare and handle food easily and safely.

Spritz bottle: You gotta have at least one plastic spray bottle for putting out fires and cooling down charcoal—more for flavored spritzes.

Zipper-lock plastic bags: You will see just how much these get used once you hit the recipe chapters (Parts 2 through 4).

 TED'S TIP

Freshly ground whole spices have more flavor than preground spices, so I recommend a mortar and pestle as part of your toolkit. Or for faster grinding, purchase a small, inexpensive coffee grinder to use for spices only.

Gadgets for the More Advanced Smoker

These aren't the tools you'll need when you start your smoking career, but they come in handy as you refine your craft.

BBQ Guru: Very simply, the BBQ Guru is a thermometer-controlled fan that attaches to the smoker. It regulates the temperature to a chosen setting by turning the fan on and off. More oxygen equals higher heat. With the high-end versions, you can control the temperature remotely, up to 600 feet away. And if the temperature drops in the middle of the night, it will fix itself or set off an alarm. With more complex versions, like the DigiQ, you can even program the heat to raise or lower at scheduled times.

Bellows: They're great to stoke a fire or to help get it going. They're not easy to find, but they are a favorite tool for pros.

BBQ Guru digital thermometer.

Cold-smoke generator: Various types of cold-smoke generators exist on the market; some are electric, others are not. Some, like the ProQ cold-smoke generator, stay inside the smoking chamber. Others, such as Smoke Daddy, Inc. cold-smoke generators, pump the smoke into the smoking chamber through a tube. High-quality cold-smoking systems like these are designed to keep the internal temperature of the smoker below 100°F.

Diffuser plates: Typically available from the manufacturer for larger rigs, these are used to provide even heat distribution under large cuts of food to be smoked, such as brisket or a big fish.

Meat grinder: If you want to make sausage, your choices include old-fashioned table-top models sold in every hardware store, or high-tech electric ones that may beckon you at big-box stores these days. You can also get a grinder attachment for a stand mixer, if you have one in your kitchen.

Meat hooks: You want something with a handle sturdy enough to haul out a whole brisket or rack of ribs from the smoker. The stainless-steel shaft needs to be long enough for reaching deep into the smoker or over hot coals so it can haul out what you need.

Meat-tenderizing press: Basically, this is a bunch of needles on a handle that you use to stab meat multiple times. By breaking up connective tissues, this tool allows for deeper penetration of marinades or brines.

Rib racks: There are multiple styles of rib racks, and in this case, you definitely get what you pay for. If you're going to smoke a lot of ribs, look for a heavy-duty rack that handles easily in a hot smoker. You want one that will hold at least four full racks, standing on their side, with clear space between each.

Rib-O-Lator: The Rib-O-Lator is a four-shelf rotisserie attachment, made entirely of stainless steel. It fits on a wide variety of gas and charcoal grills. Advantages over a standard rib rack include more cooking area, a more even cook, and less moisture loss.

Rotisserie: If your smoker will handle a rotisserie, the manufacturer generally has a rotisserie package designed specifically for the machine you are using.

Sausage stuffer: Generally your grinder will include this attachment. If you are going old school, the equipment is at the hardware store. Check out your favorite barbecue-supply store or online. Resist the urge to buy an über-cheap sausage kit. Get the best you can afford.

Smoker boxes: These are designed for use with electric, charcoal, or gas smokers or grills to allow wood chips to smolder instead of burning.

Vacuum tumbler: This accessory is the best way to get a marinade into the meat. The air is removed from the drum, which helps open up the pores of the meat so that the marinade and water can be soaked up. Tumbling allows meat to absorb 10 to 20 percent more water and spice in 20 to 60 minutes than 48 hours of traditional marinating.

TASTY TIDBIT

A kamado-style smoker has a number of specialized accessories to help with the unique design of this type of unit. These include diffuser plates, electric grill starters, tiered racks, ash tools, and grill grippers. If you research these smokers, you'll learn more about these gadgets and their uses.

Although beer and whiskey aren't really tools or accessories, I personally consider them an essential part of a smoker's toolkit. I use a lot of whiskeys (bourbon, Scotch, Tennessee, Canadian, Irish, etc.) in my smoking; it really lends itself to the smoky flavor notes I want to develop.

This is a good starter list of the most popular accessories for smokers. There are more, but some of them are just too silly to list, so use your judgment when buying accessories. Start with ones you think will make your task easier, then treat yourself to other novelty items once your basic smoking toolkit is complete. After all, if you have enough money to buy a truckload of accessories, you might want to re-evaluate and allocate some of that money to getting a more expensive, better-quality smoker. That's the piece of equipment that really matters.

The Least You Need to Know

- You don't need to break the bank when buying a smoker and accessories.
- Do your homework before buying a smoker.
- Many of the basic tools and accessories you need to get smoking are items you probably already have in your home.
- There are a ton of gadgets on the market. You don't have to go crazy and buy them all—unless you want to.

Ted's 10 Commandments for Smoking Foods

In This Chapter

- Be prepared
- Be patient
- No peeking!
- Practice makes perfect
- Take safety precautions
- Above all, have fun!

There it sits, your smoker, poised in its suit of armor ready to be fired up. You've spent the money, you've cursed your way through the assembly manual, and you just want to get the fire hot and start smoking something awesome. Buying a smoker is a big deal, and learning how to get it going for the first time is no easy feat. Just start by taking small steps, one at a time.

When it comes to smoking foods in my backyard, I have a hard-and-fast set of guidelines to help me produce the best-tasting smoked food I possibly can. These 10 commandments will help you get things rolling the first time you fire up your smoker, and every time to follow.

Commandment #1: Be Prepared

The first thing they taught us in Boy Scouts was to always "be prepared." Proper and thorough preparation is very important to successful smoking. As you decide what to smoke, you need to ask yourself: What am I hoping to achieve by smoking this food? What's the occasion? For example, smoking something in order to preserve it is much different than smoking up a great dish for a backyard barbecue or tailgate party. (By the way, my favorite tailgating dishes include ribs, Texas brisket, or a pork shoulder for pulled pork.)

Once you have a plan, it's time to get things moving forward. There are three main areas of preparation needed for good smoking:

1. Prepare the food.

2. Prepare the fire.

3. Prepare the smoker.

It may seem that these steps are obvious, but my point is that you need to plan for each of these before getting started. If you get organized for smoking properly before you start, you will save yourself time and heartache later.

Prepare the Food

Your final result out of the smoker will only be as good as the ingredients you bought to put into it. Always buy fresh, good-quality ingredients—or the best you can afford. Here are a few tips to keep in mind when shopping for foods to cook in the smoker.

> **TED'S TIP**
>
> You should be choosy when selecting your fruits and vegetables as well. Look for bright colors, firm textures, and pieces that are blemish free without any wilting. Don't be afraid to take a whiff; the produce should smell sweet and fresh. The best way to know you're getting good quality is to shop in season and locally. It's always nice to support local farmers whenever possible.

Find a great butcher who will help you pick the right cut for any occasion. Butchers can also trim to your specifications and guide you on fresh versus aged meats—so be nice! Meats with a minimum of 21 days aging are usually more tender than meat that has just been butchered. Always look for meats that are well marbled. Internal fat adds a ton of flavor and will help keep your meats moist and succulent during smoking.

A trustworthy fishmonger is another good person to have on your side, so look for a local fresh-fish market where you can buy good-quality products. Whether you're smoking salmon, tuna, mackerel, or scallops, you want your fish to be fresh, cold, and firm. Fresh will produce better results than frozen or previously frozen items.

Along with getting all your ingredients lined up, you need to review the recipe carefully. Many of my recipes have multiple stages such as brining, curing, and marinating before you even get to the smoker. Timing is very important, so make sure you allow enough time to do all necessary steps. If you want to smoke a chicken for dinner on Saturday, you will need a day for brining and a day for smoking; so plan to start the process on Friday. You may need to get organized a week ahead in some cases, especially if you are working on a big piece of meat. Get out the calendar and make a step-by-step plan!

Prepare the Fire

Before you bring your food out to the smoker, you need to prepare the fire to create smoke. Whether you're cold or hot smoking, timing is key. You need to think about how long your meat will take to smoke and organize your fuel sources and smoking woods accordingly. Make sure you have enough on hand to get you through the entire smoking time, which will be different every time depending on the type of smoker being used and the weather outside. This is another reason why you need to understand your smoker and how it works (see Chapter 2). Be sure you soak the wood chips or chunks in advance so they're ready for you when you need them (see Chapter 3).

Prepare the Smoker

Lastly, fire up your smoker (per the manufacturer's instructions). If this is your first time, please, be sure to read the owner's manual—front to back! It's not just for assembling your smoker; it teaches you the basics of using your new smoker, too. The manual has enormous value, it teaches you about what makes up your smoker, how to use it, and often includes recipes to get you started. Keep it around so you can refer to it at a later date should you run into an issue.

If you take the time to make a plan, gather your resources, and learn about your equipment, you'll be off to the best start possible—every time!

Commandment #2: Be Patient

Every aspect of smoking food takes time, that's all there is to it! Preparing the food is the easy part. Waiting for food to cure, brine, or marinate takes time. Some items could take a week or two to cure. Waiting for foods to smoke and tending the fire to maintain a consistent temperature for even smoking takes time. It takes time for charcoal to heat to the right temperature, for wood chips to soak, and for food to actually smoke. It takes time. This means you need to be patient and give each step the time needed to do each of these things properly. If you have the perseverance to wait it out, you'll discover the passion of creating truly delicious foods.

The more food in the smoker, the longer it will take to finish. Always cook with a thermometer, not a clock.

Not only are you in this for the long haul, but you need to give whatever food you're smoking a lot of attention, too. There's the basting or spritzing, maintaining the proper humidity, and keeping the temperature of your smoker consistent.

Believe it or not, as much as you need to tend to the smoker, there is still a bit of downtime. So here are some tips for passing the time while your food smokes:

- You don't have to sit right beside your unit. Get a digital thermometer that connects to your computer or cellular phone. It will alert you to any changes in the smoker's temperature or the internal temperature of the meat, giving you more freedom to move around the backyard.

- Smoke with a friend. Companionship while you smoke is always fun!

- Let your imagination run wild; think of all the different ways you can serve the food after it's pulled out of the smoker.

Me chillin' in my backyard while my meat smokes.

Waiting for good smoked foods can be very exciting. I think it's like the night before going on vacation. You just want to be there already. In this case, you just want to dig in already! Just don't let your excitement get the better of you; continue to be patient. Remember: good things come to those who wait, and oh boy, it's gonna be good!

Commandment #3: Don't Peek!

Believe me I know, easier said than done. I know how hard it is not to peek. It was one of the things I found most difficult in the beginning, too. You think to yourself: it's harmless, just a quick look to see how things are coming along …. But every time you open any part of the smoker (firebox door, lid or door to the main smoking chamber) you lose valuable sweet smoke, as well as heat (if you're hot smoking). So the more you peek, the longer it will take to smoke. For every 30 seconds the lid is off your smoker or the door is open, you can add approximately 20 minutes to the smoking time. Does it still seem harmless?

Once you have a steady smoke and steady temperature going—keep it closed! Adjust vents to maintain a constant temperature and just let the food hang out to smoke. Get dual-probe thermometers (one for the meat and one for the internal temperature of the smoker) to keep you informed about what is happening inside the smoker and prevent the need for a look-see. Every time you feel the urge to peek, take a sip of beer or your favorite beverage instead. Try setting up a "peeking jar" that you have to put money into every time you peek. At least if you break the rules, you can treat yourself to some cold beer or new accessories for your smoker. Or use the time your food is in the smoker wisely, and spend it preparing your other side dishes or basting sauces. Keep yourself busy. Remember, the less you peek, the sooner you eat!

Commandment #4: Keep 'Er Steady

Keeping your smoker running smoothly at a constant temperature is not as easy as it sounds. It is a little easier if you are using an electric or propane smoker; you can set the temperature digitally. But a charcoal or hardwood smoker is much more challenging.

When you work with a charcoal or hardwood smoker, it is important to monitor the burn time of the charcoal or wood. It may take you a while to understand what works best in your smoker. Keep track of the type of charcoal you use, i.e., lump or briquette, mesquite or hickory, blended or pure charcoal. These all burn at different temperatures and you may find that a particular charcoal works better in your smoker. You need to experiment. Once you figure out which coal works best, it will be a lot easier to manage the temperature in your smoker going forward. The same applies to your wood choice.

Most smokers have some kind of air vent. The vents are the throttles of the natural smoker. Kettle smokers usually have three vents on the bottom of the fire bowl and one on the lid. Offset barrel smokers have a door vent to the firebox and a chimney. By opening or closing the bottom and top vents, you can control the temperature. Open them wide to increase the temperature. Or close them up to varying degrees to either maintain or lower the temperature.

Before you set up your smoker, be sure to monitor the wind direction and position the smoker so the vents and firebox are not pointing directly into the wind. Excessive wind could make it harder to maintain proper low smoking temperatures or it could blow out your fire, if you're using a propane smoker.

When reloading charcoal into the smoker, remember a little goes a long way. Add small amounts of hot charcoal to your smoker, a little at a time, to keep the temperature even. Adding too many hot coals may cause your smoker to spike in temperature. Some folks like to add cold charcoal to the perimeter of the hot coals, allowing the charcoal to heat slowly. This method works well to maintain the temperature but I am not a fan of the flavor that it produces. Charcoal needs to be burned until it is white hot and beginning to form a thin layer of white ash to give off its sweetest smoke flavor. I always say that until it reaches white, it is still raw smoke. Pure smoke should be clear, or with just a hint of white; the darker the smoke, the dirtier the smoke.

The easiest way to maintain the temperature is to use a digital thermometer with a blower fan. There are many different varieties of this tool on the market, but the principal is pretty much the same for each. The fan portion of the accessory attaches to the main vent-control panel on your firebox and a thermometer probe is mounted inside the smoker. Should the temperature drop, the fan starts up and pushes a little even flow of air onto the cooling coals to help boost the internal temperature. On kamado-style grills, these mount on the front of the smoker at the bottom. On box smokers, they attach to the firebox on the side.

Commandment #5: Keep It Moist

It's important to keep the food in the smoker moist. This is especially true when smoking at a hotter temperature to ensure the meat doesn't dry out. The food just needs a mist or spritz to keep it moist and delicious. So go ahead, share your beer with the food in the smoker—it'll make you both happy. Or try injecting meats with water or other liquids—my favorite is butter. Either way it will add moisture and succulence to whatever you are smoking.

TED'S TIP

Many of the recipes in Parts 2–4 tell you to spritz or inject the meat at various points during the smoking process. Do this whenever you need to add more fuel or wood to the smoke, so you limit the number of times you have to open the smoker. Otherwise, it's just peeking with a lousy excuse—and you already know how I feel about peeking.

Humidity is an important factor in smoking foods. I like to keep my humidity levels high in the smokehouse when I hot smoke. Water smokers create humidity relatively easily from a water pan that sits above the fuel and creates steam. That steam blends with the smoke to add flavor and keep meats moist. With other smokers, humidity is created naturally through the design of the smoker. Food will release moisture and create its own humidity. A tightly sealed smoker will keep the heat and humidity in, so avoid venting if trying to maintain that humidity.

Not every food you smoke requires a high humidity level. When cold smoking cheeses, you need a dry smoking environment to keep the cheese from sweating. If it does sweat, it means the smoker is too warm. Humidity can promote mold, so if you are smoking to preserve meats, the less moisture the better. Remove excess moisture by air-drying your meats for 6 to 24 hours before smoking, thus reducing the moisture.

Always pat meats dry with paper towels to remove excess moisture from marinades. Keep meats cold and unwrapped to allow them to dry. Air-drying chicken and turkey before smoking will also produce a crispier skin, which is especially nice when eating wings or drumsticks.

Commandment #6: Keep It Safe and Clean

This is a big one: you always need to make safety a priority when smoking foods. The smoker itself can be dangerous, but you also need to take precautions when handling foods going into the smoker. There are a lot of rules in each of these areas and I'm going to do my best to teach you everything you need to know, so no one gets hurt.

Smoker Safety

Once you've purchased a smoker, you need to decide where you are going to put it. Most smokers for home use are designed to be used outdoors. So that's where you should put it! Place it at least 2 to 3 feet away from the house, and away from windows, in a well-lit and well-ventilated area. Avoid setting it up near trees, shrubs, or flowers. It's never safe to move a hot smoker, so make sure it's where you want it before you fire it up. Make sure you have nothing obstructing the path to the smoker, so you don't trip and fall into it. Always keep children and pets away from the smoker, especially the firebox. Refer to the manufacturer's instructions for more details on safe smoker placement.

Use caution when working with smokers and be sure to have fire-safety equipment on standby just in case. A fire extinguisher, a water hose, and a bucket of water are all good things to have on hand. You never know when or why a fire might get out of control. To protect yourself, you should always tie long hair back and avoid wearing long, flowing clothes. The temperature inside a smoker might not be that hot but, rest assured, the firebox gets red hot! Always wear gloves and use utensils when handling foods or the smoker itself. It's not a bad idea to have a well-stocked first-aid kit nearby to take care of minor burns and cuts.

I always recommend that you never leave your smoker unattended once you fire it up. It is always best to be close in case something happens, so you can react quickly and fix the problem. If you are not around, you risk losing control of your smoker and could end up with overcooked food, spoiled food, or even a roaring fire. It does happen, and always when you least expect it. So get comfy and stay put. I like to smoke with friends; that way someone is always watching the smoker. If you must watch the big game while your food smokes, then do what I did. I made a man cave off my smoking deck. It's fully loaded with the comforts of any garage: beer fridge, draft fridge, liquor cabinet, flat-screen TV, couch, table, chairs, and heat. Everything I need to get me through the long haul. Just make sure you enjoy your adult beverages responsibly, and don't drink so much that you can't maintain a completely safe smoking environment.

Practicing Proper Food Safety

Random cases of food poisoning are rare, but it's almost always caused by poor food-handling practices. Although you can't guarantee that you'll never get sick, you can reduce your chances by taking necessary precautions. Don't take any chances and follow these food handling tips.

SAFE SMOKING

To prevent cross-contamination of foods, never reuse brine or marinade in which you have soaked raw meat, poultry, or fish. If you want to use it for basting during cooking, make a fresh batch or set some aside before adding raw food.

The bacteria that cause foodborne illness are tiny organisms that require conditions like moderate temperature, moisture, oxygen, and a food source to survive and breed. With most micro-organisms, if you eliminate one of these things, you limit their growth. Cooking foods to the proper temperature will ensure that you eliminate the risk of most foodborne illnesses. Once you hit 140°F, you're out of the danger zone. When you reach 165°F, bacteria can no longer survive. One of the best things about smoking, generally speaking, is that by slow-cooking foods over a long period of time, it's likely the food will not only reach a safe temperature, but exceed it. A brisket is a good example: it's cooked to 185°F for slicing or 205°F for shredding. And if that weren't reassuring enough, you take it 20 to 40 degrees higher because you need it to be super tender. Done properly, smoking is a very safe way to cook.

Food safety starts at the grocery store. So here are some tips when shopping for meat, poultry, and fish:

- Always visit the meat and fish departments after you have done all your other shopping so that food spends the least amount of time out of refrigeration.

- Meat and poultry products should feel cold to the touch; if they don't feel cold, don't buy them.

- Grab extra bags in the produce department to store meat packages in to prevent juices from leaking onto other products in your shopping cart.

- Choose packages that are tightly wrapped and have no tears or punctures.

- Choose packages that are dry; liquid is an indication of temperature abuse.

- Check the "sell-by" date and make sure there is enough time to marinate, brine, or cure the product before it expires.

When buying directly from a butcher, your food will not be in packages but the same guidelines apply. Ask to confirm the sell-by dates, if necessary. The meat should be cold, dry, and without a strong odor; strong smells indicate age or improper storage.

Once you get the meat home, get it into the fridge or freezer as quickly as possible. Keeping foods cold will inhibit bacterial growth. It's also important that you maintain a safe temperature in both your refrigerator and freezer. Your refrigerator temperature should be set at 40°F or below to keep foods out of the danger zone. The danger zone, which promotes the growth of foodborne bacteria, is between 40°F and 140°F.

Food Safety Temperatures Chart

Temperature	Status of Bacterial Growth
165°F and higher	Most bacteria die within several seconds.
141°F–164°F	Perfect for holding hot foods and sauces. Bacteria aren't killed, but they don't multiply, either.
40°F–140°F **danger zone**	Bacteria thrive and multiply. Limit exposure of perishable foods to 1 hour or less.
33°F–39°F	Refrigerated food storage. Bacteria aren't killed. They multiply, but relatively slowly. Food is safe here for a limited time.
32°F and lower	Frozen food storage. Bacteria aren't killed, but they don't multiply, either.

I recommend removing meats from the foam trays they're sold in before storing in the fridge. Rinse the meat under cold water (except for ground meats), pat dry with paper towel, and then wrap loosely with wax paper. This allows the surface to dry, making it less likely that bacteria will grow. Place meat on a plate or tray to catch drippings before putting in the coldest part of the fridge. The bottom shelf is ideal because if there is a spill, it won't contaminate any other foods items below it.

Remove fresh meat and poultry from their original packaging and rewrap them tightly using freezer paper or zipper-lock plastic freezer bags before placing in the freezer. Try to remove as much air as possible to prevent condensation, which causes freezer burn. Always thaw frozen meats in the refrigerator, not at room temperature.

The following table gives some information on refrigerator storage. The recommended storage times are based on a refrigerated temperature of 37°F.

Meat, Poultry, and Fish Storage Guidelines

Food Item	Recommended Storage Time
Beef, lamb, pork, veal, and game (most cuts)	3–5 days
Ground meats	2–4 days
Variety meats (liver, heart, etc.)	1 day
Chicken, turkey, duck, and game birds	2 days
Ground poultry	1–2 days
Fish (steaks and fillets)	1–2 days
Shellfish	1–2 days

The times specified in this table are guidelines, but always use your best judgment and common sense, even if it contradicts the table. If you doubt the safety of a piece of meat, discard it. I know it's painful to throw away an expensive cut of meat, especially if you're unsure, but it's not nearly as painful as knowing you've given someone food poisoning.

One of the biggest causes of food poisoning is cross-contamination. Follow these tips to prevent it:

- Always wash your hands, cooking utensils, work surfaces, and cutting boards with hot, soapy water before and after handling raw meat, poultry, and seafood.

- Never place cooked foods on an unwashed cutting board or surface that previously held raw meat. (You can use the same cutting board, just make sure it has been thoroughly cleaned before placing cooked food on it.) The safest practice is to have several cutting boards that are assigned to specific jobs. Use one for raw meats, poultry, and fish; one for cooked foods; one for vegetables; and one for fruits and other sweet ingredients.

TASTY TIDBIT

The pink smoke-ring near the surface of smoked meat is a result of nitric oxide from the smoke interacting with hemoglobin in the meat. It's a good thing.

- Cook all meat and poultry products to safe internal temperatures to eliminate any harmful bacteria (see the following table). Using a thermometer is the only way to be certain that your meat and poultry are cooked to the proper temperature; color and clear juices are not a safe indicator of doneness.

The U.S. Department of Agriculture (USDA) says the following temperatures will produce safely cooked, but still flavorful meats.

Internal Temperatures of Safely Cooked Meats

Meat	Internal Temperature
Ground beef, veal, lamb, and pork	160°F
Beef, veal, and lamb—roasts, steaks, and chops (medium-rare)	145°F
Beef, veal, and lamb—roasts, steaks, and chops (medium)	160°F
Beef, veal, and lamb—roasts, steaks, and chops (well-done)	170°F
Pork—roasts, steaks, and chops (medium)	160°F
Pork—roasts, steaks, and chops (well-done)	170°F
Ham—raw, cooked before eating	160°F
Ham—fully cooked, to reheat	140°F
Ground chicken or turkey	165°F
Whole chicken or turkey	185°F
Chicken or turkey—breasts, roasts	165°F

For more information call the USDA Beef and Poultry Hotline at 888-MPHotline or 888-674-6854.

Get all leftovers into the fridge as soon as possible and, once they're chilled through, wrap them tightly. You can speed up the chilling process by dividing large quantities into smaller portions or spreading food out into a thin layer. Generally, meat and poultry leftovers can be stored in the refrigerator for up to 3 days and in the freezer for 1 month. And always remember the golden rule: when in doubt, throw it out!

Commandment #7: Practice, Practice, Practice

The more you practice your smoking techniques the easier they become and the better your results will taste. Take it from me! I practice a lot; in fact, every time I fire up a smoker, I consider it another practice session. Every time you smoke, it's a chance to improve on what you did last time and create new flavors that will make you and your guests deliciously happy.

There are a few things to practice in order to get really comfortable and confident with your smoker. First is learning to start the fire. Practice starting fires for charcoal or hardwood smokers in a variety of different ways. You will eventually figure out which works best for you. Some starters are designed not only to light the fuel but to do it quickly. Time how long it takes for lump charcoal to reach the perfect white-hot temperature and compare it to the timing for briquette charcoal. After it is started, learning to control the fire will make smoking food much easier, so practice adding fuel and working the vents. Remember, with charcoal, less is often more. You don't need a lot of charcoal to generate a lot of heat.

You can also experiment with different woods to create different smoke flavors and find out which sweet smoke flavor you like best. Practice with soaked and unsoaked wood chips, and compare chips to chunks or logs (see Chapter 3 for details on all the options). There's also bark and no bark to play around with. All of these factors contribute to the essence of the smoke that will flavor your foods. Try a few different combinations until you find your favorite blends.

TASTY TIDBIT

I have 100+ smokers in my backyard. For me to really understand how each smoker works I have to practice—a lot! Based on my own experimentation, I have determined the right smoker for specific foods. For example, I use my charcoal box smoker for the best pulled pork, my electronic smoker for perfect cold-smoked cheddar cheese, and my offset barrel smoker for pretty wicked ribs and wings.

Also try out various temperatures. The lower the temperature the longer it takes to smoke, and the hotter the temperature the faster it'll smoke. Both can have great results but through practice you will find a balance that best suits your tastes. Practice your recipes by making adjustments and tweaking them as you move along to create your own version of smoked perfection.

Should you run into issues during your practice sessions that you're unsure how to fix, just turn to the experts. Your smoker manufacturer's website should have a lot of information and associates to assist you. The internet is full of wonderful information and people who can help troubleshoot. There are many great smoking and barbecue professionals online who are willing to share what they know. I know I am, so check me out at tedreader.com and hopefully I can help you. Get out there and practice smoking something delicious!

A smoked prime rib of beef on olive branches in a kamado-style smoker.

Commandment #8: Take Notes

I have a fantastic memory, but as I get older I'm finding that it's not as good as it once was, so taking notes and keeping a journal of what I've done is important. It allows me to accurately recall what I did so I know what adjustments to make for next time, or how to exactly duplicate it. Keeping track of what you have done will only help make you a better smoker.

Here is an example of one of my entries:

Recipe Name: Smoked Boston Butt

Butt Weight: 13.5 lb. (1 butt, bone-in)

Brine: Basic Brine

Brine Time: 24 hours

Rub: Ted's World Famous Bone Dust BBQ Seasoning Rub, 12 hours

Wood Smoke: Blend of hickory, apple, and maple chunks (equal parts)

Soaked or Unsoaked: Soaked

Smoker: Offset Barrel Smoker

Charcoal: Basques Sugar Maple Lump Charcoal, 15 to 20 lb.

Starter: Charcoal Chimney

Spritz: Apple Jack

Injection: None

BBQ Accessory: Spray Bottle

Smoker Temperature: 200°F

Vent: Variable

Outside Temperature: 65°F

Weather: Slightly cloudy and drizzling with a slight wind from the northeast

Smoking Environment and Activity

	Hr 1	Hr 2	Hr 3	Hr 4	Hrs 5/6	Hrs 7/8	Hrs 9/10	Hrs 11/12	Hrs 13–15
Smoker temperature (°F)	220	200	235	220	200	200	200	185	225
Meat temperature (°F)	56	75	88	113	122	145	160	185	205
Spritz	x	x	x	x	x	x	x	x	x
Added charcoal		x		x		x			
Added wood	x	x	x	x	x	x	x		
Beer	x		x		x	x		x	x
Vents	open	½	open	½	¼	¼	¼	¼	¼

Always leave yourself some space on the sheet where you can jot notes and record ideas for next time as they come to you. Make notes on how it looked, how it tasted, and what you might do differently.

Take pictures of the food throughout the entire process. This will give you a more accurate account of how the meat looked during the different stages of cooking.

Commandment #9: Make It Tasty

It's easy to get lost in all the planning and variables when smoking foods, but let's not forget what our main objective is here—making tasty food! Here are some clues on how you will know if your smoked foods are tasty. It's tasty when …

- The bone twists easily from the meat on a smoked pork shoulder; it's ready for pulling.

- You come in the house and your spouse says you smell … of smoke.

- There is nothing left but empty plates and full bellies.

- A hot smoked scallop melts in your mouth like milk chocolate.

- A smoked brisket oozes juicy goodness, leaving a puddle on your plate that needs to be sopped up with some fresh bread.

- After eating your smoked feast you need a shower instead of a napkin.

- Your neighbors are drooling to come over for a nibble.

- The local firefighters show up because they saw smoke.

- Your family's eyes are rolling into the back of their heads while they tell you it was delicious.

The addition of aromatics makes for some tasty smoking, so scatter fresh herb sprigs (rosemary, thyme, or lavender) onto the hot coals in your smoker to add a flavor boost to the food you're smoking.

Commandment #10: Have Fun!

You're in this to create delicious food, but you should be having fun while you're doing it. I love food and I truly enjoy the work that goes into preparing it. Whether I'm grilling something over hot coals or smoking something low and slow, I'm always having a good time. So relax and don't get stressed out.

My barbecue rig parked in the lake. Why in the lake? Because I could. It was one very hot day and this was the easiest way to keep cool.

Smoking food in your backyard is meant to be enjoyable. The sweet smell of smoke, tending the fire, and smoking food to delicious perfection—that's what it's all about. It's a rewarding hobby and your whole family can savor the results. So enjoy yourself: grab a buddy, have a refreshing beverage, and get smoking. Cheers!

The Least You Need to Know

- Take the time to be thoroughly prepared before smoking to save time and frustration.
- Smoking foods takes a long time, so be patient and avoid peeking to maintain a constant temperature.
- Always keep safety, with both smoker and food, in mind.
- Practicing and recording your smoking adventures will help to make you a better smoker.
- A job well done is only measured by how tasty the food is and how much fun you had while preparing and smoking it.

Layering the Flavor

Smoking dries food, so that's why we take steps to combat this—like brining, marinating, and curing. Adding flavor to your food at the beginning is going to make a huge difference at the end. We slather spice rubs and pastes all over the food—and inject flavor into the food as well—to add the next layer of flavor. Finally comes sauces, bastes, and spritzes—because they're added last, these flavors are the most detectable. That's why you want to use something that complements the other flavors you've already used in the previous steps.

The marinades, cures, rubs, spritzes, and more in these chapters are good starting points for each of these techniques, and can be used for years to come. But don't be afraid to add your own personal touches or make adjustments according to your likes and dislikes. This is your rodeo and you call the shots.

Brines, Marinades, and Cures

In This Chapter

- Keeping meat tender and juicy with brines
- Imparting flavor with marinades
- Preserving meat through curing
- Recipes for flavorful brines, marinades, and cures

Slowly smoking meat—whether beef or poultry—is a slamming way to enhance the natural flavor of your beast of choice, and it's natural to want to build on those flavors. Brines, marinades, and cures help do that.

Layering and building flavor is a skill that needs constant practice. You'll never know all the possible flavor combinations out there, but don't worry—you'll have a good time experimenting. I've provided you with several recipes for layering flavors with suggested pairings at the end of this chapter, but ultimately you know your likes and dislikes better than anyone, so go with what sounds good to you. Just don't get too carried away because the goal is to enhance the meat's flavor, not mask it with seasonings.

Take your time with the flavoring steps and think them through. Make sure the next step complements the last step. If you're really into layering flavors, try keeping a smoking journal. Write down what you do each time to remember what worked so you can build on it. Be sure to also jot down what didn't work so you don't do it again! The day you were inspired to add Dr. Pepper to a marinade is as important as the day you oversalted the chicken. Each note will make you a better flavor specialist.

Brines

Brines are salty solutions that help lean meats hold their moisture and stay juicy and tender during cooking. They often have other components—such as beer, sugar, herbs, and spices—but they don't add much flavor to the end result. Salt is what penetrates and softens the protein strands, making the meat moist and tender. Lean meats without much marbling, notably poultry and pork, will hold their moisture and be more tender if brined before cooking—even if they're overcooked. Because they are so lean, I almost always recommend brining chicken and turkey, otherwise the length of time needed for smoking could severely dry them out.

First, the salt in brine draws out the water content of meat. Salt will then dissolve itself in the natural water content of meat while softening its proteins. There is a change in the actual cells of the meat as it absorbs salt through brining. It will first expel, and then draw and hold more water than it originally contained, so the meat stays moist during a long smoke.

 SAFE SMOKING

Always store raw meat in the refrigerator when brining, marinating, or rubbing.

Always use a container large enough to keep the meat submerged in the brine. You need to weigh down the meat so that it's constantly submerged because any exposed meat will breed bacteria. Position a heavy plate right side up over the meat or top with a heavy, moisture-proof object—such as a clean, foil-lined brick or a large can of tomatoes—to weigh down your meats in the brine.

Most brine times range from 12 to 24 hours. This is relative to how long it takes the brine to penetrate into and break down the meat tissues. Here is a trick you can use to save time and refrigerator space. By injecting the brine into several different areas in the meat, you can cut hours off brine time. The time varies depending on the cut and the size of the meat. A brine-injected chicken only needs 20 minutes, whereas a pork shoulder will need about 4 hours … but that's much faster than submerging for 24 hours. (See Chapter 8 to learn more about injecting meat.)

Timing your brine depends on the type of protein. Fish should be brined no longer than 30 to 90 minutes because it will become too salty. Most meats in the 6- to 10-pound range will do fine with an overnight brining of 12 to 18 hours. Large cuts of meat such as turkeys, brisket, and shoulders need a combination of injection and submersion and can be held for 18 to 24 hours (but no longer!). Brining for too long will result in the opposite of what you are going for. Eventually, the salt will draw out all the water from the meat cells and you will end up with a very dry, overly salty dinner. Refer to the table later in this chapter for guidelines on how long to brine different meats.

The standard ratio of a brine shouldn't exceed $\frac{1}{2}$ cup salt to 4 cups liquid. Always rinse meat under cold running water to wash off excess salt and dry with a paper towel before progressing with the next flavoring step.

Marinades

Marinades will tenderize meats, but they only really penetrate about $\frac{1}{8}$ inch into the flesh. That's why tough cuts get a little longer marinating time; it's the best way to ensure you get a tender end result. Keeping meat in a marinade longer isn't going to help—it's actually going to make it worse. After a certain point, the marinade will work against the meat by drawing out all the moisture, creating a tough and grainy texture. Refer to the table later in this chapter for guidelines on how long to keep meats in marinades. A good marinade can add some good, strong flavor, though. These flavors will develop in the refrigerator, but they also continue to develop during the smoking process. Fish and poultry absorb more flavor from a marinade than denser cuts like beef, pork, or lamb.

Marinades always include salt and some type of acid. The acidic component can be as simple as lemon juice or it can be wine, vinegar, citrus juices, alcohols, or even some dairy products like yogurt or buttermilk. Sugar and honey or other sweet ingredients aid in balancing out the acidic ingredients and also help produce a flavorful crust on the surface of the smoked meat. Of course, you also need other aromatic flavors like oils, herbs, spices, garlic, and/or any other flavoring agents that strike your fancy.

You can (and should!) bring out your best friend the injector to add flavor deep into the meat (see Chapter 8 for more on injectors). You can even periodically inject during a long smoke to help keep the meat moist.

SAFE SMOKING

For food safety, never inject marinade into the meat during the last half hour of the smoke, or baste with it during the last 10 minutes, to avoid any possibility of bacterial contamination.

Cures

Curing is a term basically used for saving or preserving meat. It covers processes such as drying, salting, and smoking. Applying a dry cure to meats is a way to control moisture and flavor. When applied to homemade meat products, the term often refers to preserving with salt and nitrite. I don't like using nitrites, nor do I care for some of the other commercial preservatives like ascorbate and erythorbate. Meat cured only with salt has a better flavor and will have a slightly darker color than commercially cured products, but at least its chemical free. The curing compound penetrates through meat and draws out moisture; this reduces the weight of the end product, which concentrates the flavor so a darker color results.

There are quite a few factors to consider when determining a cure's formulation and the amount of time to let a meat stand in the cure. A higher salt content in the cure mixture will speed up the process, but the larger the piece of meat, the longer it will take to cure. A fattier cut of meat will also increase the amount of time it needs to sit in the cure. And of course, the moisture content of the specific type and cut of meat will impact the amount of time it takes to cure sufficiently. The more moisture a meat has to begin with, the longer it will take. Acid or alkaline levels in the meat will also affect the amount of time it needs to stay in the cure (a lower PH level will result in a faster cure)—but we don't need to go quite that deep. The following table gives guidelines for how long to cure different meats.

The longer you want to keep the meat, the longer it will need to stay it in the cure. Meat cured strictly for preservation can be hung to dry for as long as a year. The result is a piece of meat that will be safe at room temperature for lengthy periods of time—like Italian prosciutto, for instance. However, the cures in this book are basically just another form of flavoring. When it comes down to it, we're using a mixture that includes the seasonings of a rub and the salt of a brine. We aren't going to leave the meat in a cure anywhere near as long as we would if we needed to preserve it for a year. Our purpose is to reduce the moisture in the meat and create a concentrated flavor that complements a smoky flavor. I encourage you to give it a try. Once you've mastered a couple of recipes, you may be inspired to try your own!

Timing Guidelines for Brining, Marinating, and Curing

Type of Protein	Cut	Weight (approx.)	Brine Time	Marinade Time	Cure Time
Beef	Back ribs	1½–2½ lb.	-	24 hrs	-
	Short ribs	1–2 lb.	-	24 hrs	-
	Tenderloin, whole	2 lb.	-	24 hrs	-

Type of Protein	Cut	Weight (approx.)	Brine Time	Marinade Time	Cure Time
	Tri-tip roast	2–3 lb.	-	24 hrs	-
	Top sirloin roast	10 lb.	-	24–48 hrs	-
	Prime rib roast	4–6 lb.	-	24–48 hrs	-
	Brisket, whole	8–12 lb.	24–48 hrs	24 hrs	8–12 days
	Brisket, half	4–6 lb.	24 hrs	24 hrs	6–8 days
	Flank steak	2 lb.	48 hrs	48 hrs	-
	Steak	12–16 oz. (2" thick)	-	8 hrs	-
Veal	Chop	8–12 oz.	-	4–6 hrs	-
Pork	Loin	3–5 lb.	24–36 hrs	24 hrs	-
	Shoulder	6–8 lb.	24–48 hrs	24 hrs	-
	Ribs	1½–3½ lb.	12 hrs	12 hrs	-
	Tenderloin	1½–2 lb.	12 hrs	12 hrs	3–6 days
	Belly	10–12 lb.	24–48 hrs	24 hrs	5–10 days
Lamb	Rack	1–2 lb.	-	6–8 hrs	-
	Leg (boneless)	4–9 lb.	-	24 hrs	-
	Shoulder	1–2 lb.	-	24 hrs	-
Chicken	Whole	4–6 lb.	24 hrs	24 hrs	-
	Half	2–3 lb.	24 hrs	24 hrs	-
	Breasts (boneless)	4–8 oz.	12 hrs	6–8 hrs	-
	Breasts (bone-in)	6–12 oz.	12 hrs	6–8 hrs	-
	Thighs	5–8 oz.	12 hrs	6–8 hrs	-
	Legs	4–8 oz.	12 hrs	6–8 hrs	-
	Wings (approx. 12)	1–2 lb.	12 hrs	6–8 hrs	-
	Cornish hen	1–2 lb.	12 hrs	6–8 hrs	-
	Quail	6–10 oz.	6–8 hrs	4 hrs	-
Turkey	Whole	14–18 lb.	24–48 hrs	24 hrs	-
	Breast (boneless)	5–7 lb.	12–24 hrs	12 hrs	6–8 days
	Leg/thigh	2–4 lb.	12–24 hrs	12–24 hrs	-

continues

Timing Guidelines for Brining, Marinating, and Curing   (continued)

Type of Protein	Cut	Weight (approx.)	Brine Time	Marinade Time	Cure Time
Duck	Whole	4–6 lb.	24 hrs	24 hrs	-
	Breast (boneless)	5–7 oz.	12 hrs	12 hrs	4–6 days
Fish and Seafood	Fish (fillet or steak)	8–16 oz.	30 min	15 min	2–4 days
	Shellfish	1–2 lb.	30 min	15 min	2–4 days
	Salmon, whole	5–8 lb.	12 hrs	2–3 hrs	6–10 days
	Salmon, side	2–5 lb.	12 hrs	30 min	3–4 days
	Salmon, fillet	6–12 oz.	30 min	15 min	2 days

Basic Brine

A standard brine consists of two main ingredients: water and salt. I prefer kosher salt to iodized salt, because I find it gives the brines a cleaner, less salty finish. A good rule of thumb is for every 4 cups water, add ¼ cup kosher salt, but be careful when scaling up this recipe because it can easily become too salty.

Yield:	Prep time:	Cook time:
8 cups	5 minutes	30 minutes

8 cups cold water   ¼ cup granulated sugar
½ cup kosher salt

1. Place cold water in a stockpot or large saucepan set over high heat. Cover and bring to a rolling boil. Stir in kosher salt and sugar until dissolved. Return to a boil and remove from heat.

2. Cool to room temperature. Cover and refrigerate until chilled through. Use this brine with pork or poultry.

SAFE SMOKING

Be sure to allow the brine to cool to room temperature before placing it in the refrigerator. Placing very hot items into the fridge will increase the air temperature and can cause food to spoil. Cold food into a cold container is a good, safe rule to cook by.

Apple-Honey Pig and Bird Brine

Sometimes salt and water are just not enough! I find that apple and honey add a little sweetness to any cut of pork or poultry, and fresh herbs make all the difference. So if you can get 'em, use 'em.

Yield:	Prep time:	Cook time:
12 cups	20 minutes	40 minutes

8 cups cold water

6 cups apple juice

¾ cup kosher salt

½ cup buckwheat honey

¼ cup freshly cracked black peppercorns

¼ cup chopped fresh parsley leaves

8 cloves garlic, chopped

1 medium sweet onion, chopped

1 (3-in.) cinnamon stick

2 TB. chopped fresh rosemary leaves

2 TB. chopped fresh thyme leaves

1 TB. crushed red pepper flakes

1 tsp. cumin seeds

1. Combine cold water and apple juice in a stockpot or large saucepan set over high heat. Cover and bring to a rolling boil. Stir in kosher salt, buckwheat honey, black peppercorns, parsley, garlic, sweet onion, cinnamon stick, rosemary, thyme, red pepper flakes, and cumin seeds. Return to a boil; remove from heat.

2. Cool to room temperature. Cover and refrigerate until chilled through. Use this brine with pork or poultry.

TED'S TIP

Experience has shown that allowing the brine to chill for 24 hours before pouring over your pork or poultry of choice really allows the flavors to meld, resulting in a more flavorful end result.

Juicy Citrus Brine

This brine is chock-full of fresh fruit, making it pretty intense. All those bright and fresh flavors marry beautifully with the smoke to make a memorable meal. Enjoy!

Yield:	Prep time:	Cook time:
16 cups	45 minutes	40 minutes

1 ripe pineapple, peeled, cored, and chopped

8 cups cold water

4 cups white grape juice

3 oranges, zested and juiced

3 lemons, zested and juiced

3 limes, zested and juiced

3 green onions, chopped

2 to 3 red Thai or bird chile peppers, chopped

¾ cup kosher salt

½ cup firmly packed light brown sugar

¼ cup chopped fresh thyme leaves

2 TB. freshly cracked black pepper

1 TB. minced fresh ginger

1. Place pineapple chunks in a blender. Purée, adding up to ½ cup cold water, until smooth. Transfer to a stockpot or large saucepan, and add remaining 7½ cups cold water and white grape juice; set over high heat. Cover and bring to a rolling boil.

2. Stir in zests and juices of oranges, lemons, and limes; green onions; red Thai chile peppers; kosher salt; light brown sugar; thyme; black pepper; and ginger. Return to a boil; remove from heat.

3. Cool to room temperature. Cover and refrigerate until chilled through. Use this brine with pork, poultry, and seafood.

TED'S TIP

You don't need to set aside a lot of time for using this brine because pineapple juice is very acidic and therefore breaks down meat proteins very quickly. I recommend a maximum of 20 minutes for seafood; 4 to 6 hours for chicken, duck, and other game; and 8 to 12 hours for turkey. As for pork and other cuts of hearty meat, I recommend no longer than 12 hours or else this brine will devour your meat—and not in a good way!

Maple Whiskey Brine

The flavors of maple and whiskey work wonderfully together. Use a whiskey that's a little sweeter, like bourbon or a Tennessee whiskey.

Yield:	Prep time:	Cook time:
12 cups	10 minutes	30 minutes

12 cups cold water

4 cups Tennessee whiskey

2 cups maple syrup

½ cup packed light brown sugar

2 TB. mustard seed

2 TB. freshly cracked black pepper

1 TB. cracked coriander seed

4 cloves garlic, minced

¾ cup kosher salt

1. Combine cold water, Tennessee whiskey, maple syrup, light brown sugar, mustard seed, black pepper, coriander seed, and garlic in a stockpot or large saucepan set over high heat. Cover and bring to a rolling boil. Stir in kosher salt until dissolved. Return to a boil and remove from heat.

2. Cool to room temperature. Cover and refrigerate until chilled through. Use this brine on beef, game, poultry, and pork (especially brisket, tri-tip, and pork loins).

Variation: Boiling whiskey in the brine cooks off the alcohol, which produces a less boozy flavor. If the kick of alcohol is what you're looking for, add whiskey after kosher salt and remove from heat immediately.

Dark Ale Marinade

Nice, dark ales with a smooth drinking flavor are the best choice for this marinade. The more bitter ales will overpower the meat you're smoking, and the goal is to enhance the meat's flavor, not take over.

Yield:	Prep time:
5 cups	20 minutes

2 (12-oz.) bottles dark ale

1 cup malt vinegar

4 cloves garlic, minced

2 jalapeños, minced

2 bay leaves

1 large yellow onion, minced

¼ cup Worcestershire sauce

2 TB. fresh, coarsely ground black pepper

2 TB. packed light brown sugar

2 TB. vegetable oil

1 TB. kosher salt

2 tsp. hot English prepared mustard

1. In a large bowl, stir dark ale, malt vinegar, garlic, jalapeños, bay leaves, yellow onion, Worcestershire sauce, black pepper, light brown sugar, vegetable oil, kosher salt, and English mustard until well combined and sugar has dissolved.

2. Store, tightly covered, in the refrigerator for up to 1 week. Use this marinade with red meats.

TED'S TIP

Always have plenty of cold beer on hand. This way you'll be able to resist the temptation to drink the marinade—you can leave that for the meat and just grab yourself a fresh, cold one!

Cubano Mojo Marinade

Seville oranges give this marinade true Cuban flavor. The robust flavor of the cumin with the chile peppers makes a great combination, but it's the addition of citrus that makes it a real tropical experience.

Yield:	Prep time:
2 cups	20 minutes

1 cup Seville orange juice	2 tsp. granulated sugar
¼ cup lemon juice	2 tsp. freshly ground black pepper
¼ cup olive oil	1 tsp. ground cumin
1 head fresh garlic, finely minced	1 tsp. kosher salt
½ cup chopped fresh oregano leaves	1 tsp. crushed red pepper flakes

1. In a large bowl, combine orange juice with lemon juice, olive oil, garlic, oregano, sugar, black pepper, cumin, kosher salt, and red pepper flakes until well combined.

2. Store, tightly covered, in the refrigerator for up to 1 week. Use this marinade with chicken and seafood.

Variation: Seville oranges, which have a slightly bitter flavor, or sour oranges work best for this recipe. If they're not available, replace with ¾ cup fresh orange juice and ¼ cup fresh lime juice.

TED'S TIP

Try using orange charcoal and citrus wood chips to smoke your chicken or seafood—it really adds to the tropical flavors.

Dragon Marinade

The combination of hot chiles with the sweetness of hoisin sauce and mirin makes this marinade very spicy, but you can control the level of heat by adjusting the amounts of spicy ingredients. For a tame marinade, reduce the amount of fresh chiles, chili sauce, and/or hot sauce. If you like it crazy-spicy, just add more of all those ingredients—but be careful not to pop your top!

Yield:	Prep time:
1¼ cups	20 minutes

1 cup finely chopped fresh cilantro leaves

½ cup naturally brewed soy sauce

¼ cup fresh lime juice

3 green onions, finely chopped

2 to 3 red Thai or bird chile peppers, minced

2 TB. hoisin sauce

2 TB. rice wine vinegar

1 TB. light brown sugar

1 TB. vegetable oil

1 TB. mirin (rice wine)

2 tsp. sambal red chile sauce

2 tsp. Thai Sriracha hot sauce

½ tsp. fish sauce (optional)

1. In a large bowl, stir cilantro, soy sauce, lime juice, green onions, red Thai chile peppers, hoisin sauce, rice wine vinegar, light brown sugar, vegetable oil, mirin, sambal red chile sauce, Thai Sriracha hot sauce, and fish sauce (if using) until well combined.

2. Store, tightly covered, in the refrigerator for up to 2 weeks. Use this marinade with fish, chicken, beef, and pork.

SAFE SMOKING

Be sure to wear rubber gloves when handling hot chile peppers because oil from the peppers will penetrate your skin and stay there for a while. Often people wash their hands and later rub their eyes, which causes an intense burning. If you ever get the actual juice or seeds of a chile in your eyes, fill a large bowl with about 3 quarts cold water. Add a few tablespoons of baking soda to the water and stir until dissolved. Plunge your face into the water and blink your eyes until the pain subsides. The baking soda helps neutralize the acid of the pepper and relieves the sting. Unfortunately I've had to use this trick a few times in my career and it works.

Smoked Garlic Marinade

Forget adding liquid smoke to your marinades—this is the real deal! Smoking the garlic adds an intense, smoky dimension to the marinade and therefore to whatever you are marinating. Fresh herbs balance everything out by adding a touch of sweetness.

Yield:	Prep time:
2 cups	20 minutes

1 cup vegetable juice cocktail

½ cup balsamic vinegar

¼ cup chopped fresh basil leaves

¼ cup chopped fresh oregano leaves

¼ cup chopped fresh parsley leaves

¼ cup chopped fresh thyme leaves

24 cloves Smoked Garlic, puréed (see Smoked Prime Rib Demi-Glace Burgers with Smoked Garlic and Onions recipe in Chapter 10)

2 TB. olive oil

2 TB. honey

1 tsp. crushed red pepper flakes

1 tsp. kosher salt

1 tsp. freshly cracked black pepper

1. In a large bowl, stir vegetable juice cocktail, balsamic vinegar, basil, oregano, parsley, thyme, Smoked Garlic, olive oil, honey, red pepper flakes, kosher salt, and black pepper until well combined.

2. Store, tightly covered, in the refrigerator for up to 1 week. Use this marinade with ribs, pork chops, chicken, or turkey.

TED'S TIP

Take smoked garlic cloves and roast them slowly in olive oil until soft and tender. Smash and use them to season mashed potatoes, other marinades, pastes, or even salad dressings.

Honey Riesling Wine Marinade

With its refreshingly sweet, fruity flavor, this marinade is so yummy you might be tempted to drink it! It also doubles as a great dressing for grilled vegetables and fresh green salads.

Yield:	Prep time:
3 cups	20 minutes

2 cups Riesling wine

½ cup mixed chopped fresh herbs, such as sage, parsley, thyme, and cilantro leaves

¼ cup fresh lemon juice

¼ cup olive oil

¼ cup honey

4 cloves garlic, minced

1 stalk lemongrass, smashed and finely chopped

1 green onion, chopped

1 hot red chile pepper, minced

2 TB. Dijon mustard

2 TB. white balsamic vinegar

1 tsp. minced ginger

1 tsp. kosher salt

1 tsp. freshly cracked black pepper

1. In a large bowl, stir Riesling wine, mixed herbs, lemon juice, olive oil, honey, garlic, lemongrass, green onion, hot chile pepper, Dijon mustard, white balsamic vinegar, ginger, kosher salt, and black pepper until well combined.

2. Store, tightly covered, in the refrigerator for up to 1 week. Use this marinade with beef, pork, poultry, fish, seafood, or any protein.

TED'S TIP

In general, marinate pork or beef for 6 to 8 hours or overnight, poultry for 4 to 6 hours, and fish or seafood for only 15 to 20 minutes.

Whiskey and Cola Marinade

One of my favorite beverages is a whiskey on the rocks with a splash of cola. The cola in this marinade quickly breaks down the fibers of the meat to tenderize it, and the whisky imparts a smoky rich flavor.

Yield:	Prep time:
2 cups	20 minutes

2 (11.5-oz.) cans cola	2 TB. chopped fresh sage leaves
1 cup Tennessee whiskey	1 tsp. freshly cracked black pepper
¼ cup chopped fresh parsley leaves	6 cloves garlic, minced
3 TB. Worcestershire sauce	Dash hot sauce
2 TB. vegetable oil	Pinch ground cinnamon

1. In a large bowl, stir cola, Tennessee whiskey, parsley, Worcestershire sauce, vegetable oil, sage, black pepper, garlic, hot sauce, and cinnamon until well combined.

2. Store, tightly covered, in the refrigerator for up to 2 weeks. Use this marinade with tough cuts, such as beef ribs, short ribs, brisket, skirt and flank steaks.

Variation: Many soft drinks make great marinade bases. Try ginger ale, orange soda, lemon-lime soda, or even grape soda!

SAFE SMOKING

The sugars and acids in cola break down meat protein very quickly, so 24 hours is the maximum you should marinate meat in this mixture. Any longer and the cola will break the meat down too much, resulting in an unpleasant and grainy texture.

Basic Cure

Try using flavored salts in your cure recipe to change the flavor of your meat. Smoked salt, lemon salt, and chile-infused salts are just three of the many varieties of flavored salts available.

Yield:	Prep time:
1½ cups	5 minutes

1 cup kosher salt	2 tsp. ground white pepper
½ cup granulated sugar	2 tsp. celery salt

1. In a large bowl, stir kosher salt, sugar, white pepper, and celery salt until well combined.

2. Store in an airtight container in a cool, dry, and dark place for up to 4 months. Use this cure on fish, chicken, pork chops, pork belly, or duck.

TASTY TIDBIT

A cure is essential in removing moisture from meat, which is what allows meats to be preserved. Cures are applied in small quantities: approximately 3 to 6 percent of the total weight for meats, and less for seafood and shellfish.

Fish Cure

Sweet and salty flavors are blended with the heat of the black pepper and the smokiness of the alcohol. This cure works well with salmon and other fish or shellfish. If you would like to omit the alcohol from this recipe, replace the same volume with a juice that isn't too acidic, like apple juice.

Yield:	Prep time:
5 cups	15 minutes

1½ cups kosher salt

4 cups chopped fresh dill

1 cup granulated sugar

¼ cup fresh, coarsely ground black pepper

3 TB. grated lemon zest

½ cup cognac, brandy, Armagnac, rum, or whiskey

1. In a large bowl, stir kosher salt, dill, sugar, black pepper, and lemon zest until well combined.

2. Generously rub mixture over 4 pounds of fish and drizzle with cognac. Let stand for 2 days for every 1 inch of thickness. Use this cure on salmon, tuna, trout, mackerel, or halibut.

Variation: For a **Margarita Cure,** replace lemon zest with lime zest, dill with fresh cilantro, and cognac with *reposado* tequila. Or for a **Harvey Wallbanger Cure,** replace lemon zest with orange zest, dill with equal parts thyme and parsley, and use an orange-flavored vodka for drizzling.

TED'S TIP

This cure is a guide to use when experimenting. Stick with the volumes, but change up the ingredients. Try light brown sugar, maple syrup, or honey in place of granulated sugar. Mix up the herbs and types of citrus to see what delicious concoction you come up with!

Aromatic Cure

The pairing of allspice and thyme truly enhances the flavor of mild proteins. There's just something about warm spices with smoky flavor that warms my heart—and belly!

Yield:	Prep time:
2¼ cups	15 minutes

1 cup kosher salt	1 TB. celery salt
¾ cup granulated sugar	1 tsp. ground allspice
1 TB. freshly ground black pepper	1 tsp. dried thyme leaves
1 TB. ground white pepper	1 tsp. dry mustard powder
1 TB. onion powder	1 tsp. cayenne
1 TB. garlic powder	½ tsp. ground nutmeg

1. In a large bowl, stir kosher salt, sugar, black pepper, white pepper, onion powder, garlic powder, celery salt, allspice, thyme, dry mustard powder, cayenne, and nutmeg until well combined.

2. Store in an airtight container in a cool, dry, and dark place for up to 4 months. Use this cure with poultry, halibut, or pork belly.

TED'S TIP

A little bit of this cure goes a long way, so don't overdo it. Rub the cure into the meat, pressing firmly so that it adheres well to the meat.

Rubs, Pastes, and Injections

In This Chapter

- Seasoning rubs
- Wet rubs and pastes
- Adding flavor with injections
- Tasty recipes for rubs, pastes, and injections

There are literally hundreds of commercial rubs and pastes on the market. You can begin your smoking career by playing with these but, as you will see in this chapter, making your own is not rocket science; it's as simple as throwing a few spices together in a bowl. You also get to control the salt and there are never any scary preservatives added. And after you see how easy it is to follow these recipes, I hope you'll be inspired to create your own signature rub!

Rubs

A rub is a dry mixture of spices, dried herbs, sugar, and salt that gets massaged into meats before smoking to add flavor. Its purpose is to enhance the flavor of meat without overwhelming or masking its natural flavor. Rubs tend to have salt and sugar as their base and commercial rubs in particular are very high in salt—up to 50 percent. I've kept the sugar and salt low in the rub recipes in this chapter so they have more versatility. Too much salt will just dry out the meat and, if used on a brined piece of meat, could make the whole thing way too salty; besides, salt's not that good for us. Sugar is used to balance the flavors of the other ingredients, but I don't like to use too much because it can cause the outside of the meat to char. I also like to keep the dry herb content low for the same reason.

A rub should be applied to meat in abundance and massaged with a bit of vigor. Take care not to have uneven areas of heavily rubbed flesh and bare spots; cover the meat evenly and completely—even cover the back-side of ribs where it's all bone. Gently push your fingers under the skin of poultry to rub directly onto the flesh, because the seasoning won't go through the skin to flavor the meat itself. But do rub the skin as well so you have a crispy flavored exterior to protect the flavored flesh beneath. Set aside rubbed meats for anywhere from 30 minutes to overnight to allow the spices to permeate the surface of the meat.

There are a few things to remember when you decide to create your own dry rub recipes: Start simply, because balance is key. You don't want one flavor to take over the whole mixture; you want a nice combination of ingredients to make a new flavor. A dry rub must never contain anything fresh; no chopped herbs or minced garlic. Fresh ingredients will decrease the longevity of the mixture and the flavors will continue to develop and become too strong. Here is a beginner's recipe to use as an outline:

- 1 tsp. salt
- 1 tsp. sugar
- 2 TB. sweet paprika
- 1 TB. dry mustard powder
- 1 tsp. black pepper
- 1 tsp. cayenne
- 1 tsp. garlic powder
- 1 tsp. onion powder
- 2 tsp. dry herb or spice #1
- 2 tsp. dry herb or spice #2
- 2 tsp. dry herb or spice #3

Stick to the proportions but try adding creative variety to the specified ingredients, like using hickory or smoked salts, cane or Demerara sugars, different herbs and spices, more or less heat, and so on. Be brave but remember our mantra: less is more. Rubs can be stored in an airtight container for 3 to 6 months in a cool, dark place. You don't want them hanging around any longer than 6 months because the flavor in spices tends to diminish over time.

Pastes

A paste is created when oil or another liquid ingredient is added to a rub. You can also specifically create a wet seasoning mixture, which is sometimes called a wet rub or a slather. A paste will adhere to the meat a little better than a dry rub but it tends to deliver a milder flavor. Pastes are also commonly used on lean cuts to add moisture along with flavor. A paste is applied like a rub—thoroughly massaged into the meat with a nice, even coating. Once it's applied, place the meat in a zipper-lock plastic bag and refrigerate for anywhere from 20 minutes (for seafood) to 24 hours (for large cuts of meat). The best paste consistency is thick enough to stay on the meat while it sits but thin enough to slather on with your hands or a mop.

SAFE SMOKING

Be very careful not to contaminate rubs and pastes with raw meat. Put what you intend to use in a bowl and work out of that, and throw away whatever is left in the bowl. Once you have touched a rub or paste with raw meat, it is *never* safe to use it again!

The following table lists some of the common ingredients that I always keep in my kitchen. It's meant to be a starting point and inspiration for your own spice mixtures but, as I say over and over, your only limitation is your own imagination. Some of the best flavors I found by accident. For instance, I learned that when you slather mayonnaise all over a salmon fillet before putting it in the smoker or use peanut butter as the base for a pork-loin paste, the flavor will blow you away! Experimenting also taught me that maraschino cherry juice makes a great component to a pork paste, too.

You can even go so far as to toast and grind your own spices. Toasting whole spices before grinding is always a good idea; it releases all the natural oils in the spices and allows their true flavors to come through.

Purchase raw spices at a reputable store where you can be sure they're fresh. Low and slow applies here as well. Keep the temperature of your oven no higher than 325°F, but I prefer 275°F. Spread spices in a thin, even layer on a baking sheet and don't overload the tray. Roast them just until you begin to smell the fragrance of the spice. Do not burn them! There is no salvation for burnt spices, so if you take them too far in the oven, just throw them away and start again. Let them cool to room temperature and grind them. You can use a mortar and pestle but a good coffee grinder is also handy for this purpose. Just make sure you have one dedicated to spices and one dedicated to coffee, unless you like cumin-flavored coffee.

Dried spices can be stored in an airtight container for 6 to 9 months in a cool, dark place. Spices will lose their intensity over time, so you might want to consider grinding them as you need them. Dried herbs should be stored for no more than 3 to 4 months.

Pastes should always be stored, tightly covered, in the refrigerator. A general rule of thumb is that pastes that contain oil should last a good 3 weeks in the fridge. Pastes without oil are usually only good for 5 to 7 days.

Smoker's Basic Spice Rack

Dry Ingredients	Wet Ingredients
allspice, ground or whole	anchovies
anise seed, ground or whole	assorted sodas and colas
black pepper, ground or whole	beer
cayenne	bourbon
celery salt	chipotle peppers in adobo sauce
chili powder	cider vinegar
cinnamon, ground and sticks	hoisin sauce
coriander, ground or whole	honey
cumin, ground or whole	horseradish
curry powder	lemon juice
dried ancho pepper	lime juice
dried chipotle powder	maple syrup
dried lemon zest	mixed fresh herbs
dried oregano leaves	mustards: Dijon, yellow, spicy
dried sage leaves	oil, vegetable and olive
dried thyme leaves	orange juice
dry mustard powder	oyster sauce
garlic powder or granulate	puréed garlic
ginger, ground	puréed jalapeño
lemon pepper	puréed onion
nutmeg, ground or whole	soy sauce
onion powder or granulate	whiskey
salt, kosher and sea	wine, red and white
sugar, granulated and brown	Worcestershire sauce

Injections

Injectors are sometimes called a smoker's best friend. The injector is not just for brining and adding moisture; it also aids in the efforts to layer and enhance flavor. An injector can be filled with so many different liquids. You can use the same mixture the meat was brined or marinated in, to reinforce the flavor profile. Or you can use an entirely different recipe for the injection that will complement the brine, marinade, rub, and paste already used. It's all about the layers and what you like!

In a BBQ competition, you will often see the old pros injecting their championship meats during the long, slow smoke. It's because they know this is what will help bring home that title!

Ted's World-Famous Bone Dust BBQ Seasoning Rub

I've been making my Bone Dust BBQ Seasoning Rub for over 20 years now and it has a great following. The combination of 13 different seasoning ingredients is easy to make but has a wonderfully complex flavor.

Yield:	Prep time:
2½ cups	15 minutes

½ cup paprika	2 TB. hot dry mustard powder
¼ cup chili powder	1 TB. freshly ground black pepper
3 TB. kosher salt	1 TB. dried basil leaves
2 TB. ground coriander	1 TB. dried thyme leaves
2 TB. garlic powder	1 TB. ground cumin
2 TB. granulated sugar	1 TB. cayenne
2 TB. curry powder	

1. In a large bowl, stir paprika, chili powder, kosher salt, coriander, garlic powder, sugar, curry powder, hot dry mustard powder, black pepper, basil, thyme, cumin, and cayenne until well combined.

2. Store in an airtight container in a cool, dry, and dark place for up to 4 months. Use this rub on ribs, pork, chicken, or turkey.

Crazy Cajun Rub

The land of the Cajun is a very rhythmic place and it's loaded with great flavors. This rub will give food a smoky twist before it even hits the smoker and the cayenne will add a nice kick of heat.

Yield:	Prep time:
1¼ cups	15 minutes

3 TB. cayenne

2 TB. kosher salt

2 TB. sweet paprika

1 TB. smoked paprika

1 TB. granulated sugar

1 TB. hot dry mustard powder

1 TB. freshly ground black pepper

1 TB. freshly ground white pepper

1 TB. garlic powder

1 TB. onion powder

2 tsp. ground cumin

1 tsp. dried oregano leaves

1 tsp. dried thyme leaves

1 tsp. ground coriander

½ tsp. dried sage leaves

1. In a large bowl, stir cayenne, kosher salt, sweet paprika, smoked paprika, sugar, hot dry mustard powder, black pepper, white pepper, garlic powder, onion powder, cumin, oregano, thyme, coriander, and sage until well combined.

2. Store in an airtight container in a cool, dry, and dark place for up to 4 months. Use this rub on veal, pork, chicken, fish, beef, or lamb.

TASTY TIDBIT

Smoked paprika traditionally comes from Spain or Hungary. Made from the freshest peppers and smoked using oak wood, smoked paprika has a distinct, aromatic flavor and brilliant red color. It can be found in most major grocery stores and specialty food shops in the spice aisle.

Garlic-Herb Fresh Rub

Most rubs are dry, so they have a long shelf life. This fresh rub won't last nearly as long but the flavor is great and it adds brightness that dry rubs don't, so give it a shot. It rocks!

Yield:	Prep time:
¾ cup	20 minutes

½ cup coarse-ground sea salt

2 TB. chopped fresh chives

2 TB. chopped fresh oregano leaves

2 TB. chopped fresh parsley leaves

2 TB. chopped fresh thyme leaves

1 TB. freshly ground black pepper

1 TB. freshly ground white pepper

1 TB. granulated sugar

8 cloves garlic, minced

1. In a large bowl, toss sea salt, chives, oregano, parsley, thyme, black pepper, white pepper, sugar, and garlic until well combined.

2. Store in an airtight container in the refrigerator for up to 5 days. Use this rub on beef, veal, lamb, or chicken.

Variation: Change up the types or quantities of the fresh herbs to create new flavor combinations. Try cilantro, mint-basil or sage, or thyme-oregano. Be creative!

TED'S TIP

Always wash and dry your herbs well before using them in a recipe. A salad spinner is a great tool to dry fresh herbs.

Jamaican Jerk Rub

If you've been to Jamaica and had a real taste of jerk-seasoned food, you know what the flavor is all about. The heat from Scotch bonnet peppers, green onion, thyme, and Jamaican allspice is what makes jerk food.

Yield:	Prep time:
1 cup	15 minutes

2 TB. ground allspice

2 TB. cayenne

2 TB. dried ground habañero pepper or Scotch bonnet pepper

1 TB. kosher salt

1 TB. freshly ground black pepper

1 TB. granulated sugar

1 TB. granulated onion

1 TB. garlic salt

1 TB. dried thyme leaves

1 tsp. dry mustard powder

½ tsp. ground nutmeg

¼ tsp. ground cinnamon

1. In a large bowl, stir allspice, cayenne, habañero pepper, kosher salt, black pepper, sugar, onion, garlic salt, thyme, dry mustard powder, nutmeg, and cinnamon until well combined.

2. Store in an airtight container in a cool, dry, and dark place for up to 4 months. Use this rub on pork, chicken, or fish.

TED'S TIP

Whisk the juice of 1 lime with 3 tablespoons Jamaican Jerk Rub and 1 tablespoon olive oil for a quick paste to rub on pork, chicken, or fish.

Memphis Rib Rub

In Memphis, Tennessee, ribs are traditionally served dry—that's right, without sauce. Just a great rub and sweet smoke is all that's needed to create some of the finest-tasting ribs in the country. Many people like saucy ribs, but a true rib lover will always be down for a tasty dry rack. Sauce is for dipping!

Yield:	Prep time:
2 cups	10 minutes

½ cup paprika

3 TB. kosher salt

2 TB. packed light brown sugar

2 TB. onion powder

1 TB. freshly ground black pepper

1 TB. celery salt

2 tsp. cayenne

2 tsp. garlic powder

1 tsp. dried oregano leaves

1 tsp. dried thyme leaves

1 tsp. ground cumin

1 tsp. ground coriander

½ tsp. allspice

1. In a large bowl, stir paprika, kosher salt, light brown sugar, onion powder, black pepper, celery salt, cayenne, garlic powder, oregano, thyme, cumin, coriander, and allspice until well combined.

2. Store in an airtight container in a cool, dry, and dark place for up to 4 months. Use this rub on ribs, pork butt, or chicken.

TASTY TIDBIT

There are a lot of great BBQ restaurants with dry ribs in Memphis, but one of the most famous is Charles Vergos' Rendezvous restaurant (hogsfly.com) located in the alley, downstairs, at 52 South Second Street. Put this place on your bucket list because the ribs are a little salty and a little sweet; you can just taste the tradition. Add a couple cold ones and this place is a real Memphis treat!

Tandoori Rub

Tandoori is traditionally grilled quickly on a hot BBQ, but I like to think that cooking it in a smoker is a nice way to combine old flavors with new techniques. Make sure you rub the meat 24 hours prior to smoking in order to get that rich red color that is synonymous with tandoori.

Yield:	Prep time:
1 cup	10 minutes

½ cup paprika	1 TB. granulated sugar
3 TB. ground cumin	1 TB. ground cardamom
2 TB. cayenne	1 TB. ground cinnamon
2 TB. ground coriander	1 TB. freshly ground black pepper
1 TB. kosher salt	1 tsp. ground cloves

1. In a large bowl, stir paprika, cumin, cayenne, coriander, kosher salt, sugar, cardamom, cinnamon, black pepper, and cloves until well combined.

2. Store in an airtight container in a cool, dry, and dark place for up to 4 months. Use this rub on pork ribs or chicken.

TED'S TIP

Stir ¼ cup Tandoori Rub with 1 cup yogurt to use as a marinade for chicken, pork ribs, or lamb.

Mediterranean Spice Rub

This rub is loaded with flavorful ingredients. There's garlic (and lots of it), red pepper, sun-dried tomato, onion, herbs, and fennel. The big seasoning boost comes from chicken stock powder, which really amps up the meatiness of the chicken. This rub is tasty and versatile, so make a big batch because you're going to use it all up!

Yield:	Prep time:
2 cups	10 minutes

½ cup dehydrated minced garlic

¼ cup kosher salt

¼ cup packed light brown sugar

2 TB. dehydrated sweet red pepper flakes

2 TB. finely chopped sun-dried tomato (about 3 pieces)

2 TB. MSG-free chicken soup–base powder

2 TB. fresh, medium-ground black pepper

2 TB. dehydrated minced onion

1 TB. dried parsley flakes

1 TB. dried basil leaves

1 TB. dried oregano leaves

1 TB. fennel seeds, coarsely ground

2 tsp. dried thyme leaves

2 tsp. cayenne

1. In a large bowl, stir dehydrated garlic, kosher salt, light brown sugar, sweet red pepper flakes, sun-dried tomato, chicken soup–base powder, black pepper, onion, parsley, basil, oregano, fennel seeds, thyme, and cayenne until well combined.

2. Store in an airtight container in a cool, dry, and dark place for up to 4 months. Use this rub on ribs, pork, chicken, veal, beef, fish, or seafood.

TED'S TIP

Combine this rub with some olive oil and use as a paste for rack of lamb before smoking. It can even be combined with olive oil and vinegar to make a salad dressing.

Cinnamon Chipotle Rub

Cinnamon adds a sweet and nutty flavor to your meats that's really nice. Try this rubbed on scallops; it'll bring a whole new meaning to the word delicious.

Yield:	Prep time:
1 cup	15 minutes

½ cup ground chipotle powder

¼ cup ground cinnamon

2 TB. sweet paprika

2 TB. granulated sugar

2 TB. packed light brown sugar

2 TB. ground cumin

2 TB. ground allspice

1 TB. ground cloves

1 TB. ground ginger

1 TB. garlic powder

1 TB. kosher salt

1. In a large bowl, stir chipotle powder, cinnamon, sweet paprika, granulated sugar, light brown sugar, cumin, allspice, cloves, ginger, garlic powder, and kosher salt until well combined.

2. Store in an airtight container in a cool, dry, and dark place for up to 4 months. Use this rub on chicken, ribs, pork, and seafood.

TED'S TIP

Grinding your own cinnamon sticks gives a much sweeter perfume to the rub, so avoid the preground stuff and go for a more natural flavor.

Smoked Sea Salt

The smoker gives the salt a sweet and slightly nutty flavor. It is robust and an easy way to naturally add smoke to your favorite recipes instead of using liquid smoke.

Yield:	Prep time:	Cook time:
4 cups	2 minutes	4 to 6 hours

4 cups coarse sea salt

1. Preheat the smoker for cold smoking per manufacturer's instructions to maximum 125°F; the colder the better.

2. Spread sea salt in an even layer on a foil-lined smoke rack and place in the smoker.

3. Smoke, gently stirring the salt every hour, for 4 to 6 hours or until salt is smoky brown and has a distinct smoke flavor; cool.

4. Store in an airtight container in a cool, dry, and dark place for up to 4 months. Use on prime rib roast, leg of lamb, steaks, chops, chicken, or turkey.

TED'S TIP

Using an electric box smoker is an easy way to smoke salt. You can also smoke salt in a heavy-bottom cast-iron pan over an open fire. Just make sure you set aside a good amount of time because it takes a while and you need to stir it frequently. Haven't got the time to smoke salt? Look for a variety of smoked seasoning salts in specialty food and grocery stores.

Hot 'n' Spicy BBQ Paste

Sometimes you just want to kick it up a notch, and this paste will sure do the trick. For the best flavor and to really give your food that spicy kick, allow the meat to marinate for at least 24 hours prior to smoking.

Yield:	Prep time:
1 cup	30 minutes

¼ cup Memphis Rib Rub (recipe earlier in this chapter)

4 cloves garlic, minced

3 chipotle chiles in adobo sauce, minced

2 fresh red jalapeños or red chile peppers

1 green onion, minced

2 TB. chopped parsley

2 TB. olive oil

1 tsp. dried pequin chile pepper

1. Place Memphis Rib Rub, garlic, chipotle chiles, red jalapeños, green onion, parsley, olive oil, and pequin chile pepper into a food processor. Pulse, adding up to 1 tablespoon water if needed, until very smooth.

2. Store in an airtight container in the refrigerator for up to 1 week. Rub this paste onto pork ribs, chops, shoulders, and poultry.

TASTY TIDBIT

You can find canned chipotle chiles in adobo sauce in Hispanic specialty food stores, as well as in the Mexican section of most major grocery stores.

Margarita Paste

Nothing is more refreshing than a margarita on a hot summer's day when working over a hot smoker. So while you have all the ingredients out, mix up a pitcher to enjoy with family and friends while the smoker does its thing. The sweet, smoky flavor of tequila contrasts well with the tang of fresh lime.

Yield:	Prep time:
1½ cups	30 minutes

½ cup chopped fresh cilantro leaves

¼ cup fresh lime juice

2 oz. amber tequila

2 to 3 jalapeños, minced

2 large cloves garlic, minced

2 TB. kosher salt

2 TB. olive oil

2 TB. honey

1 TB. packed light brown sugar

1 TB. freshly cracked black pepper

1 tsp. grated lime zest

1 tsp. prepared mustard

1. In a large bowl, stir cilantro, lime juice, amber tequila, jalapeños, garlic, kosher salt, olive oil, honey, light brown sugar, black pepper, lime zest, and mustard until well combined.

2. Store in an airtight container in the refrigerator for up to 1 week. Rub this paste on chicken, pork, or seafood.

TED'S TIP

Use this paste to rim a margarita glass instead of salt for a savory and delicious twist on a classic cocktail!

Java-Java Paste

Coffee isn't just for your morning pick-me-up or to drink with cakes and pastries. The sweet and savory flavor combination of this rub is a bit out there (would you expect anything less from me?), but it is awesome—trust me!

Yield:	Prep time:
2 cups	20 minutes

½ cup mocha-flavored coffee beans

¼ cup French vanilla–flavored coffee beans

6 cloves garlic, minced

½ cup chopped mixed fresh herbs, such as parsley, cilantro, sage, and thyme leaves

¼ cup freshly cracked black pepper

¼ cup olive oil

2 TB. molasses

2 TB. good-quality balsamic vinegar

1 TB. packed light brown sugar

Kosher salt

1. Combine mocha coffee beans and French vanilla coffee beans in a zipper-lock plastic bag. Use a heavy-bottom saucepan to crush the beans into small granules, but don't crush them too finely.

2. In a large bowl, add coffee bean mixture, garlic, mixed herbs, black pepper, olive oil, molasses, balsamic vinegar, light brown sugar, and kosher salt to taste.

3. Store tightly covered in the refrigerator for up to 2 weeks. Use this paste on steaks, chops, prime rib, or rack of lamb.

TED'S TIP

I find it best to make this rub at least a day ahead so the coffee beans soften and release more flavor.

Chive Butter Injection

This combination of sweet, fresh chives and rich, creamery butter will make anything more delicious. I first used this injection on slow-smoked chicken breasts and they were awesome. The key to this recipe is to let the chives steep in the melted butter. This extracts the wonderful green chlorophyll, which makes this butter bright green!

Yield:	Prep time:	Cook time:
1 cup	40 minutes	1 hour

1 cup chopped fresh chives

½ tsp. salt

½ tsp. lemon juice

1 cup (2 sticks) unsalted butter

1. Place chives in a large bowl and sprinkle with salt and lemon juice. Let stand for 30 minutes or until softened.

2. Melt unsalted butter in a medium saucepan set over medium-low heat. Add chive mixture and reduce the heat to low. Cook, stirring often, for 1 hour or until chives are very soft and fragrant.

3. Blend mixture, using a hand blender, until smooth. Strain mixture through a fine mesh sieve, pushing as much of the pulp through as possible; discard solids.

4. Suck up mixture with an injector, plunge the needle into meat, and press plunger to release. Use this injection with poultry, fish, or seafood.

Variation: Replace the chives with any fresh herbs; dill, parsley, sage, rosemary, basil, or oregano will all give your smoked foods a buttery herb boost.

TED'S TIP

A simple herbed butter mixture like this one is great when injected into the breast of your holiday turkey. The increase in internal fat of the bird will make the meat moist and juicy.

Rum Runner's Maple Injection

I love the combination of spiced rum and maple syrup. Although we are using it as an injection, this mixture can also be drizzled as a finishing touch on so many things. What makes it really special is adding butter, which makes just about everything so much tastier.

Yield:	Prep time:	Cook time:
1 cup	10 minutes	10 minutes

1 cup maple syrup

4 oz. spiced rum

2 oz. fresh orange juice

½ tsp. kosher salt

½ tsp. finely ground black pepper

1 cup (2 sticks) unsalted butter, cut into cubes

1. Combine maple syrup, spiced rum, orange juice, kosher salt, and black pepper in a medium saucepan set over medium heat. Cook until steaming but not boiling (you don't want to boil off the alcohol in the rum). Remove from the heat.

2. Whisk in unsalted butter, a couple of cubes at a time, until well combined.

3. Suck up mixture with an injector, plunge the needle into meat, and press plunger to release. Use this injection on beef, pork, or poultry.

TED'S TIP

Spring for real maple syrup; it's worth the coin, because the flavor will make all the difference in this recipe. Stay away from the artificial table syrups—they just won't cut it.

Basting, Saucing, and Spritzing

In This Chapter

- When to baste and when to back off
- The wonderful world of BBQ sauce
- A little spritz adds flavor
- Let's get saucy: recipes to slather on your meats

So we've brined our meat, marinated it, injected it, and rubbed it. Now it's time for the next step in flavor layering: basting, saucing, and spritzing. These layers are added at the smoker and if done properly are the *pièce de résistance*.

Then again, this is also the place where a beautifully prepared piece of meat can be ruined by an improperly applied baste or sauce, or even by adding anything at all—they're not always necessary. One of the places I often find I'm arguing about this is when smoking ribs. If all the other steps are done well, ribs don't always need sauce. Putting sauce on almost seems like a disguise to the meat. Sometimes serving the sauce on the side as a dunk is the better option.

Basting with Caution

In the smoking world, a baste is usually referred to as *the mop*. Every committed smoker has a few of these miniature cotton string doohickeys. The cotton strings absorb lots of liquid and gently apply the sauce to the meat's surface. You don't want to baste too often because every time the smoker's door is opened almost 50 percent of the heat and smoke escapes. This causes a fluctuation in the cook time and ultimately can affect the quality of the end result. Basting or mopping is not always necessary when you have a fatty meat with lots of marbling or a nice fat cap, unless, of course, your mop is part of your plan to build flavor. Lean meats and poultry should definitely be basted to create a nice, crisp skin.

Many of the recipes in this chapter include a basting mixture developed specifically for that particular flavor profile. However, you can baste with a variety of mixtures. Use your favorite BBQ sauce, homemade or prepared, and just thin it out with some water, beer, wine, or liquor. You want a nice thin mixture that you can apply in thin, even layers. You can even use a marinade (if it hasn't come in contact with raw meat) that isn't too acidic.

It is a good idea to keep the baste mixture hot while smoking; just set it over low heat on the back burner. This can decrease the possibility of any foodborne illness. It's also a good practice to leave the mop submerged in the simmering baste for at least 90 seconds after using it on partially cooked meats. Likewise, it's also best to wait until halfway through the smoking time to start basting. Leave the lid closed until then—no matter what! You don't want to lose any heat while that smoke is first being laid down on your meat. For long-smoked meat, I would then give it a good juicy mop every 45 minutes until the last 30 minutes. That's when I would lay on whatever sauce I wanted to glaze it with.

SAFE SMOKING

It may be getting boring, but it can't be said enough: refrigerate your bastes and sauces until you are ready to use them. Never dip your brush or mop directly into the sauce container. Pour the sauce you intend to use in a bowl and work from there; if there's any left in the bowl when you're done, discard it.

BBQ Sauces from Around the World

BBQ sauces come after basting and, when smoking, you should apply the sauce—and leave it to take on a glaze—about 30 minutes before the meat is ready to come off the smoker.

BBQ sauces—whatever their origin or style—tend to have a high sugar content. It's nothing more than a seasoned, sweet and sour liquid. In Kansas City, it's tomato based with sweet and smoky notes. In Memphis, it's tomato based with some zing and heat. They're both the thickness of ketchup. In the Carolinas, the sauce is thin and yellow from a vinegar and mustard base. In the Deep South, they use mayonnaise-based sauces.

Whatever the style, they all break down similarly. It starts with a base, such as ketchup, mustard, mayonnaise, or vinegar. Next there's something to sweeten it, such as granulated sugar, molasses, or even cola. Then the sweetness needs to be balanced out with an acid like lemon juice or vinegar, or an alcohol like beer or wine. Next, you want to bulk it up and make it pourable with something like orange juice, apple juice, or even Dr. Pepper. Lastly, season it with dry and liquid ingredients such as Worcestershire sauce, garlic powder, or even a bit of your favorite rub or paste. The sauce should be smooth, but don't let this limit your creativity. Throw in chopped fruits and vegetables. Sauces can be puréed with a hand or regular blender, or a food processor. After you try a few of the recipes in this chapter you'll get a feel for the formula and hopefully have the confidence to venture farther afield.

Large cuts like pork shoulder, destined to become luscious pulled pork, don't necessarily require glazing. While I recommend adding a light coating of sauce to ribs and chicken wings or thighs, I also like to just put a couple of big bowls of sauce on the table because sometimes there's nothing better than a good, self-serve dunk.

Sauces are meant to be finishing touches. They should never be a slap dash. You want them to provide the final complement to what you have spent as much as 24 hours preparing. Remember, you need to keep this part of the process to the last 30 minutes or less; just enough time to heat it and make it sticky and visually appetizing to one and all. If you overdo it, you'll just end up with your head in your hands and a sticky, burnt mess.

A Spritz Can Make All the Difference

If you've ever watched a BBQ documentary or a televised BBQ competition, then you've probably noticed the pros spraying their meats with a mysterious mixture. The old pros in Memphis can be seen whipping open the smoker really quick to spray the meat with something and then closing the doors just as quickly. Some of them are spraying apple juice, which is commonly used on a whole hog or ribs.

It's becoming very popular because you can do it fast, which limits the amount of heat lost. It's also another way to load up the flavor. You can do something as simple as apple juice or orange juice, but you can use all sorts of ingredients. Some use reserved marinade (as long as it didn't come in contact with raw meat) or you can create a special spritz designed to complement all your other flavoring steps. Check out the recipes that follow for inspiration on what to fill your squeeze bottle with.

Kansas City BBQ Sauce

Some folks say that when it comes to BBQ sauce for your smoked meats it is all about the Kansas City style. Considered the sauce capital of the USA, Kansas City BBQ Sauce has four main characteristics: it's thick, it's rich with tomato flavor, it's a bit sweet, and it also has a bit of a spicy kick. This is my version and I think it's pretty darn good!

Yield:	Prep time:	Cook time:
8 cups	15 minutes	1 hour, 15 minutes

¼ cup bacon fat (pan drippings) or butter

1 cup diced sweet onion, such as Vidalia or Maui sweet

4 large cloves garlic, minced

4 cups ketchup

1 cup tomato paste

1 cup tomato juice

1 cup packed light brown sugar

½ cup molasses

⅓ cup Worcestershire sauce

¼ cup cider vinegar

2 TB. Ted's World-Famous Bone Dust BBQ Seasoning Rub (recipe in Chapter 8)

1 tsp. kosher salt

1 tsp. freshly ground black pepper

1 tsp. cayenne

¼ tsp. hickory-flavor liquid smoke

Hot sauce

1. Heat bacon fat in a large saucepan set over medium heat. Add sweet onion and garlic. Sauté for 3 to 5 minutes or until onion is softened but not browned.

2. Add ketchup, tomato paste, tomato juice, light brown sugar, molasses, Worcestershire sauce, cider vinegar, Ted's World-Famous Bone Dust BBQ Seasoning Rub, kosher salt, black pepper, cayenne, hickory-flavor liquid smoke, and hot sauce to taste.

3. Simmer, stirring occasionally, for 1 hour or until thick. Purée, using a hand blender, until smooth. Push mixture though a fine mesh sieve; discard solids.

4. Store in an airtight container in the refrigerator for up to 2 weeks. Use this sauce on pork ribs, pulled pork, brisket, chicken, or turkey.

TED'S TIP

This recipe is a great base to use when experimenting and creating your own custom BBQ sauce, or to use as the prepared BBQ sauce in other recipes later in this book.

Bourbon-Wasabi BBQ Sauce

This is a bit of a weird combination but it is truly delicious. The blend of bourbon, soy, and hot wasabi with the added sweetness of brown sugar is delicious when basted on smoked food.

Yield:	Prep time:	Cook time:
3 cups	15 minutes	10 minutes

1 TB. vegetable oil

1 cup finely diced onion

8 cloves garlic, minced

1 cup packed light brown sugar

⅓ cup dark soy sauce

2 TB. sweet rice vinegar

2 TB. honey

2 TB. molasses

1 TB. hot prepared horseradish

1 tsp. Worcestershire sauce

½ tsp. freshly ground black pepper

½ cup ginger ale

2 tsp. cornstarch

1 tsp. wasabi powder

2 oz. bourbon whiskey

1. Heat vegetable oil in a medium saucepan set over medium heat. Add onion and garlic. Cook, stirring often, for 3 to 5 minutes or until onion is softened but not browned.

2. Add light brown sugar and stir until smooth. Stir in dark soy sauce, sweet rice vinegar, honey, molasses, hot horseradish, Worcestershire sauce, and black pepper. Bring to a boil.

3. Meanwhile, in a medium bowl, whisk ginger ale, cornstarch, and wasabi powder until smooth. Add to the saucepan, stirring rapidly, until well combined. Return mixture to a boil, reduce heat to low, and simmer for 1 minute or until thickened; remove from heat. Add bourbon; cool completely.

4. Store in an airtight container in the refrigerator for up to 2 weeks. Use this sauce on beef ribs, short ribs, prime rib, lamb, or chicken.

> **TED'S TIP**
>
> Don't have time to fire up the smoker? This BBQ sauce is also delicious on plain old grilled steaks.

Four-Ingredient Cherry Cola BBQ Sauce

When it comes to making BBQ sauce, some recipes are difficult and others are easy—like this one. Only four ingredients and they're all easy to find! They aren't typical BBQ sauce ingredients, but they sure do taste good when you mix them all together.

Yield:	Prep time:
4 cups	15 minutes

2 cups cherry pie filling
½ cup light brown sugar
¼ cup low-sodium soy sauce

1½ cups flat cola, at room temperature

1. In a medium bowl, whisk cherry pie filling, light brown sugar, and soy sauce until well combined. Add flat cola in a slow steady stream, whisking constantly, until completely combined.

2. Store tightly covered in the refrigerator for up to 2 weeks. Use this sauce with brisket, pork butt, or poultry.

TED'S TIP

Lemon pie filling makes a great barbecue sauce, too. Go ahead, experiment a bit; you never know what you may come up with!

Apple Butter BBQ Glaze

The combination of sweet apple and maple with tangy ketchup and spicy jalapeños makes this sauce really flavorful and a hit with just about everybody.

Yield:	Prep time:	Cook time:
5 cups	30 minutes	40 minutes

3 TB. butter

½ cup minced onion

2 red jalapeños or red chile peppers, chopped

2 cloves garlic, crushed

2 cups applesauce

2 cups ketchup

½ cup apple juice

½ cup apple butter

¼ cup maple syrup

3 TB. apple cider vinegar

½ tsp. kosher salt

½ tsp. freshly ground black pepper

1. Melt butter in a medium saucepan set over medium heat. Add onion, red jalapeños, and garlic. Cook, stirring, for 3 to 5 minutes or until mixture is softened.

2. Stir in applesauce, ketchup, apple juice, apple butter, maple syrup, apple cider vinegar, kosher salt, and black pepper. Simmer, stirring occasionally, for 20 minutes or until thickened.

3. Purée mixture using a hand blender until the texture resembles applesauce. Push mixture though a fine mesh sieve; discard solids.

4. Store in an airtight container in the refrigerator for up to 2 weeks. Use this glaze on ribs or mixed in with BBQ pulled pork, chicken, or turkey.

TASTY TIDBIT

A red jalapeño is the same as the more common green variety; it's just been left on the plant longer in order to ripen completely. This makes the pepper's heat a little more intense.

Memphis-Style BBQ Sauce

The best way to describe Memphis-style BBQ sauce is that it's a little spicy, a little sweet, and loaded with flavor. It has a bit of a kick that comes from the cayenne but it's not too hot. The sauce also balances itself with a nice tang from vinegar and prepared mustard. You're gonna love it!

Yield:	Prep time:	Cook time:
5 cups	20 minutes	10 minutes

2 TB. butter	⅓ cup packed light brown sugar
½ cup diced onion	¼ cup Worcestershire Sauce
3 large cloves garlic, minced	2 tsp. black pepper
1½ cups tomato paste	1 tsp. salt
¾ cup white vinegar	1 tsp. cayenne
½ cup yellow prepared mustard	1 tsp. celery salt
¼ cup cider vinegar	1 tsp. dry mustard powder

1. Melt butter in a medium saucepan set over medium heat. Add onion and garlic. Sauté for 3 to 5 minutes or until onion is softened but not browned.

2. Stir in tomato paste, white vinegar, yellow mustard, and cider vinegar.

3. Add light brown sugar, Worcestershire sauce, black pepper, salt, cayenne, celery salt, and dry mustard powder. Simmer, stirring frequently, for 5 minutes or until thickened.

4. Purée the mixture using a hand blender until smooth. Push the mixture though a fine mesh sieve; discard solids.

5. Store in an airtight container in the refrigerator for up to 2 weeks. Use this sauce with ribs and chicken or drizzle it on your shredded pulled pork before serving.

TED'S TIP

Use an injector and try injecting this sauce into chicken, turkey, or pork!

Carolina Sweet Mustard Sauce

The smell of smoke coming from a BBQ joint in the Carolinas always makes me crave their sweet mustard sauce. It's bright yellow from prepared mustard and turmeric, and the sweetness of apple offsets the kick of mustard. Slop it on just about anything—it's sure to brighten up your day.

Yield:	Prep time:	Cook time:
3 cups	15 minutes	30 minutes

2 TB. butter

2 medium yellow bell peppers, seeded and diced

2 hot yellow banana peppers, chopped

1 small onion, finely chopped

4 cloves garlic, minced

½ cup prepared mustard

½ cup honey

¼ cup granulated sugar

¼ cup cider vinegar

¼ cup apple juice

1 tsp. turmeric

1 tsp. freshly ground black pepper

½ tsp. ground cumin

½ tsp. cayenne

Kosher salt

1. Melt butter in a medium saucepan set over medium-high heat. Add yellow bell peppers, yellow banana peppers, onion, and garlic. Sauté for 3 to 5 minutes or until peppers and onion are softened but not browned.

2. Reduce the heat to medium. Stir in mustard, honey, sugar, cider vinegar, apple juice, turmeric, black pepper, cumin, and cayenne; bring to a boil. Reduce the heat and simmer, stirring occasionally, for 20 to 30 minutes or until reduced by one third. Season to taste with kosher salt.

3. Purée using a hand blender until smooth; strain. Cool completely.

4. Store in an airtight container in the refrigerator for up to 2 weeks. Use this sauce on chicken, pulled pork, or ribs.

Variation: For a seriously spicy sauce, omit banana peppers and replace them with yellow or orange Scotch bonnet or habañero peppers.

Lemon-Ginger Wine Spritz

The sweet buttery flavor of Riesling wine is so fresh tasting when blended with fresh lemon juice and ginger ale!

Yield:	Prep time:
4 cups	5 minutes

2 cups Riesling wine	1 cup flat ginger ale
1 cup white grape juice	2 TB. fresh lemon juice

1. Use a funnel to fill a spray bottle with Riesling wine, white grape juice, flat ginger ale, and lemon juice. Shake to mix well.

2. Store in the refrigerator for up to 1 week. Use this spritz on poultry, fish, seafood, or pork.

TED'S TIP

I like to set the spray nozzle to mist so I can give foods just a fine spray. Spritz about 6 to 8 inches away from the food in an even layer. Be careful of the stream setting on the bottle, as it can puncture your foods, especially delicate fish or seafood.

Cherry-Pom Spritz

This spritz, a blend of cherry and pomegranate juices with pomegranate-infused liqueur, is best with red meats. It gives meat a nice mahogany color and adds a rich, smooth sweetness.

Yield:	Prep time:
4 cups	5 minutes

1 cup cherry juice	1 cup pomegranate-infused liqueur
1 cup pomegranate juice	1 cup cold water

1. Using a funnel, fill a spray bottle with cherry juice, pomegranate juice, pomegranate-infused liqueur, and cold water. Shake to mix well.

2. Store in the refrigerator for up to 1 week. Use this spritz on beef, lamb, or game.

Variation: Substitute cherry juice with cranberry or blueberry juice.

TASTY TIDBIT

You can often find fresh cherry-pomegranate juice blends in the fresh refrigerated juice section of your grocer's produce department.

Honey-Herb Spritz

For this spritz I like to add fresh sprigs of rosemary—or just about any herb I have on hand—to the spray bottle so the flavor infuses into the orange juice and honey. The longer you let the spritz stand, the more herb flavor will come through.

Yield:	Prep time:
4 cups	5 minutes

1 to 2 sprigs fresh rosemary, thyme, oregano, basil, mint, or sage

2 cups warm water

1 cup pulp-free orange juice

1 cup liquid honey

1. Stuff rosemary into a spray bottle, keeping as many leaves on the stem as possible.

2. Using a funnel, fill the spray bottle with warm water, orange juice, and liquid honey. Shake to mix well. Let stand for at least 4 hours or up to overnight to allow the flavors to infuse.

Meat, Meat, and More Meat ... and Fish

The word *meat* doesn't just refer to beef; it's used as a blanket term for any protein that comes from an animal: beef, veal, pork, lamb, game, poultry, fish, and seafood. I'm drooling just thinking about all the wonderful meats I've brought home from my butcher and put in my smoker!

There are many cuts of meat out there, but in these chapters I explain most of them so you'll understand what you're asking for when you head to the butcher shop or grocery store. Start simple, maybe a pork butt, and work your way up to the more advanced cuts, like brisket or ribs. Don't worry; it won't be long before you know exactly what you're doing. The recipes in Part 3 are sure to inspire you to get out there and smoke something delicious!

Blazing Beef

In This Chapter

- Different cuts of beef
- What you need to know to buy beef
- Mouthwateringly good beef recipes

If there's one thing you gotta know about me, it's that I'm a meat guy. I love meat. There is nothing more satisfying than setting a perfectly smoked, juicy, crusted piece of beef before your family and friends. It's that first cut, through the dark fragrant crust into a juicy pink interior bringing forth a geyser of rich, natural juices, which draws stares of awe from your table. All the work you've done—brining, marinating, rubbing, stoking of coals, basting, glazing, and spritzing—is suddenly so worth it. Amid the oohs and ahhs, your chest puffs out a little and you sit back to enjoy the sounds of cutlery rattling, slurping, and munching. That's what smoking meats means to me.

None of this is possible, though, if you don't get the right cut of meat. If you can, find a good old-fashioned butcher, one who doesn't just present you with plastic-wrapped bundles. They're still out there; it just takes a little research on your part. Find someone you can talk with face to face and build a relationship with. Once you do, hang on to him! You want the guy who understands exactly what you're looking for when you tell him you want a brisket flat, totally trimmed and cleaned for the smoker, but with some of the fat left intact. Before you find a butcher, you need to have a good understanding of meat on your own, so let's get started.

Breaking Down the Different Cuts of Beef

There are four basic major (primal) cuts into which beef is separated: chuck, loin, rib, and round. Generally, cuts from the chuck and round are less tender and require moist heat or long, slow cooking—like smoking! The loin and rib are more tender, so they can be cooked with dry heat methods such as broiling or grilling. The less-tender cuts are typically the ones that end up in the smoker most often, but that's not to say that a smoked steak isn't worth the time. It's obviously going to take longer than grilling it, but a smoked prime rib or 2-inch-thick rib eye steak can transport you to heaven for a short while.

The main thing that affects the tenderness, marbling (the delicate veins of fat running through the meat), and flavor of meat (all meats) is where it comes from on the animal. An area that gets worked hard in the day-to-day activities of an animal's life is going to be tougher with less marbling, but it also has more flavor. The tenderloin doesn't really do much; that's why you, as the cook, don't have to do much to it because it's going to melt in your mouth no matter what—unless you overcook it! However, the round, shank, and chuck work hard to move the cow around and keep its head up, so they become tough but loaded with beefy flavor.

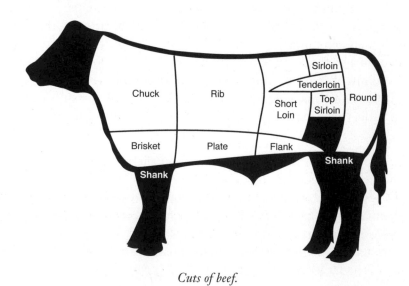

Cuts of beef.

Forequarter

The following are the cuts that come from the front half of the cow and some of the different names they are often referred to as:

- **Chuck:** Includes bone-in chuck steaks, arm and blade roasts (the blade is also known as a flat-iron steak), boneless clod steaks and roasts, and chest short ribs. These are very tough pieces of meat and well suited to the art of the smoker.

- **Rib:** These include short ribs, prime rib, and rib eye steak.

- **Brisket:** This is a very coarse-textured muscle. The heavy layer of fat and sternum or breastbone are removed before selling. It's often sold in a flat-cut half and point-cut half and is used for stewing meat, barbecue, corned beef, and pastrami.

- **Shank:** This is the toughest of all cuts and is most often used for stews and soups.

- **Plate:** This is where the rest of the short ribs come from, as well as pot roast and outside skirt steak. The remaining meat is usually ground because it's cheap, tough, and fatty.

Hindquarter

The following are cuts that come from the back half of the cow, which is where most of the popular steaks come from:

- **Short loin:** T-bone and porterhouse steaks are cut from short loin if bone-in, or New York strip if boneless.

- **Sirloin:** Produces top sirloin and bottom sirloin, including tri-tip roast.

- **Tenderloin:** If it's removed as a separate subprimal, it can be cut into filet mignon, tournedos, and tenderloin steaks or can also be left whole as a roast—which is pricey but magnificent. When it's cut with the bone in, it becomes part of T-bone and porterhouse steaks.

- **Round:** Provides top, bottom, and eye-of-round steaks and roasts.

- **Flank:** Is basically used for flank steak or inside skirt steak.

The most important thing to remember when selecting a cut and recipe is that it's going to affect the time needed to smoke. A tender cut won't take nearly as long as a tough cut, but you're going to be nursing the smoker for a while to check the meat so it doesn't overcook. So grab a beer (or a six-pack) and get comfy because perfection takes time ... but it's soooo worth it!

Beef Buying Basics with Your Buddy Ted

The names for various cuts vary regionally and nationally. This can become confusing when using a cookbook. I'm from Canada, and there a boneless top-loin steak is called a strip-loin steak. In the United States, this same steak may be called a Kansas City steak, a New York strip steak, a hotel-cut strip steak, an ambassador steak, or a club sirloin steak, just to name a few.

When buying beef, read the label; it should list the primal cut somewhere, so even if the name of the cut is different from what I've called for you'll know if it's from the tender or tough region of the cow. Smoking was initially practiced as a way of making cheap or even discarded cuts edible. Over time they've became more than just edible, they have become the glorious institution of American barbecue!

Now just because a cut is tough doesn't mean it's not good quality. All beef is graded, and there are three main grades: USDA Prime, USDA Choice, and USDA Select. Very little USDA Prime makes it to retail sale because less than 2 percent of all graded beef achieves the Prime status and the majority of it goes to the restaurant industry. I always recommend you buy the best you can afford and there is absolutely no shame in choosing the less tender pieces or the Choice or Select grades. The cooking method is what will raise them to another level. Select is the easiest grade to find and it's about 5 to 7 cents a pound cheaper than Choice. It has the least amount of marbling so it will benefit the most from the brining and/or marinating techniques discussed in Chapter 7.

TASTY TIDBIT

Beef is often overlooked as a healthy source of protein. It's actually loaded with 14 essential nutrients, including zinc and vitamin D, which most people don't get enough of in their daily diets.

Another thing to look for when shopping for beef is color. The meat should be bright cherry red without any gray spots. If it's vacuum packed the meat won't be bright red, but if it's fresh it'll turn bright red about 5 to 10 minutes after opening the package. Good beef should be firm to the touch, not mushy. The packaging should be fairly dry because excess moisture in the tray usually indicates temperature abuse. Loin and rib cuts should have marbling running through the flesh and there shouldn't be a lot of big clumps of fat.

Be sure to match your selected cuts with the right cooking method and flavor combinations. For example, tender cuts need shorter smoking times and more delicate flavors, while tougher cuts need longer smoking times and can take on more robust flavors. The following recipes will give you some ideas about how to smoke and add great flavor to a good variety of beef cuts.

Shredded Beef Sandwiches with Chimichurri Mayonnaise

I use flank steak for this recipe because it's a fairly lean cut of beef and has great beefy flavor. Ask your butcher to cut a steak with as much external fat as possible. The flank is marinated for 24 hours in a mixture of beer, lime, garlic, and red pepper flakes, and slowly smoked over hardwood oak, making this a very robust dish.

Yield:	Prep time:	Cook time:	Serving size:
1 steak	24 hours, 30 minutes	4½ hours	¼ steak

1 flank steak (about 2 lb.)

1 (12-oz.) bottle of pilsner-style beer

1 lime, halved and juiced

8 large garlic cloves, smashed and roughly chopped

2 TB. olive oil

1½ tsp. crushed red pepper flakes

1 tsp. coarsely ground black pepper

½ tsp. ground cumin

½ cup (1 stick) butter, softened

¼ cup cream cheese or goat cheese, softened

½ cup mayonnaise

¼ cup chopped fresh parsley leaves

2 green onions, finely chopped

2 cloves garlic, minced

½ tsp. finely ground black pepper

Pinch cayenne

Pinch ground cumin

Kosher salt

1. Use a sharp knife to remove the silver skin or sinew from the steak, leaving as much of the fat intact as possible. Place steak in a large zipper-lock plastic bag. Add pilsner beer and all but 1 teaspoon lime juice, along with lime halves, roughly chopped garlic, olive oil, 1 teaspoon red pepper flakes, coarsely ground black pepper, and cumin. Seal the bag, pressing out as much air as possible, and gently massage to evenly coat the steak. Marinate in the refrigerator, turning the bag every 4 to 6 hours, for 24 hours.

2. Preheat the smoker per manufacturer's instructions to 180°F to 210°F, using oak wood chunks or chips soaked in water.

3. Arrange steak on a smoking rack. Insert thermometer probe into the thickest portion of the steak. Set the internal temperature for 150°F. Smoke for 2½ to 3 hours or until internal temperature is achieved.

4. Transfer steak to a cutting board and brush all over with all but 2 teaspoons of softened butter. Wrap tightly in 6 layers of heavy-duty plastic food wrap. (Yes, I said 6 layers. Nice and tight please!) Then wrap in 2 layers of heavy-duty foil.

5. Return steak to the smoker and reinsert meat probe thermometer into the center of the wrapped meat. Set the internal temperature for 200°F. Smoke for 2 hours or until internal temperature is achieved.

6. Meanwhile, in a medium bowl, whisk cream cheese and mayonnaise until smooth. Stir in parsley, green onions, minced garlic, finely ground black pepper, remaining ½ teaspoon red pepper flakes, cayenne, cumin, and remaining 1 teaspoon lime juice until well combined. Season with kosher salt to taste. Store Chimichurri Mayonnaise in an airtight container in the refrigerator for up to 3 days.

7. Transfer wrapped steak to a large bowl. Remove wraps, being careful of the steam, and transfer steak to a second bowl. Shred the steak into fine strands using tongs, two forks, or in my case, hands of steel. Toss the shredded meat with remaining 2 teaspoons butter and enough of the cooking juices to moisten. Serve immediately with Chimichurri Mayonnaise. I like to serve it on soft onion buns with lettuce, steak tomatoes, and shaved red onion.

Variation: Instead of shredding the steak, smoke it until the internal temperature reaches 135°F for rare. Skip the wrapping and let it rest for 5 minutes before slicing it very thinly. Pile the sliced beef high on pillowy rolls and garnish however you like. There you go—two recipes in one. Bonus!

TED'S TIP

Now let's set the record straight: I am a firm believer in never wrapping food that goes in the smoker, but this is my one exception. Wrapping the flank steak in plastic and foil allows the meat to sit in its butter bath and soak up all those valuable juices. This maximizes flavor and creates a shreddable tenderness.

Korean Bulgogi Smoked Top Sirloin Roast

Bulgogi means *fire meat*, but the name actually refers to the way it is cooked, not the spiciness of the marinade. This marinade is sweet and savory and typically combined with beef. Adding smoke just makes this popular dish even better, in my opinion.

Yield:	Prep time:	Cook time:	Serving size:
1 roast	30 minutes	5 hours	¹⁄₁₂ roast

¼ cup hoisin sauce

2 cups packed light brown sugar

2 cups chopped fresh cilantro leaves

3 cloves garlic, minced

2 green onions, finely chopped

1 red Thai chile, finely chopped

½ tsp. coarsely ground black pepper

2 TB. sesame seeds

1 TB. soy sauce

1 TB. rice wine vinegar

1 TB. minced ginger

1 tsp. kosher salt

½ tsp. sesame oil

1 top sirloin beef roast (about 6 to 8 lb.)

1. In a medium bowl, stir hoisin sauce, light brown sugar, cilantro, garlic, green onions, red Thai chile, black pepper, sesame seeds, soy sauce, rice wine vinegar, ginger, kosher salt, and sesame oil until well combined. Paste can be stored in an airtight container in refrigerator for up to 2 weeks.

2. Preheat the smoker per manufacturer's instructions to 180°F to 225°F using maple, oak, or cherry or a blend of all three woods.

3. Pat roast dry with paper towel. Rub paste all over roast. Place roast into the smoker. Insert thermometer probe into the center of roast. Set the internal temperature for 140°F for medium-rare to medium doneness. Smoke for 5 to 6 hours or until internal temperature is achieved.

4. Remove from smoker and tent with foil; let stand for 15 minutes. Using a sharp slicing knife, thinly slice roast. Serve on toasted buns, drizzled with your favorite BBQ sauce, or try the recipe for Bourbon-Wasabi BBQ Sauce in Chapter 9.

TED'S TIP

A top sirloin is a relatively lean cut of beef, so you don't want to take it past medium doneness. It's terrific when sliced super thin, hot or cold, and piled high to make delicious sandwiches. If you like a juicier surface, you can spritz the roast while it smokes to keep it moist. I actually prefer not to spritz this recipe because I like a dryer smoke, which creates a crisp outside crust with a moist and juicy center.

Four-Pepper–Crusted Beef Tenderloin with Armagnac Butter Injection

The Szechuan peppercorns in this recipe have a unique aroma with a slight lemon flavor. They're really not as spicy as other peppercorns but they do create a bit of a tingle on your tongue. You can find Szechuan peppercorns at Asian markets, specialty food stores, and well-stocked grocers.

Yield:	Prep time:	Cook time:	Serving size:
1 roast	30 minutes	1½ hours	⅙ roast

3 oz. Armagnac

1 TB. olive oil

8 cloves garlic, minced

2 tsp. hot English mustard

2 tsp. honey

¼ cup mixed chopped fresh herbs, such as parsley and rosemary leaves

2 TB. cracked black peppercorns

2 TB. cracked pink peppercorns

2 TB. cracked white peppercorns

2 TB. cracked Szechuan peppercorns

1 TB. kosher salt

½ cup (1 stick) butter

1½ to 2 lb. trussed center-cut beef tenderloin roast

1. In a medium bowl, stir 2 ounces Armagnac, olive oil, garlic, hot English mustard, honey, and mixed herbs until well combined.

2. In a separate bowl, toss black peppercorns, pink peppercorns, white peppercorns, and Szechuan peppercorns with kosher salt; set aside.

3. Melt butter in a small saucepan set over medium-low heat. Stir in remaining 1 ounce Armagnac; set aside and keep warm.

4. Preheat the smoker per manufacturer's instructions to 250°F, using a blend of oak and mesquite that has been soaked in water.

5. Baste tenderloin with most of the herb-garlic mixture, and then rub it with the peppercorn mixture, pressing firmly to adhere. Inject with most of the butter mixture.

6. Insert thermometer probe into the center of roast. Set the internal temperature for 135°F for rare or 145°F for medium doneness, and place in the smoker.

7. Brush with remaining herb-garlic mixture. Close the door and smoke for 1½ to 2 hours or until desired internal temperature is achieved. Inject with remaining butter mixture—during the smoking process, this will keep the tenderloin moist and succulently delicious. Remove from smoker and allow roast to rest for 5 to 10 minutes. Slice and serve.

TED'S TIP

Beef tenderloin is considered the best cut of beef because it's tender and very lean. The absence of fat makes it susceptible to becoming tough and dry if overcooked, so it's best served rare to medium-rare.

Coffee-Porter N.Y. Strip Steaks with Blue Cheese–Pecan Butter

My favorite cut of steak is from the strip loin or short loin. I like my steaks nice and thick; 2 inches tall and weighing in at about 16 ounces each—gotta love it! One steak of this size will easily feed two to three people. Also, cutting the steaks thick will keep them from getting overcooked during smoking. The richness of the coffee and the bold flavor of the porter complements the full flavor of these smoky steaks.

Yield:	Prep time:	Cook time:	Serving size:
4 steaks	4 hours, 30 minutes	1½ hours	½ thinly sliced steak

4 New York boneless strip steaks (about 2 in. thick and 1 lb. each)

1 cup fresh-brewed coffee, chilled

1 (12-oz.) bottle porter-style beer

½ cup (1 stick) unsalted butter, softened

½ cup creamy blue cheese, softened

¼ cup crushed pecans

1 TB. chopped fresh parsley leaves

½ tsp. freshly ground black pepper

Kosher salt

½ cup Java-Java Paste (recipe in Chapter 8)

1. Arrange steaks in a single layer on a glass dish. Add coffee and porter-style beer, turning to coat steaks evenly. Cover and refrigerate, turning steaks each hour, for 4 hours.

2. Meanwhile, in a large bowl, blend unsalted butter with blue cheese until smooth. Stir in pecans, parsley, and black pepper. Season with kosher salt to taste. Store in an airtight container in the refrigerator for up to 3 days.

3. Preheat the smoker per manufacturer's instructions to 250°F, using a blend of pecan and maple woods soaked in water.

4. Remove steaks from coffee-porter marinade; discard excess and pat steaks dry with paper towel. Rub Java-Java Paste all over the steaks, pressing firmly to make it adhere well.

5. Arrange steaks, evenly spaced, on the smoker rack. Insert thermometer probe into the center of a steak. Set the internal temperature for 135°F for medium-rare doneness. Close the door and smoke for 1½ to 2 hours or until desired internal temperature is achieved.

6. Transfer steaks to a cutting board and tent with foil; let stand for 10 minutes. Slice thinly on the bias and serve fanned out on a plate topped with a spoonful of the blue cheese–pecan butter. Serve immediately.

TED'S TIP

Leftover smoked steaks make great sandwiches. Slice it thinly and serve with any leftover blue cheese–pecan butter. This spread on toasted baguettes or rolls is wonderfully delicious.

Prime Rib with Whiskey Mist and Hot Horseradish Mustard

Nothing beats a good old-fashioned prime rib roast, but let me tell ya: it's that much better when it's smoked! Slow things down and smoke this baby right to give it all the "meat respect" and love it deserves.

Yield:	Prep time:	Cook time:	Serving size:
1 roast	30 minutes	3 hours	⅙ roast

½ cup minced garlic

2 TB. freshly cracked black pepper

2 TB. kosher salt plus more as needed

3 TB. olive oil

1 prime rib roast with 6 bones (about 10 to 12 lb.)

½ cup plus 1 tsp. Tennessee whiskey

¼ cup Worcestershire sauce

¼ cup hot Dijon mustard

1 TB. hot prepared horseradish

½ tsp. freshly ground black pepper

1. In a medium bowl, blend garlic, cracked black pepper, and 2 tablespoons kosher salt; add olive oil to form a paste. Rub paste all over roast, pressing firmly so it adheres.

2. Use a funnel to fill a spray bottle with ½ cup Tennessee whiskey and Worcestershire sauce. Shake to mix well; set aside.

3. Preheat the smoker per manufacturer's instructions to 250°F to 280°F, using whiskey barrel–oak smoke chunks or chips that have been soaked in water.

4. Arrange roast on a smoker rack. Insert thermometer probe in center of roast. Set the internal temperature for 135°F to 145°F for rare to medium-rare doneness.

5. Smoke, spritzing with whiskey mixture every 30 minutes, for 3 to 4 hours or until desired internal temperature is achieved.

6. Meanwhile, in a medium bowl, blend Dijon mustard, horseradish, ground black pepper, and remaining 1 teaspoon whiskey. Season with kosher salt to taste; set aside.

7. Transfer roast to a cutting board and tent loosely with foil; rest for 10 to 15 minutes. Carve prime rib and serve with mustard sauce.

> **TED'S TIP**
>
> For a prime rib that will really melt in your mouth, ask your butcher to hook you up with a roast that has been dry aged for at least 21 days.

Cherry Whiskey–Smoked Eye-of-Round

Eye-of-round is one of the lesser-known smoked meats, which is truly a shame. Here's the lowdown on this cut: it's tough, lean, and best when served thinly sliced or shaved. So make sure you always use a brine or marinade, never cook it past medium, and always use a razor-sharp knife to slice it as thinly as possible.

Yield:	Prep time:	Cook time:	Serving size:
1 roast	24 hours, 30 minutes	2½ hours	⅙ roast

1½ cups cherry whiskey or brandy

1 cup water

1 eye-of-round beef roast (about 4 lb.)

½ cup Brisket Rub (see Big Beefy Texas-Style Smoked Brisket recipe in Chapter 15)

1 cup cherry juice

1 cup cola

1. Use a funnel to fill a spray bottle with 1 cup cherry whiskey and water. Shake to mix well; set aside.

2. Rub roast with ¼ cup Brisket Rub. Place the roast in a large zipper-lock plastic bag. Top with cherry juice, cola, and remaining ½ cup cherry whiskey. Seal the bag, removing as much air as possible, and refrigerate for 24 hours, turning the bag every 4 to 6 hours.

3. Prepare the smoker according to manufacturer's instructions to 200°F to 225°F, using oak and cherry woods soaked in water.

4. Remove roast from marinade and discard excess. Rub roast with remaining ¼ cup Brisket Rub. Arrange roast on a smoking rack.

5. Insert thermometer probe into center of roast. Set the internal temperature for 140°F to 145°F for medium doneness. Close the door and smoke, spritzing occasionally with the cherry whiskey mixture, for 2 to 3 hours or until desired internal temperature is achieved.

6. Transfer roast to a cutting board and tent loosely with foil. Let stand for 10 minutes. Thinly slice or shave the roast using a shape knife. Serve immediately on toasted rolls with desired garnishes.

TED'S TIP

Keep your knives honed with a sharp edge by giving them a few passes on a sharpening steel before each use. Knives are the most important tool in the kitchen, and a sharp blade will always make kitchen prep and slicing easier.

Smoked Beef Ribs with Chocolate Stout and Horseradish Baste

The flavor of chocolate with the boldness of a strong stout makes these beef ribs sing with deliciousness. Ask your butcher for really meaty beef ribs. Special order them if you have to; the extra cost will be worth it. Try to get racks with eight bones so all your efforts can feed a crowd. Nothing beats watching your family gnaw on sweet, smoky bones trying to suck off every last bit of the tender meat.

Yield:	Prep time:	Cook time:	Serving size:
3 racks of ribs	24 hours, 30 minutes	6 hours	3 bones

3 racks meaty beef back ribs (about 4 lb. each)

6 (12-oz.) bottles chocolate-infused stout or porter

¾ cup Big Beefy Brisket Rub (recipe with brisket recipes in Chapter 15)

½ cup (1 stick) unsalted butter

½ cup Worcestershire sauce

3 TB. beef or veal *demi-glace*

2 TB. packed light brown sugar

1 TB. prepared hot horseradish

4 cloves garlic, minced

1 tsp. chopped fresh rosemary leaves

1. Place ribs in a large container and top with 5½ bottles chocolate-infused stout, making sure ribs are submerged. Cover and refrigerate for 24 hours. Remove ribs from stout and pat dry with paper towel. Rub Big Beefy Brisket Rub all over ribs; set aside.

2. Meanwhile, combine remaining ½ bottle stout, unsalted butter, Worcestershire sauce, beef demi-glace, light brown sugar, hot horseradish, garlic, and rosemary in a small saucepan set over medium-low heat. Cook, stirring constantly, until butter is melted and mixture is well combined; set aside.

3. Preheat the smoker per manufacturer's instructions to 220°F, using oak, maple, hickory, or cherry woods with a good amount of humidity.

4. Insert thermometer probe into meatiest part of rib without touching the bone. Set the internal temperature for 185°F. Close the door. Smoke, basting frequently with sauce, for 6 to 8 hours or until internal temperature is achieved and bones move freely. Remove from smoker and serve immediately.

Variation: Speed up the process by wrapping the ribs in two layers of foil after the initial 4 hours of smoking. Smoke for an additional 2 hours or until set temperature is achieved. I prefer to smoke the old-school way and not wrap the meat, but sometimes you need to give it a bit of a push.

DEFINITION

A **demi-glace** is a classic French sauce made from reduced beef or veal broth. You can buy prepared demi-glace from boutique grocers.

Smoked Prime Rib Demi-Glace Burgers with Smoked Garlic and Onions

If there was ever a burger to stop people dead in their tracks, this is it. The beef demi-glace center is just part of what makes this burger so juicy; the prime rib helps, too. Have plenty of napkins on hand because this is a chin-dripping burger, and then get ready for a lot of pats on the back.

Yield:	Prep time:	Cook time:	Serving size:
8 burgers and	2 hours	5 hours	1 burger and
1 cup horseradish sauce			1 TB. horseradish sauce

2 large sweet onions, peeled and cut into eight wedges

24 large garlic cloves, peeled

3 lb. ground prime rib, chilled

1 cup crispy fried onions

1 tsp. Worcestershire sauce

2 tsp. Dijon mustard

Kosher salt

Freshly ground black pepper

8 (1-tsp.) demi-glace cubes (for this recipe, portion out 1 teaspoon into 8 ice cube molds and chill until solid)

15 sprigs fresh rosemary

½ cup whipped cream cheese

¼ cup sour cream

¼ cup mayonnaise

1 TB. hot prepared horseradish

1 tsp. chopped fresh chives

8 burger buns, toasted

1 cup Boursin cheese or herbed goat cheese, softened

4 cups arugula

1. Preheat the smoker per manufacturer's instructions to 220°F, using oak, mesquite, pecan, hickory, or apple wood. (I've found that the Bradley Smoker produces the best burgers but any smoker will do the job.)

2. Arrange sweet onions and garlic on separate racks and place in the smoker. Smoke for 3 hours or until onions are tender (garlic will still be firm); cool completely. Reserve onions to garnish smoked burgers. Set garlic aside. (Onions and garlic can be smoked up to 2 days in advance.)

3. Preheat the smoker to 250°F to 260°F per manufacturer's instructions using mesquite, oak, or hickory, or try a blend of mesquite, pecan, and oak woods.

4. Mince garlic cloves into a fine paste. Place in a large bowl with the ground prime rib, crispy fried onions, Worcestershire sauce, and Dijon mustard. Season with kosher salt and black pepper to taste. Mix gently until well combined.

5. Divide meat mixture into 8 equal portions (approximately 6 ounces each) and form into baseball-shaped burgers. Using your finger, poke a hole into the center of each burger. Place a demi-glace cube into the center and mold the meat around to enclose the cube. Chill for 1 hour to allow the meat to rest.

6. Line the wire rack of the smoker with fresh rosemary sprigs. Arrange burgers, evenly spaced, on top of rosemary and place in the smoker. Insert thermometer probe into one of the burgers. Set the internal temperature for 160°F for fully cooked beef. Close the door and smoke burgers for 1½ to 2 hours or until desired internal temperature is achieved. If you are grinding your own meat and want to see a little red, go for it. I like my burgers at medium doneness (about 145°F).

7. Meanwhile, in a medium bowl, blend whipped cream cheese, sour cream, mayonnaise, horseradish, and chives. Season with kosher salt and black pepper to taste. Transfer to a small serving dish and chill until ready to serve or up to 3 days.

8. Remove burgers from smoker. Spread bottom of each toasted bun with horseradish cream and top each with burger, smoked onion, Boursin cheese, and arugula. But hey, these are your burgers; dress 'em any way you like!

TED'S TIP

Freshly ground prime rib is always the best. If you don't have a grinder at home, get the butcher to do it for you before you leave the shop. Don't let him give you a hard time about it, either—you're paying top dollar for this cut, so he should make sure you're satisfied!

Santa Maria Tri-Tip with Cabernet Wine Mop

The tri-tip roast comes from the bottom sirloin and gets its name from its triangular shape. Look for a roast that is well marbled with a good amount of external fat. This fat will help keep the roast moist as well as flavor the meat. And keep a close eye on the temperature so you don't overcook this delicate piece of meat.

Yield:	Prep time:	Cook time:	Serving size:
1 roast	4 hours, 30 minutes	3 hours	¼ or ⅙ roast

2 cups cabernet sauvignon wine

¼ cup plus 2 TB. good-quality red wine vinegar

2 TB. minced roasted garlic (about 12 cloves)

1 TB. soy sauce

2 TB. chopped fresh parsley leaves

2 tsp. crushed red pepper flakes

¼ cup plus 2 TB. olive oil

Kosher salt

15 fresh rosemary sprigs

3 TB. coarsely ground black pepper, plus more to taste

1 beef tri-tip roast

1 large sweet onion, peeled and quartered

2 ripe avocados, peeled, pitted, and diced (reserve pit)

3 green onions, chopped

Pinch cayenne

1. In a large bowl, stir cabernet, ¼ cup red wine vinegar, garlic, soy sauce, parsley, and red pepper flakes until well combined. Add ¼ cup olive oil in a slow, steady stream while whisking until fully incorporated. Season with kosher salt to taste; set aside.

2. Tie rosemary sprigs together, using kitchen twine, to make a brush that resembles a feather duster; set aside.

3. Preheat the smoker per manufacturer's instructions to 180°F to 210°F, using vine cuttings or red wine–barrel wood staves, chunks, or chips soaked in water.

4. Rub black pepper all over roast, pressing firmly so it adheres. Place roast on smoking rack. Insert thermometer probe into center of roast. Set the internal temperature for 135°F to 145°F for medium-rare to medium doneness. Smoke, basting every 20 to 30 minutes with reserved wine mixture using rosemary brush, for 3 to 4 hours or until desired internal temperature is achieved.

5. Meanwhile, preheat grill to medium-high heat, about 400°F to 500°F. Grill sweet onion quarters, turning occasionally, for 10 to 15 minutes or until onions are tender and lightly charred; cool and thinly slice.

6. In a large bowl, combine sweet onion slices with avocado, remaining 2 tablespoons red wine vinegar, and remaining 2 tablespoons olive oil. Add green onions and season with kosher salt, black pepper, and cayenne to taste. Place avocado pit in the mixture to help keep the mixture from oxidizing, cover, and keep refrigerated.

7. Transfer roast to a cutting board. Loosely tent with foil and rest for 10 minutes. Carve the roast across the grain into thin slices. Serve immediately with reserved avocado mixture.

> **TED'S TIP**
>
> If you're lucky enough to live near a vineyard, you should check with them in the early spring to figure out when they'll be trimming their grape vines. These cuttings can bring great flavor to your smoked meats. They're also great as skewers for grilling meats. I'm lucky I live in an Italian neighborhood, so in the spring there are plenty of vine cuttings lining the street for easy picking.

Texas Cowboy Beef Jerky

When I think of beef jerky I think of a hard-working cowboy on the open range, and a cowboy's favorite snack is beef jerky. Good jerky should be dry and require a firm hard bite to tear or rip off a piece. Jerky is made with a lot of salt, so even though it's high in protein and low in carbs, the sodium is through the roof. So make this an every-once-in-a-while treat, not a daily habit.

Yield:	Prep time:	Cook time:	Serving size:
12 oz.	1 hour	36 hours	2 oz.

1 beef eye-of-round roast (about 2 to 3 lb.)

2 cups Maple Whiskey Brine (recipe in Chapter 7)

¼ cup maple syrup

1 TB. soy sauce

2 TB. freshly ground black pepper

1. Using a sharp knife, trim all visible fat and sinew from outside of roast. Place roast in the freezer for 2 hours or until slightly frozen but still soft enough to slice. Using a meat slicer or a very sharp carving knife, cut roast into ¼-inch slices, across the grain.

2. Lay a sheet of plastic wrap, about a 12-inch square, on a flat work surface. Arrange 2 slices of beef on the square and top with a second piece of plastic wrap. Using a meat mallet, gently pound slices until they're an even thickness and a little thinner than when you started; repeat with remaining beef. Remember, the thicker the slices, the longer it's going to take to dry them out.

3. In a medium bowl, combine Maple Whiskey Brine, maple syrup, and soy sauce. Dip each slice of beef in marinade and place in a large casserole dish; top with any remaining marinade. Cover and refrigerate, turning once daily, for 2 to 3 days.

4. Preheat the smoker per manufacturer's instructions to 140°F, using oak, mesquite, hickory, pecan, maple, or a combination of the woods. Keep the humidity level to a minimum; do not fill the water pan in your smoker (if you have one).

5. Remove beef from marinade; discard excess. Pat each slice dry with paper towels. It is important that beef is very dry because the smoke will not penetrate the meat if there is any moisture on it. Lay slices in a single layer, evenly spaced, on wire smoker rack(s). Sprinkle with black pepper and place in the smoker.

6. Smoke for 8 to 12 hours or until beef is dry and has reduced in size by about 60 percent.

7. Remove jerky from smoker and cool completely. Serve immediately, or transfer to an airtight container and store in the refrigerator for up to 6 weeks.

TASTY TIDBIT

Jerky can be made from pretty much any type of meat that can be sliced thinly and air-cured. Most of us are familiar with beef jerky, but historically, it was made from buffalo, deer, elk, and antelope. Now, it's become trendy to dry turkey, salmon, ostrich, or even moose. Back in the day, jerky was dried in the sun, but we're not quite so rustic nowadays.

Glorious Pork

In This Chapter

- Different cuts of pork
- The 411 on making sausage
- Makin' bacon
- Ribs, ribs, and more ribs
- Delicious pork recipes

Does anything offer the smoker more versatility than the humble pig? Every cut off a pig is smoker friendly, right down to the tail—although that's an acquired taste. To me, there is just nothing better than pulled pork shredded from the butt as soon as it's removed from the smoker. Glistening with juicy fat, a fragrant pile of moist meaty morsels is like an aphrodisiac. Who can resist? It's that ratio of fat to meat and the adaptable mild flavor of the meat that makes pork a perfect meat for smoking. You can spice it sweet or savory, or hot as hell. Pork can take it all!

I could rhapsodize for three pages on how I love pork or we can just agree right now that pork is the perfect choice for the smoker. So let's dive in and dissect this glorious animal to learn about all its beautiful cuts, tough and tender alike.

Assorted Pork Cuts

The tender cuts of pork, like beef, come from the rib and loin. The best cuts come from higher up on the animal, thus the old saying "high on the hog." The shank and shoulder muscles give us the toughest cuts.

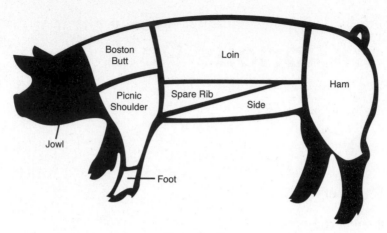

Cuts of pork.

Here's how the different cuts break down:

- **Boston butt:** Also called *pork butt*, it comes from the upper shoulder, which consists of parts from the neck, shoulder blade, and upper arm. It's moderately tough with a good deal of connective tissue … but after 12 or 16 hours in the smoker, it turns into some pretty tasty pulled pork. It can also be cut into steaks or ground for sausages.

- **Pork shoulder:** Also called *picnic shoulder*, this cut is pretty tough and is usually cured and/or smoked. It is also used for making ground pork or sausage meat. It's not ideal, but the pork shoulder can be roasted as well.

- **Pork loin:** Hogs are bred to have extra long loins, so that they can have up to 17 ribs—unlike beef and lamb, which only have 13 ribs. The entire pork loin can be smoked, bone-in or boneless. It can also be cut into individual chops or cutlets. The tenderloin is taken from the rear of the pork loin, and baby-back ribs come from the upper rib cage area of the loin.

- **Ham:** The back legs of the hog is where we get fresh, smoked, or cured hams.

- **Ham hock:** Is taken from the joint at the shank end of the ham, where it joins the foot; it's used extensively in southern U.S. cuisine.

- **Pork belly or side:** The pork belly, or pork side, is where we get pancetta and bacon!

- **Pork spare ribs:** Are taken from the belly side of the ribs where they join the breastbone. Tougher than back ribs, spare ribs are best prepared by smoking very slowly over a low temperature.

- **Pork jowl:** Is mostly used to make sausages, although it can also be cured and made into bacon. In Italian cooking, cured pork jowl is referred to as *guanciale.*

- **Feet:** Pork feet can be cured and/or smoked or even pickled. Pig feet are a key ingredient in traditional Mexican *menudo.*

TED'S TIP

A smoked ham hock is a fabulous addition to all kinds of comfort foods. Keep a ready supply to stir into a pot of baked beans, split pea soup, rice and beans, chili, or succotash.

All You Need to Know About Sausage

Let's talk sausage! But first, let me ask you a question: What is a sausage? Do you really know? A sausage is a pile of chopped or ground meat with added fat and seasoning, or ground seafood with fat and seasoning, or even ground vegetables with fat and seasoning. That's it. No real mystery, no secret ingredients with weird names, although you can definitely find those sorts of sausages in a retail setting. So if you can make a meatloaf, you can make a sausage. You just need to add the stuffing step. You might be surprised to find out it's actually kinda fun!

You'll only need one piece of equipment beyond what you probably already have in your kitchen. You could go out and buy an expensive sausage stuffer at a good kitchen or restaurant supply store. But if your wife has one of those stand mixers that comes in every color of the rainbow then you're in luck! A good-quality, high-powered stand mixer almost always has a grinder/sausage attachment available. If not, and the pocketbook still protests, you can still get an affordable, hand-crank meat grinder at a hardware store. You know, like the kind your grandmother would attach to the table to grind beef. Whatever you end up with, just make sure it has coarse- and fine-grinding plates so you can experiment with different textures.

Grinding your own meat is not absolutely necessary, but it's very satisfying. Especially if you want to get fancy and combine various meats with exotic seasonings. When making sausages, it's okay to let your imagination take over; you may come up with really creative flavor and texture combinations. Read my recipe for a basic Smoked Polish Sausage later in this chapter, and you'll get a sense of how straightforward the process can be.

Whether you grind the meat yourself, have your butcher grind it, or buy the packaged stuff from the supermarket, there are a few things to remember to ensure success. First, last, and always, stick to this rule: keep it cold! Everything—from the meat, to the tools, to all the additional ingredients—must always be kept cold. I even chill the grinder attachment. If you're grinding or stuffing a lot, break the meat up into separate packages so you never have too much out of the fridge at a time. Besides the safety issue, which is always paramount, the chilled components will ensure the meat emerging from the grinder will be firm and compact, falling out in tight little nuggets or tubes.

To produce tender sausage out of your smoker, aim for a meat-to-fat ratio of 80/20, or even up to 70/30. Since a lot of that fat melts away during smoking, your sausage won't be greasy. I like to add about ½ cup cold water with a bit of crushed ice to every 5 pounds of meat filling when I mix it. This ensures that the filling maintains a good chill that will help it through the stuffer. Handle the meat very gently and wear latex gloves so you don't warm the mixture with your hands.

Once you have perfected my recipe, you can venture farther afield. There are many classic sausage recipes to inspire you: bratwurst, hot and sweet Italian, even breakfast sausages. Or take a page from us chefs, who have opened this one up wide. You'll see creative combos like chicken and apple, lamb and mango chutney, rabbit with pistachio, and so on. I love to put cheese in my sausages. As I always say, your only limitation is your imagination.

Once you have your cold meat mixture and your grinder is set up for stuffing, you need casing. There are 2 basic kinds of casings: natural and collagen. Natural casings are made from the intestines of hogs, sheep, and cattle. These are by far the most popular. They are packed in dry salt or brine, so you need to flush them with water and soak them before you use them. They come in different sizes, so select whatever makes sense for what you're making. Beef casings are the biggest and used for things like bologna or mortadella. These are tough casings and can be handled fairly roughly.

Collagen casings are an edible by-product of animal hide—usually cattle—and can come in a variety of sizes and colors. When you stuff this casing, the meat adheres to it very tightly, making it difficult to peel away. Collagen is quite delicate, so once stuffed try not to handle it too much. A normal collagen casing is not the ideal casing for a smoked sausage because it doesn't always support the weight of sausage when hung in a smoker. You can purchase extra-thick collagen casings that will stand up to the smoker, and they're much easier to use without a lot of preparation. There are pros and cons for both types of casings. It comes down to personal preference in the end.

TASTY TIDBIT

Texas hot links are possibly one of the most famous smoked sausages around. Charlie Hasselback made them in 1897 in the storeroom of his general store. They grew in popularity as a quick lunch, dinner, or take-out option for house-wives; it wasn't long before they were available nationwide. Over a century later and they're still made the exact same way Charlie made them.

Follow the steps for making Smoked Polish Sausage later in this chapter and you'll learn the basics of stuffing and smoking sausage. Master this method and then you'll know what works and what doesn't when making your own sausage. Then you can add your own personal touches.

Let's Talk Bacon

Okay, I admit, I'm not the most modest guy. But in this case, ask my friends—I make awesome bacon! Without fail, it's the one thing my friends will ask for when they come mooching. So now I'm a meat guy, a sausage guy, and a bacon guy.

Bacon is easily one of the most heavily processed products in the modern marketplace. It's made in huge plants where speed to market is the goal above all others. The curing solutions for mass-produced bacon contain synthetic nitrates in excess, despite the wealth of health concerns connected to this additive. Nitrates are used to help ensure food safety by preventing botulism, which is one of the deadliest foodborne illnesses. And all those synthetic nitrates give you the bright pink, slimy product that we've all come to know as bacon. But it doesn't have to be that way. Once you've made your own bacon and tasted the true luscious smoky notes, you will never be able to eat the prepackaged stuff again.

Follow my recipe for Maple Smoked Bacon later in this chapter, step by step. Once you have a feel for making bacon, you can experiment and put a bit of yourself in it by adding your own personal touches to the cure. I promise you, once you have bitten into my smoked bacon, you'll find yourself on the hunt for more bacon recipes. Anyone who knows my cookbooks knows I have a huge crush on bacon.

When I make bacon, I will usually make at least a whole pork belly's worth. After it's come out of the smoker I portion it out and wrap it well to freeze. It will last in the freezer for up to 3 months (any longer and it will start to taste a bit rancid—but my batches never last longer 3 months, anyway!). In the fridge, it's good for about 2 weeks, which is not as long as the store-bought stuff. But I ask you: who has bacon in the fridge for more than 2 weeks? If I know it's there, I am thinking of ways to use it!

At first, when you read the recipe, you're going to think I'm crazy because on paper, it looks like way too much work. Although it takes 7 days, in terms of actual effort, it's less than 30 minutes worth of work. Patience is the word! While it is curing, you don't have to do anything but wait. Then it's only going to be in the smoker for something like 3 hours, and voilà—homemade bacon!

TASTY TIDBIT

The term "bringing home the bacon" comes from the sport of catching a greased pig at country fairs. The winner kept the pig, and therefore brought home the bacon. Now that's a sport I could really get into!

Rockin' Ribs

Ribs are one of the things I am best known for. In my other life, I'm a corporate development chef for one of the largest rib producers in North America. You may have eaten some of my work in a restaurant chain or retail store we sell to. There's nothing—and I mean nothing—as good as a rack of baby-back ribs pulled from the smoker after about 4 or 5 hours of serious slow-smoking tender love and care. The aroma, the taste, and the texture as you bite into a rib and feel the meat pull away from the bone with just the tiniest bit of effort is unparalleled. If the bone can be pulled out of a rack with no resistance at all, it's overcooked. After that first bite, take a long look at the gorgeous pinky red ring the smoke leaves and try not to suck on the bone … but of course, you will.

When you decide to succeed at perfect ribs, that's when you really need a butcher you can trust. Making friends with your butcher is the best way to guarantee success on the smoker. A good butcher will open a case of ribs and let you choose the best three or four slabs. A good butcher will also help by preparing special cuts and ordering exotic meats. Be kind to your butcher and she will be kind to you!

Preparation is 99 percent of success when smoking. A huge part of that preparation is choosing the right ribs—but first you need to know what you are looking for. So here's the breakdown of all the ribs out there, pork and otherwise:

- **Pork spare ribs:** These ribs are cut from the side where they attach to the breastbone and there is usually soft bone brisket attached. This soft bone brisket should be removed. Spare ribs with large clumps of fat should be avoided. The flap of meat that runs down to the last three ribs can be left or trimmed and cooked separately. Butchers used to discard this cut as it was very tough and no one thought the average consumer could do anything with it—but we know better, don't we? These ribs were made for the smoker. They have the perfect ratio of fat to meat that's perfect for the smoker, but too fatty and tough for the grill. After 4 hours in the smoker, the fat will melt into the meat, making it rich and tender.

- **Pork baby-back ribs:** These ribs are from the strip of rib bones the butcher gets when boning a whole loin. The button bones are the tailpiece of the rack and should be removed. Back ribs are a chef's favorite pick because they are so versatile. They cost more because they have a higher meat-to-bone ratio and they contain some of the tenderloin and loin meat. They are the tenderest cut and can do very well on the grill. In the smoker you have to be very careful not to overcook back ribs. They can be so tender the bones just fall out when you go to lift a rack.

- **Pork country-style ribs:** These ribs are very meaty but tough, making them another rib born for the smoker. They come from the rib end and usually only have a few bones attached.

- **Pork St. Louis ribs and Kansas City ribs:** St. Louis ribs are spare ribs trimmed to have the sternum bone, cartilage, and rib tips removed. Kansas City ribs are an even more closely trimmed spare rib because the hard bone is removed.

There are various other cuts in the pork rib category, such as rib tips, riblets, and button ribs. These ribs are basically a way to sell every last morsel of the rib section of an animal but they are not necessarily smoker friendly. We don't cover them in this book but you are welcome to investigate on your own; you may find something you really like. Me, I'm a baby-back guy.

Now I know we're in the pork chapter, but we're already talking about ribs, so let's go over the other types of ribs out there:

- **Beef ribs:** These are huge ribs cut from the loin. They can be very meaty but they can also be very fatty and full of tough cartilage. Long, slow cooking in the smoker turns them into something to behold. When you eat a really good plate of these huge ribs, there is no way you won't be dripping with juices and have such a dirty face you'll be in need of a shower—but you'll have no regrets! My recipe for Smoked Beef Ribs with Chocolate Stout and Horseradish Baste in Chapter 10 could very well change your life.

- **Lamb ribs:** These are cut from the forequarter of the lamb. (That's the front.) The rack is oblong in shape with layers of fat and lean meat. Lamb ribs are sweet and rich with flavor.

- **Bison ribs and venison ribs:** These ribs are also cut from the loin of the animal. They can be absolutely delicious, but as with all game, they require a little extra TLC. Game tends to be extremely lean so you will see my game rib recipes involve adding a lot of moisture. Game takes a longer time in the smoker and tolerates stronger flavors than more domesticated meats. Game ribs are not always easy to find at the local grocery store. But your friend the butcher will know where to get these; she can order them for you. I do love that Cranberry-Orange Honey Glaze in Chapter 12 on venison ribs!

I know we got a bit off topic, since this chapter is an ode to the pig—my favorite of all the animals. Shhh, don't tell the others, though.

Back to buying ribs. Ribs, no matter what kind, should show a healthy layer of meat all over the slab. There shouldn't be any bones showing on the slab. These are called shiners. You only want to see the bones peeking out at the ends. Check carefully for shiners with back ribs because they're produced if poorly butchered. With spare ribs there will be cartilage and the split breastbone attached; there will also be heavy fat over the last three bones. Remove the cartilage and the heavy fat trimmed, but only the excess on those last three bones; you need the rest for the smoker.

TASTY TIDBIT

Did you know national bacon day is the first Saturday before Labor Day? So get ready to smoke some bacon and eat it all day—breakfast, lunch, dinner, and midnight snack!

You'll find lots of how-to info that you need to prepare ribs in my rib recipes in this chapter and in Chapter 15. But there is one thing that needs a special mention to guarantee success: Remove the membrane! Please! The thick membrane that covers the back of your rack of ribs—no matter what kind—must go, otherwise the seasoning and smoke will not penetrate it. This step makes or breaks your ribs. Some people score it in a diamond shape. That's cheating and it just produces a lot of very chewy bits because it's tough and inedible. It's not hard to remove, just work your fingers under the membrane at one end and once it's loose enough grasp it with a paper towel (it's very slippery), and slowly and firmly pull it off the back in one big piece. Once you've done two or three, you'll wonder what all the fuss was about.

Pork T-Bones with Smoked Strawberry and Rhubarb Compote

Big, thick, meaty pork T-bone chops are ideal for serving your friends and family. Paired with a compote of tender smoked strawberries, this dish is unique and delicious.

Yield:	Prep time:	Cook time:	Serving size:
4 pork chops and 3 cups compote	30 minutes	2 hours	1 pork chop and 3 TB. compote

4 (2-in.) thick pork T-bone chops, tenderloin intact

¼ cup honey

½ cup Ted's World-Famous Bone Dust BBQ Seasoning Rub (recipe in Chapter 8)

1 pt. fresh strawberries, hulled

2 large stalks fresh rhubarb, peeled and coarsely chopped

⅓ cup granulated sugar

⅓ cup packed light brown sugar

½ cup apple juice

1 TB. fresh lemon juice

½ tsp. finely grated lemon zest

2 TB. prepared gourmet-style BBQ sauce

1 tsp. cold unsalted butter

Kosher salt

Freshly ground black pepper

1. Preheat the smoker per manufacturer's instructions to 250°F using cherry, pecan, hickory, apple, or oak wood.

2. Working on one side at a time, brush pork chops with honey and sprinkle with Ted's World-Famous Bone Dust BBQ Seasoning Rub; press the seasoning into the meat. Place pork chops on smoker rack.

3. Insert thermometer probe into the thickest part of one pork chop close to the bone. Set the internal temperature thermometer for 145°F to 150°F for medium to medium-well doneness. (You can do less if you wish. I personally like the chops at 140°F.) Smoke chops for approximately 2 to 3 hours or until desired internal temperature is achieved.

4. Meanwhile, lay strawberries on a rack and place in the smoker. Smoke for 30 minutes or until dull in color; cool slightly. Combine rhubarb, granulated sugar, light brown sugar, and apple juice in a medium saucepan set over medium heat. Cook, stirring occasionally, for 10 to 12 minutes or until rhubarb is soft. Add lemon juice and lemon zest. Stir in gourmet-style BBQ sauce and smoked strawberries.

5. Reduce the heat to medium-low. Cook, stirring occasionally, for 10 to 12 minutes or until strawberries have softened and the compote has thickened. Stir in unsalted butter and season with kosher salt and black pepper. Set aside and keep warm.

6. Remove pork chops from smoker. Serve immediately topped with smoked strawberry and rhubarb compote. Compote can be stored tightly covered in the refrigerator for up to 1 week.

> **TED'S TIP**
>
> Smoked Strawberry and Rhubarb Compote spooned over vanilla ice cream rocks! Seriously, try it.

Fire Ball Spritzed–Extra-Meaty Back Ribs with Smoked Honey Glaze

You know you have smoked good ribs when you can pull the bone cleanly from the meat without too much resistance. This is the first sign that you have done a pretty good job. It's the sign that lets you know the ribs are ready to devour and they're going to be moist and succulent and taste of the sweet smoke.

Yield:	Prep time:	Cook time:	Serving size:
4 racks ribs	24 hours, 40 minutes	6 hours	½ or full rack

2 cups apple juice

1 cup cold water

½ cup cinnamon schnapps liqueur

¼ cup hot sauce

4 racks meaty pork back ribs (about 2½ lb. each)

1 cup plus 1 tsp. Cinnamon Chipotle Rub (recipe in Chapter 8)

1 cup Smoked Honey (recipe in Chapter 17)

1. Use a funnel to fill a spray bottle with apple juice, cold water, cinnamon schnapps liqueur, and hot sauce. Shake to mix well. Spritz can be stored in the refrigerator for up to 1 week.

2. Remove membrane from the bone side of each rack. Rub 1 cup Cinnamon Chipotle Rub all over both sides of each rack. Arrange in a container, cover, and refrigerate for 24 hours.

3. Preheat the smoker per manufacturer's instructions to 200°F to 230°F using hickory, oak, maple, or mesquite.

4. Insert thermometer probe into meatiest part of rib without touching the bone. Set the internal temperature for 185°F. Close the door. Smoke, spritzing every hour with the apple juice mixture, for 6 to 8 hours or until internal temperature is achieved and bones move freely but stay in place.

5. Remove ribs from smoker, brush with Smoked Honey, and sprinkle with remaining 1 teaspoon Cinnamon Chipotle Rub. Serve immediately with plenty of napkins—it's gonna get messy!

TED'S TIP

This spritz is a bit spicy, so make sure you don't spritz into the wind. Spritz safety 101: always spritz with the wind at your back. Use this spritz on poultry, pork ribs, pork chops, fish, or seafood.

Smoked BBQ Ribs with Redneck White Sauce

This recipe may seem lengthy but it has a lot of useful and versatile components. It not only gives you the basics for smoking side ribs—which you can execute with any flavoring accompaniments—but it also includes a great rub and sauce recipe that can be used in several different applications.

Yield:	Prep time:	Cook time:	Serving size:
2 racks ribs	25 hours	6 hours	¼ to ½ rack ribs

2 whole racks pork side ribs (about 5 to 6 lb. each)

8 cups Apple-Honey Pig and Bird Brine, icy cold (recipe in Chapter 7)

1 cup packed light brown sugar

½ cup granulated sugar

½ cup paprika

¼ cup celery salt

¼ cup onion salt

¼ cup ground black pepper

2 TB. chili powder

1 TB. dry mustard powder

1 TB. smoked paprika

2 tsp. ground ginger

2 tsp. plus pinch cayenne

1 tsp. poultry seasoning

8 (12-oz.) cans your favorite beer, slightly warm

1 TB. unsalted butter

¼ cup diced sweet onion

2 cloves garlic, minced

¼ cup 35 percent whipping cream

½ cup ranch dressing

½ cup mayonnaise

1 TB. grated Parmesan cheese

1½ tsp. lemon juice

1½ tsp. cracked black pepper

½ tsp. prepared horseradish

½ tsp. Worcestershire sauce

½ tsp. kosher salt

1 TB. chopped fresh parsley leaves

½ tsp. chopped fresh thyme leaves

1. Place ribs in a large, deep container. Pour Apple-Honey Pig and Bird Brine over ribs, cover, and refrigerate, turning every 8 hours, for 24 hours.

2. In a medium bowl, stir light brown sugar, granulated sugar, paprika, celery salt, onion salt, black pepper, chili powder, dry mustard powder, smoked paprika, ginger, 2 teaspoons cayenne, and poultry seasoning until well combined. This Kansas City–style rub can be stored in an airtight container in a cool, dry, and dark place for up to 4 months.

3. Sprinkle about ½ cup rub all over each rack of ribs. Place in a clean container, cover, and refrigerate overnight.

4. Preheat the smoker per manufacturer's instructions to 220°F to 235°F with high humidity, using hickory, maple, mesquite, or oak wood, or a blend of your favorites.

5. Arrange ribs, bone side down and evenly spaced, on a smoker rack. Go ahead and use a rib-rack accessory here, if you have one. Insert thermometer probe into the meatiest section of a rack without touching bone. Set the internal temperature thermometer for 185°F.

6. Smoke, drizzling with a warm beer every hour (that's half a can of beer per rack, every hour) for 8 to 10 hours, or until bones move freely but not so much that they fall off the meat. Be sure to adjust the dampers as required and keep the humidity level high in the smoker.

7. Meanwhile, melt unsalted butter in a medium saucepan set over medium heat. Add sweet onion and garlic. Sauté for 3 to 5 minutes or until onion and garlic are softened but not browned. Pour in whipping cream and bring to a boil, stirring frequently.

8. Reduce the heat to low. Whisk in ranch dressing and mayonnaise. Whisk in Parmesan cheese, lemon juice, black pepper, horseradish, Worcestershire sauce, kosher salt, and remaining pinch cayenne. Cook for 10 minutes, stirring constantly, or until thickened. Remove from heat and stir in parsley and thyme. Sauce can be stored in an airtight container in the refrigerator for up to 1 week.

9. Once internal temperature is achieved, remove ribs from smoker and sprinkle with a little extra spice mixture. Serve immediately with warm sauce on the side.

TED'S TIP

The spice mixture is a Kansas City–style rub that is also great when used with pork shoulder, chops, beef, or chicken. The sauce, which I call Redneck White Sauce, is also very versatile. You can serve it with grilled chicken or even pour over biscuits and mashed potatoes. It's also great with fried chicken!

Maple Smoked Bacon

The quest to smoke my own bacon started years ago because I was tired of buying commercial bacon that's injected with a ton of water and just splatters all over my kitchen—plus it's not very tasty. I started using a ready cure but it's packed full of unnatural ingredients to preserve the bacon and give it that beautiful pink color we all know and love so much. I wanted something more natural, even if it meant losing the pink color. So I developed a cure without all the scary nitrates and nitrites to use on fresh pork bellies. This bacon doesn't last as long as the commercial stuff and it has a grayish hue instead of pink, but it tastes great and you can feel good about eating it.

Yield:	Prep time:	Cook time:	Serving size:
1 pork belly	5 days	36 hours	2 to 3 slices

3 cups kosher salt

1 cup packed dark brown sugar

1 cup maple syrup

½ cup Ted's World-Famous Bone Dust BBQ Seasoning Rub (recipe in Chapter 8)

2 tsp. pure vanilla extract

1 fresh pork belly of uniform thickness, rind removed (about 10 to 12 lb.)

1. In a medium bowl, stir kosher salt, dark brown sugar, maple syrup, Ted's World-Famous Bone Dust BBQ Seasoning Rub, and vanilla extract until well combined. Store in an airtight container in the refrigerator for up to 6 months.

2. Cut pork belly into three manageable pieces, about 10 inches long each. Rinse under cold water and pat dry with paper towel. Place in a large (not metal) container and refrigerate.

3. Rub about ½ cup maple cure all over each piece of pork belly in an even layer. Sprinkle a handful of salt mixture on the bottom of the container and place a piece of pork belly on top. Sprinkle top of pork belly with another handful of cure, rubbing the cure into the flesh. Add another pork belly and repeat until all pieces have been seasoned with maple cure.

4. Cover and place in the refrigerator for 5 to 10 days, depending on the thickness of the pork belly and how salty you like it. I find about 6 to 7 days works nicely.

5. Each day, be sure to spoon the liquid that has accumulated in the bottom of the container over the pork belly.

6. Remove pork from container and pat dry with paper towel. Arrange bellies on a cooling rack in a rimmed baking sheet and store uncovered in the fridge for 3 to 4 days or until good and dry.

7. Preheat the smoker for cold smoking per manufacturer's instructions to 85°F or less.

8. Insert thermometer probe into center of belly. Set the internal temperature for 145°F. Smoke for at least 24 hours or until flesh is firm and pork belly is a rich, brownish-red color and the internal temperature is achieved. Bacon can now be thinly sliced and used as desired.

9. If you prefer double-smoked bacon, just increase the smoker temperature to 135°F and smoke for an additional 8 hours or until the internal temperature is 150°F to 160°F. Remove from smoker and cool completely. Wrap in cheesecloth or butcher's paper and refrigerate until needed. Do not wrap in plastic wrap, as the plastic will promote moisture and cause your bacon to spoil. Bacon will keep for 2 weeks in the refrigerator or for up to 3 months if vacuum sealed and frozen.

TED'S TIP

Store bacon in a large piece and cut slices as needed; this will prevent mold. Should mold spores start to appear on the belly, simply cut them off and replace the wrapping.

Smoked Peameal with Bloody Mary Injection

Peameal bacon is a Canadian thing. What Americans call back bacon and what Canadians call back bacon are two very different things: U.S. back bacon is a boneless pork loin that's smoked and fully cooked with a similar texture to ham. Canadian back bacon is pork loin cured in a brine and then crusted in fine cornmeal. It can be roasted whole or sliced to pan fry or grill. This recipe is a combination of our respective versions for a friendly cross-border treat.

Yield:	Prep time:	Cook time:	Serving size:
1 pork loin roast	30 minutes	4 hours	⅛ roast

1½ cups tomato juice

½ cup pepper-flavored vodka

1 TB. Worcestershire sauce

2 tsp. celery salt

1 tsp. hot sauce

1 tsp. kosher salt

½ cup (1 stick) cold butter, cut into cubes

1 boneless cured pork loin peameal roast with cornmeal crust (about 3 lb.)

4 TB. Ted's World-Famous Bone Dust BBQ Seasoning Rub (recipe in Chapter 8)

1. Combine tomato juice, pepper-flavored vodka, Worcestershire sauce, celery salt, hot sauce, and kosher salt in a medium saucepan set over medium heat. Cook for 5 minutes or until mixture begins to bubble; remove from heat.

2. Whisk in cold butter, a few cubes at a time, until well combined; cool completely. Measure out 1 cup and reserve.

3. Rinse roast under cold water to remove cornmeal crust and pat dry with paper towel. Place roast in a zipper-lock plastic bag. Pour tomato juice mixture over roast, keeping 1 cup reserved. Seal the bag, removing as much air as possible, and gently massage. Refrigerate, turning twice, for 24 hours.

4. Preheat the smoker per manufacturer's instructions to 240°F using hickory, maple, or apple wood.

5. Remove roast from marinade; discard excess marinade. Sprinkle Ted's World-Famous Bone Dust BBQ Seasoning Rub all over roast; set aside. Suck up reserved 1 cup tomato juice mixture into your injector and inject roast in several places.

6. Place roast in the middle of the smoker rack. Insert thermometer probe into the center of the roast. Set the internal temperature thermometer for 160°F. Close the lid and smoke for 3 to 4 hours or until internal temperature is achieved. Remove from the smoker and tent loosely with foil; let stand for 5 minutes. Carve and serve immediately.

TED'S TIP

Pile slices of smoked peameal on fresh-baked biscuits with the Smoked Frittata with Grape Tomatoes and Cheese (recipe in Chapter 17) for an outstanding breakfast!

Smoked Ozark Sirloin

This may seem abnormal to you, but trust me when I say there is just something so comforting about a log of smoked bologna. Food doesn't always have to be fancy, and smoking is definitely all about flavor, even with something as simple as bologna.

Yield:	Prep time:	Cook time:	Serving size:
1 bologna log	5 minutes	1½ hours	⅛ log

3 lb. pork, beef, chicken, or turkey bologna log (about 4 in. wide and 8 in. long)	Beer, wine, or ginger ale for spritzing

1. Preheat the smoker per manufacturer's instructions to 250°F using hickory wood.

2. Arrange bologna in the smoker. Insert thermometer probe into the center of the log. Set the internal temperature for 160°F. Smoke, spritzing occasionally with beer for 1½ to 2 hours or until internal temperature is achieved.

3. Transfer bologna to a cutting board and slice into thin or thick rounds. Drizzle with your favorite mustard or BBQ sauce and serve immediately.

TED'S TIP

The folks in Arkansas call this an Ozark Sirloin. Here in Canada we call it Newfie steak. My favorite way to serve it is thinly sliced on top of a grilled cheese sandwich with pickled onions and a drizzle of ketchup!

Smoked Spam

You might think smoking Spam is weird, but it's really a great vehicle for smoke, taking on a sweet smoky flavor that adds a new dimension to this popular canned meat. I've pan-fried Spam with eggs for breakfast, added it to grilled cheese sandwiches, and grilled it to make a quick and easy burger. I've deep-fried little cubes until crispy to use as croutons in salads and soups, and now I'm smoking it!

Yield:	Prep time:	Cook time:	Serving size:
12 ounces	2 minutes	3 hours	3 ounces

1 (12-oz.) tin Spam

1. Chill the tin of Spam in the refrigerator for 24 hours.

2. Preheat the smoker for cold smoking with ice packs per manufacturer's instructions to 85°F or colder using hickory wood.

3. Open tin and carefully remove Spam in one piece. Place in the smoker and smoke for 2 to 3 hours or until it's a smoky golden brown.

4. Remove Spam from smoker and refrigerate until chilled. Slice and serve in any way your little Spam-loving heart desires!

TASTY TIDBIT

Did you know the state of Hawaii sells more tins of Spam than any other state in the United States and that Korea is the largest consumer of Spam in the whole world?

Smoked Polish Sausage

Polish sausage, also known as *kielbasa* (all sausage in Poland is called kielbasa), is made from pork mixed with fresh garlic and marjoram. For this recipe, I have slightly modified the classic with the addition of some hot pepper for a bit of heat. I like my sausage to bite back!

Yield:	Prep time:	Cook time:	Serving size:
20 (4-oz.) sausages	2 hours	4 hours	1 sausage

5 lb. boneless pork butt, cut into 1-in. chunks (80 percent lean)

8 large cloves garlic, minced

1 TB. pickling salt

2 tsp. freshly ground black pepper

2 tsp. granulated dried garlic

2 tsp. dried marjoram leaves

1 tsp. crushed red pepper flakes

½ tsp. cayenne

2 TB. cold water

1 cup finely crushed ice

Hog or collagen sausage casings, soaked in cold water

1. Set up the meat grinder according to manufacturer's instructions. Arrange pork chunks on a parchment-lined baking sheet and place in the freezer for 30 minutes or until very cold but not frozen.

2. In a medium bowl, stir minced garlic, pickling salt, black pepper, granulated garlic, marjoram, crushed red pepper flakes, and cayenne until well combined; set aside.

3. Grind pork using the medium plate on the meat grinder. Place ground meat in the refrigerator for 30 minutes to rest. (Tip: clean your meat grinder now; it saves time and aggravation later.)

4. Set up the sausage stuffer according to manufacturer's instructions. Take pork out of the refrigerator and sprinkle spice mixture evenly over the surface. Pour cold water over crushed ice and add to meat mixture. Mix thoroughly with your hands until all ingredients are evenly distributed.

5. Using the sausage stuffer, portion the pork mixture into hog casings. You decide the length of the sausage; I personally like sausages about 6 to 7 inches in length. Arrange sausage on a parchment- or butcher paper–lined baking sheet; refrigerate. The sausages are now ready for any preparations.

6. Preheat the smoker for cold smoking per manufacturer's instructions to 125°F using oak or maple wood.

7. Hang sausage from hooks, if you have them (this ensures even smoking and doesn't cause rack markings), or arrange them, evenly spaced, on a smoker rack. Place sausages in the smoker. Heat and dry out sausages for 30 minutes without any added smoke. Insert thermometer probe into the center of a sausage and set the internal temperature for 165°F.

8. Start adding in the smoke and maintain the 125°F temperature. Smoke sausages for 2 hours. Increase the smoker temperature to 165°F, and continue to smoke for 3 to 4 hours or until internal temperature is achieved. Remove sausages from smoker and cool completely. Transfer to a container and refrigerate for up to 2 days or freeze for up to 2 months.

9. To serve, just preheat your grill to medium heat. Cook sausages for 3 to 5 minutes per side or until heated through and lightly charred.

10. Serve with your favorite sausage condiments. I like 'em with mayo, hot mustard, sauerkraut, red onion, and a crispy, garlicky dill pickle.

TED'S TIP

You're going to need a meat grinder with a medium grinding plate and a sausage stuffer. So if you don't have these things, see if you can borrow them. Your butcher should sell sausage casings, but you can also get them at specialty food service operations, as well as specialty food stores. Also, if you know your butcher really well, you can ask him to prepare a meat mixture for sausages using a spice recipe you like. But you have to ask really nicely!

Delicious Lamb and Wild Game

In This Chapter

- The difference between domestic and imported lamb
- Different cuts of lamb
- Cooking basics for lamb and wild game
- Smoky recipes for lamb and wild game

A lot of people are afraid to cook lamb. I think they have this idea that it's difficult to cook, so they don't want to experiment with an expensive cut of meat because they could screw up and waste their money. Well even though I'm a chef, I can tell you that lamb is one of the easiest meats for the average Joe to cook. No kidding. There's really nothing more straightforward than slathering some garlic, mustard, and maybe some rosemary all over a boned leg, tying it up in a roll, and throwing it on the grill. You just have to sear it first; then move it over to indirect heat, close the lid, and 45 minutes later your family thinks you're a god. It really is that easy.

Guess what? It's no harder to smoke lamb, and boy is it worth the time. Lamb, more than any other meat, comes with its own built-in baste. Lamb fat is dense and sweet. If you've cooked any lamb at all, you know how quickly that fat will set up (harden) away from heat. But it melts just as fast, especially in the heat of the smoker where it keeps that young meat moist, tender, and über juicy.

My favorite ways to prepare lamb include marinating and grilling leg of lamb on the rotisserie, smoking a boneless leg, or my absolute favorite, smoking a whole baby lamb. I remember one occasion in my backyard when the aroma from the lamb in the smoker just completely overwhelmed us. We began picking at it "just for a taste" and suddenly, we were like wild animals—pulling the lamb apart by hand, grabbing rolls to sandwich the meat and sop up the juices. By the time we got ourselves back under control there was not much left but a pile of bones. Forget carving it properly to put it on the table and eat like human beings—that fragrant lamb demanded we dive in right then and there, and we weren't sorry!

Domestic vs. Imported Lamb

New Zealand and Australia are major exporters of lamb to North America. Most American lamb is raised in Texas, California, Wyoming, South Dakota, Colorado, and Utah. North American lamb is often marketed as having milder flavor than imported because it's fed a combination of mixed grains and mixed grasses, whereas imported breeds are fed only grass, which gives the meat a stronger flavor. It's really only noticeable in older imported lamb because the imported young lamb is comparable to most North American lamb. The choice is totally personal, both are good products, but I have to say, I don't want to eat lamb that has been disguised to taste like beef—what's the point?

Assorted Lamb Cuts

Just like with any other animal, it's essential to know where the cut comes from in order to determine how to prepare it and what flavors to use.

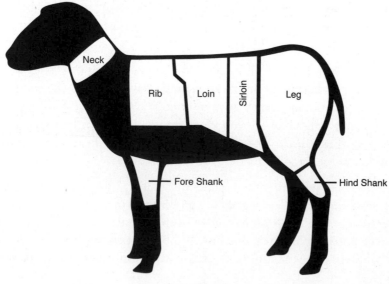

Cuts of lamb.

Lamb primal cuts include the following:

- **Lamb shoulder:** Sold with or without the bone and often used for roasts, lamb shoulder becomes incredibly tender when it's slow smoked.

> **TED'S TIP**
>
> Square-cut lamb shoulder is a square-shaped cut containing arm, blade, and rib bones. Ask your butcher to special order it for you before they cut it into chops.

- **Lamb rib:** Sometimes called a hotel rack, this primal cut is where we get lamb rib chops, lamb crown roast, and rack of lamb. Depending on the size of the ribs, a lamb chop may actually have two ribs on it. A rack prepared in the smoker will quite literally show you what "melts in your mouth" actually means.

- **Lamb breast:** This cut contains a lot of cartilage and other connective tissues, so it is one of the few cuts that should be cooked with moist heat. Lamb breast is also used to make ground lamb. It definitely lends itself to smoking methods; a slow-smoked breast can make sensational pulled lamb.

- **Lamb neck:** Another tougher cut (as far as lamb is concerned) with a lot of cartilage, the lamb neck is best used for making lamb stew or smoked for pulled lamb.

- **Lamb shank:** The shank is the lower section of the animal's leg, and it's extremely tough and full of connective tissue, so the best cooking method for this cut is braising. (Note: lamb has a foreshank and a hindshank, which come from the foresaddle and hindsaddle respectively. The hindshanks are just a bit meatier.) Lamb shanks braised in the smoker combines two great techniques creating an amazing texture and smoky flavor.

- **Lamb loin:** This is where we get the lamb-loin roast and lamb-loin chops, both tender cuts that are best prepared using dry heat. The entire lamb loin can also be cooked on the grill.

- **Lamb sirloin:** Sometimes considered part of the leg primal cut, but it can also be prepared separately. It is frequently cut into chops or steaks.

- **Lamb flank:** As with beef flank, lamb flank can be tough unless cooked with moist heat. Lamb flank is also used for making ground lamb.

- **Lamb leg:** The leg of lamb can be cut into leg chops, though more frequently it is prepared whole. Roasted leg of lamb is one of the most common preparations, although braised leg of lamb is also popular in some cuisines. As smoking gains in popularity lamb legs are in big demand.

Lamb and Wild Game Basics

We all know that a lamb is a young sheep but there are rules around what can officially be called lamb. Lamb may not be older than 1 year. A younger lamb is milder in flavor and more tender meat than older lamb. The lamb commonly found in supermarkets is anywhere from 6 weeks to 1 year old. After 1 year, it becomes mutton and begins to take on a stronger, almost gamey, flavor.

TASTY TIDBIT

Owensboro, Kentucky, is the undisputed capital for lamb and mutton barbecue, and home to the annual International Bar-B-Q Festival in May. Unlike the Kansas City Barbeque Society competitions that feature pork, chicken, and beef, Owensboro is all about chicken, mutton, and burgoo (a thick soup made with mutton, beef, chicken, and vegetables).

Many people only think of two cuts when they think of cooking lamb: rack of lamb and leg of lamb. But just about every cut of lamb is pretty tender (the animal wasn't alive long enough to develop old, tough meat). Because lamb is so tender, most cuts of lamb can be cooked using dry heat, even when the corresponding cut of beef or pork might not. You can apply any cooking method to lamb that you would to beef or pork but just remember, it isn't going to take as long because the meat is younger. There's a recipe for Owensboro Smoked Lamb Shoulder later in this chapter, and you'll notice it has the same steps the pork shoulder and even the beef brisket do, but the smoking time is way less. The main goal with smoking lamb is to achieve a great smoky flavor and not overcook the meat until it's too dry. A lamb can be slow smoked to 145°F, which will give you a glorious medium-rare meat.

Lamb meat has almost no marbling so the fat tends to encase it and not run through it like its older brother, mutton. Lamb meat can definitely benefit from a good 6 to 8 hours of marinating before you rub it, but it doesn't really need brining. Take it easy on really strong flavors that can overpower the mild meat. Trust me, people who say lamb tastes really strong have probably been eating mutton and didn't know it.

The same cannot be said of game. Game tends to have a strong earthy flavor and must be cooked accordingly. While the venison and bison cuts we see in the marketplace come from farmed animals, they still have true game flavor because of the way they're raised. Their feed is controlled, which makes the gamey flavor a bit more mild, but they are allowed to run free as they would in the wild. This means they get a good amount of exercise, which results in their meat having very little fat. Bison is actually one of the healthiest meats you can eat. It's much leaner and higher in protein than beef. By the way, "gamey" flavor is really just a blanket term for a strong meat flavor. You'll see in my recipes that my standard method for preparing game is to marinate, rub, and cook game meats over low and slow smoke.

The basic form of bison and venison is identical to that of beef, so check out Chapter 10 for information on the various cuts. You can use the same general techniques as you would on beef when you're experimenting with different cuts of game meat. Just remember to multiply by at least 50 percent for everything; for example, a longer marinade time, a longer sit with the rub, and a longer smoke time. Additionally, the flavors you use can be stronger than you would pair with beef.

Smoking game, to my mind, is one of the very best ways to prepare and eat it. It's also a good way to introduce it to someone who's never tasted it. In addition to smoked lamb ribs, I have given you rib recipes for both venison and bison. Once you've nailed the recipes in this chapter, don't be afraid to spread your wings and try other cuts on your own.

SAFE SMOKING

Be sure to review the safety and handling information in Chapter 6 if you will be cooking with actual wild game. It's important to know how to handle it properly. Low and slow is still the mantra, but please make sure you use your thermometer and cook all wild game to the proper temperature (170°F) to ensure that no one gets sick.

Smoky Rack o' Lamb with Goat Cheese

This recipe uses classic flavors that blend beautifully with lamb: garlic, Dijon mustard, and rosemary—a perfect example of "if it ain't broke, don't fix it"! Served with hot smoked creamy goat cheese, this recipe is sure to be a hit.

Yield:	Prep time:	Cook time:	Serving size:
4 racks lamb	30 minutes	1 hour	½ rack lamb

½ cup (1 stick) unsalted butter

4 TB. Dijon mustard

1 TB. chopped fresh rosemary leaves

2 cloves garlic, minced

1 cup panko breadcrumbs

¼ cup grated Parmesan cheese

3 TB. olive oil

3 TB. chopped fresh parsley leaves

Kosher salt

Freshly ground black pepper

4 frenched lamb racks (about 1½ lb. each)

4 oz. creamy goat cheese

1. Combine unsalted butter, 2 tablespoons Dijon mustard, rosemary, and garlic in a medium saucepan set over medium heat. Cook until butter is melted; keep warm.

2. In a medium bowl, toss panko breadcrumbs, Parmesan cheese, olive oil, parsley, and remaining 2 tablespoons Dijon mustard until well combined. Season with kosher salt and black pepper to taste. Set aside, stirring occasionally.

3. Preheat the smoker per manufacturer's instructions to 200°F to 250°F, using oak, maple, or pecan wood.

4. Season lamb all over with kosher salt and black pepper. Arrange lamb, evenly spaced, on a smoker rack. Insert thermometer probe into the thickest portion of lamb without touching bone. Set the internal temperature for 140°F. Smoke, basting with butter mixture every 15 minutes, for 1 to 1½ hours or until desired internal temperature is achieved.

5. Meanwhile, place goat cheese in the freezer for 20 minutes. Line a smoker rack or tray with foil and top with semifrozen goat cheese. Place cheese in the smoker 30 minutes before lamb is ready to come out. Goat cheese is ready when it begins to melt and starts to take on a golden brown color. The cheese should be soft to the touch but not fluid. Remove cheese from the smoker and place in a bowl. Whip with a whisk until smooth; keep warm.

6. When lamb reaches 120°F, brush again with butter mixture and coat each rack in a thin layer of the breadcrumb mixture. Continue to smoke until internal temperature is achieved. Remove from smoker and tent loosely with foil; let stand for 5 minutes. Cut lamb racks into single-bone chops and top with a dollop of warm goat cheese. Serve immediately.

TED'S TIP

Once cut into chops, the lamb can be served in a variety of ways. Arrange 2 to 3 chops on a bed of mashed potatoes or creamy polenta for an impressive entrée. Or arrange on a platter and pass around at a cocktail party as an elegant *hors d'oeuvre*, often called lamb lollipops because the frenched bone resembles a long, white candy stick.

Owensboro Smoked Lamb Shoulder

My inspiration for this recipe comes from Owensboro, Kentucky, known as the BBQ-mutton capital of the United States. Mutton is pretty strongly flavored and can be tough, too, so for this recipe I opted to use spring lamb instead—which has a much sweeter flavor that's usually more appealing. My favorite way to serve this is piled high on warm crusty rolls with a tall glass of sweet Kentucky bourbon!

Yield:	Prep time:	Cook time:	Serving size:
2 roasts	45 minutes	6 hours	⅙ roast

15 sprigs fresh rosemary

½ cup plus 3 TB. freshly ground black pepper

¼ cup plus 3 TB. packed light brown sugar

¾ cup Worcestershire sauce

6 TB. kosher salt

3 TB. olive oil

12 cloves garlic, minced

2 tsp. ground allspice

1 tsp. cayenne

2 square-cut, bone-in lamb shoulder roasts (about 4 to 5 lb. each)

2 cups lamb or beef stock

1 (12-oz.) bottle strong, dark beer

1 cup white vinegar

2 TB. crushed red pepper flakes

1 cup (2 sticks) unsalted butter

1. Use kitchen twine to tie rosemary sprigs together to make a brush that resembles a feather duster; set aside.

2. In a medium bowl, stir ½ cup black pepper, ¼ cup light brown sugar, ¼ cup Worcestershire sauce, 3 tablespoons kosher salt, olive oil, garlic, allspice, and cayenne until well combined; set aside.

3. Using a sharp knife, score a diamond pattern into the fat cap of each roast that's about 1 inch thick and ¼ inch deep. Rub paste all over each roast, pushing the seasoning into the cuts. Transfer roasts to a large pan and cover with plastic wrap. Refrigerate for 24 hours. Remove roasts from the refrigerator and allow to come to room temperature.

4. Combine lamb stock, dark beer, white vinegar, red pepper flakes, remaining 3 tablespoons black pepper, remaining 3 tablespoons light brown sugar, remaining ½ cup Worcestershire sauce, and remaining 3 tablespoons kosher salt in a large saucepan set over high heat. Bring to a rolling boil and remove from heat. Whisk in unsalted butter a tablespoon at a time until well combined. Measure out 1 cup and reserve.

5. Preheat the smoker per manufacturer's instructions to 200°F to 230°F, using oak or oak bourbon-barrel–stave chips or chunks.

6. Insert thermometer probe into the thickest portion of a roast. Set the internal temperature for 200°F. Smoke, basting with beer mixture using the rosemary brush every 30 minutes for 2½ to 3 hours or until internal temperature is achieved and bones move very freely.

7. Carefully transfer roasts to a large pan. Let stand until just cool enough to handle. Pull out the bones; discard or reserve for another use, such as a smoky lamb stock. Remove and discard big hunks of fat if preferred. (Or leave in some fat based on how rich you would like the final dish to be.)

8. Using your finger or two forks, shred the meat into thin strands. Stir in enough of the reserved beer mixture to moisten. Season with additional kosher salt and black pepper. Serve immediately.

TED'S TIP

Place a foil drip pan under the roasts while smoking to catch the drippings. Add the drippings to the shredded meat with the beer mixture before serving for extra lamb goodness.

Smoked Lamb Ribs with Garlic-Ginger-Lemon Soy Baste

Lamb ribs can be very fatty, so to cut the richness I use a tart and salty rub and basting mixture. The flavors of the soy sauce, garlic, ginger, and lemon juice help to balance the richness but don't mask the flavor of the lamb.

Yield:	Prep time:	Cook time:	Serving size:
8 racks	30 minutes	5 hours	⅔ rack

8 racks lamb ribs (about 12 to 16 oz. each)

¼ cup freshly cracked black pepper

¼ cup molasses

12 cloves garlic, minced

5 TB. olive oil

4 TB. soy sauce

4 TB. lemon juice

1 TB. chopped fresh rosemary leaves

2 tsp. minced ginger

1 tsp. crushed red pepper flakes

½ tsp. kosher salt

1 tsp. sambal red chili sauce

1 green onion, minced

1. Trim ribs of excess silver skin, sinew, and fat; set aside.

2. In a medium bowl, stir black pepper, molasses, garlic, 3 tablespoons olive oil, 2 tablespoons soy sauce, 2 tablespoons lemon juice, rosemary, 1 teaspoon ginger, red pepper flakes, and kosher salt until well combined. Rub all over ribs. Place in a container and cover. Refrigerate, turning and spooning pooled liquids over ribs, for 24 hours.

3. Preheat the smoker per manufacturer's instructions to 235°F with a moist humidity level, using oak or hickory wood.

4. Arrange ribs, evenly spaced, on the smoker rack. Smoke for 3 hours or until bones move fairly freely. Transfer to a heatproof work surface. Brush ribs all over with remaining 2 tablespoons olive oil. Wrap tightly in two layers of heavy-duty foil.

5. Return ribs to smoker and continue to smoke at 235°F for an additional 2 hours or until bones pull cleanly from the meat. Remove ribs from smoker and cool slightly.

6. Meanwhile, in a medium bowl, stir remaining 2 tablespoons soy sauce, remaining 2 tablespoons lemon juice, remaining 1 teaspoon ginger, sambal red chili sauce, and green onion until well combined; set aside.

7. Preheat the grill to medium heat, about 350°F to 400°F. Cut rib racks into 2 to 3 bone portions. Grill ribs, basting with green onion mixture, for 3 to 4 minutes per side or until ribs are lightly charred and heated through. Serve immediately.

> **TED'S TIP**
>
> Lamb ribs can be quite fatty, and that can cause flare-ups during grilling. You can prevent this by searing ribs over high heat and then finishing and basting over indirect heat until caramelized, rather than scorched.

Smoked Veal Chops with Blackberry Butter

The key to this recipe is to smoke the veal chops quickly to keep them moist and succulent and allow the richness to stand out. This is one place you definitely don't want to overcook anything, so keep a close eye on the thermometer. When buying veal, look for milk-fed veal because it is more tender and moist compared to grain-fed veal, which is a little tougher. Also, ask your butcher to french the veal chops for you, which means he cleans the bones and leaves them nice and long for an elegant presentation.

Yield:	Prep time:	Cook time:	Serving size:
4 veal chops	30 minutes	1½ hours	1 veal chop

4 milk-fed, bone-in veal chops (about 1½ to 2 in. thick and 12 to 16 oz. each)

2 cups buttermilk

1 sprig fresh thyme

6 black peppercorns, cracked

1 cup brandy

1 cup water

2 cinnamon sticks (about 3 in. long)

1 cup fresh blackberries

½ tsp. granulated sugar

Pinch kosher salt

4 tsp. freshly ground black pepper

1 tsp. chopped fresh thyme leaves

½ cup (1 stick) unsalted butter, softened

Pinch ground cinnamon

1. Place veal chops in a large zipper-lock plastic bag. Add buttermilk, thyme, and 1 teaspoon black peppercorns. Seal bag, squeezing out as much air as possible, and refrigerate for at least 6 hours or up to overnight.

2. Meanwhile, prepare the spritz. Using a funnel, pour brandy and water into a spray bottle. Add cinnamon sticks and shake well. Store in the refrigerator until needed.

3. In a small bowl, toss blackberries, sugar, and kosher salt; let stand for 15 minutes. Mash blackberry mixture until almost smooth. Stir in 1 teaspoon black pepper, thyme, unsalted butter, and cinnamon until well combined. Refrigerate until needed or up to 2 weeks.

4. Preheat the smoker per manufacturer's instructions to 200°F to 250°F, using a blend of pecan and oak or maple and cherry woods.

5. Remove chops from marinade; discard excess marinade. Pat veal chops dry with paper towel. Season chops with remaining 3 teaspoons black pepper on all sides. Arrange chops, evenly spaced, on a smoker rack.

6. Insert thermometer probe into the thickest portion of a chop without touching bone. Set the internal temperature for 135°F to 145°F for medium-rare to medium doneness. Smoke, spritzing with brandy mixture every 15 to 20 minutes, for 1½ hours or until desired internal temperature is achieved.

7. Remove chops from smoker and place on a platter. Loosely tent with foil and let stand for 5 minutes.

8. Serve chops garnished with a dollop or two of blackberry butter.

TED'S TIP

This blackberry butter is just fantastic with so many things. Try it as a garnish for your favorite grilled or smoked chicken recipes. Spread it on toast to have for breakfast, or have it with pancakes and waffles.

Smoked Bison Short Ribs with Black Currant–BBQ Sauce

The combination of red wine, cinnamon, and black currants works really well with the strong bison flavor. First you marinate, then you rub, and then you smoke—that's a lot of flavor layers!

Yield:	Prep time:	Cook time:	Serving size:
6 racks ribs	25 hours	6 hours	¾ to 1 rack ribs

2½ cups Shiraz wine

¼ cup Concord grape juice

6 cloves garlic, minced

3 TB. mixed chopped fresh herbs, such as rosemary, thyme, and parsley leaves

3 TB. olive oil

3 TB. balsamic vinegar

2 TB. packed light brown sugar

1 TB. fresh coarsely ground black pepper

1 TB. prepared horseradish

1 tsp. Worcestershire sauce

1 cup fresh black currants, blueberries, or blackberries

¼ cup granulated sugar

¼ cup cassis (black currant liqueur)

2 TB. hot red pepper jelly

6 racks bison short ribs (about 1½ lb. each)

¼ cup Cinnamon Chipotle Rub (recipe in Chapter 8)

1. In a medium bowl, stir Shiraz wine, Concord grape juice, garlic, mixed herbs, olive oil, balsamic vinegar, light brown sugar, black pepper, horseradish, and Worcestershire sauce until well combined. Can be stored tightly covered in the refrigerator for up to 1 week.

2. Combine black currants, granulated sugar, cassis, and hot red pepper jelly in a medium saucepan set over medium heat. Bring to a boil and reduce the heat. Simmer, stirring occasionally, for 20 minutes or until currants are extremely soft. Using a hand blender, purée sauce mixture until smooth. Add another splash of cassis if the sauce is too thick.

3. Place ribs in a zipper-lock plastic bag and pour in Shiraz marinade. Seal bag, removing as much air as possible. Refrigerate for 24 hours. Remove ribs from marinade and pat dry with paper towel; discard excess marinade. Remove or score membrane of the ribs. Rub Cinnamon Chipotle Rub all over ribs. Hold in the refrigerator.

4. Preheat the smoker per manufacturer's instructions to 200°F using oak or wine-barrel staves.

5. Arrange ribs, evenly spaced, on the smoker rack; smoke for 4 hours. Transfer ribs to a heatproof surface and baste with black currant sauce. Wrap tightly in two layers of heavy-duty foil and return to the smoker.

6. Increase smoker temperature to 235°F. Smoke for an additional 2 hours or until bones move very freely. Remove from smoker and carefully open foil pouch. Serve with any remaining black currant sauce.

Variation: Replace the bison ribs with beef short ribs, venison, or elk ribs.

TED'S TIP

You should select a good-quality Shiraz for the marinade, but it doesn't have to be anything super pricey. Just pick something you would want to drink with the meal you smoked using the marinade. It can also be used with chicken, turkey, fish, shellfish, pork, or beef.

Venison Ribs with Cranberry-Orange Honey Glaze

The sweet and tart flavor of the cranberries mixed with the orange and honey makes for a delicious glaze on these smoked, meaty ribs. If you aren't the hunting sort, venison and other game ribs can be found in specialty meat shops. This recipe also works well with elk or bison ribs.

Yield:	Prep time:	Cook time:	Serving size:
4 racks ribs	30 minutes	8 hours	⅓ to ¼ rack

4 racks venison or elk ribs (about 1½ to 2 lb. each)

6 TB. Crazy Cajun Rub (recipe in Chapter 8)

2 (12-oz.) bottles strawberry or raspberry lambic-style beer

½ cup cranberry sauce

½ cup cranberry jelly

¼ cup cranberry juice

¼ cup orange marmalade

¼ cup honey

1 TB. apple cider vinegar

1 tsp. crushed red pepper flakes

1. Using a sharp knife, remove membrane from back of ribs or score backside in a diamond pattern. Rub Crazy Cajun Rub all over ribs. Arrange ribs on a baking sheet, cover with plastic wrap, and refrigerate for 24 hours.

2. Pour strawberry lambic-style beer into two glasses and let stand until slightly flat. Give them a stir to remove a few of the bubbles. Using a funnel, transfer beer to a spray bottle; set aside.

3. Combine cranberry sauce, cranberry jelly, cranberry juice, orange marmalade, honey, apple cider vinegar, and red pepper flakes in a medium saucepan set over medium heat. Cook for 5 to 10 minutes or until heated through and well combined; set aside.

4. Preheat the smoker per manufacturer's instructions to 200°F to 230°F, using oak, hickory, maple, pecan, or cherry wood.

5. Arrange ribs, bone side down, and evenly spaced on a smoker rack. Insert thermometer probe into the meatiest portion of rib without touching bone. Set the internal temperature for 180°F to 185°F. Smoke, basting with cranberry mixture and spritzing with beer, for 4 to 6 hours or until internal temperature is achieved and bones move very freely.

6. Remove from smoker and baste one last time with cranberry mixture. Cut into two-bone portions and serve immediately.

TED'S TIP

Don't worry if this or any other rib recipe makes a bit more than you need for one meal. Just refrigerate leftovers; to reheat, toss the ribs on a hot grill, basting with remaining cranberry mixture or your favorite BBQ sauce, until lightly charred and heated through.

Smokin' Chicken and Other Poultry

In This Chapter

- Chef 101: chicken and poultry basics
- The two kinds of poultry available
- Different cuts of poultry
- Recipes for chicken and other poultry

Is there anything you can't do with chicken? I know people who only eat chicken, and while it's not my chosen lifestyle, I can appreciate the loyalty. It is one of the most versatile proteins—well, all poultry is versatile.

Chicken and Poultry Basics

I like to buy whole birds—chickens, turkeys, or ducks—because then I can cut them the way I like. Quail, pheasant, and other game birds are usually only available whole. If I want a "Supreme of Chicken" I don't have to explain what that is to a grocery store butcher.

I get to use up all the so-called waste to make homemade stock, too. Homemade stock is easy to make and so worth it. Just throw whatever chicken scraps you have (backbone, wing tips, carcass, etc.) into a large pot. Add a few ribs of celery, a couple carrots, and an onion. Fill the pot with cold water and bring to a gentle simmer. Don't boil or stir the stock; otherwise, it'll get cloudy. Let it simmer for 1½ hours, then strain and discard solids. Put it back on the stove to simmer for another hour to concentrate the flavors, and that's it! I pour mine into ice cube trays or small containers and freeze. I can just thaw a small amount when I need it to use as an injection or add to sauces and gravies for a flavor boost.

Keep in mind, there is a difference between stock and broth. Stock is exactly what I have just described; there aren't any additional seasonings, like salt or pepper. Broth—especially store-bought broth—can be very salty, so limit where you use it and how much you add to your recipes. Using stock gives the cook more control and allows you to decide when to add salt and how much to use. Most chefs prefer to use stock but I do call for broth sometimes, so read the recipes carefully to make sure you have the right ingredient.

When you're choosing poultry for the smoker, look for nice plump birds with a broad, well-formed breast that's even on both sides. The thighs should also be plump-ish. Use a finger to press down on the flesh; it should feel firm, not soft and mushy. The skin should be tight and strong with no discolorations or blemishes. There should be no pinfeathers or broken bones sticking out. Make sure there isn't too much fat clinging to the "pope's nose" (the stubby knob at the rear of a bird where the tail feathers used to be) or under the thigh skin. A little is okay but pulling big clumps of fat out of the body cavity is annoying—and who wants to pay for fat and extra skin instead of actual meat?

Fresh chicken should not have an odor; you should have to put your face close to the bird to catch the slightly sweet, clean fragrance. If there is a sour or off odor coming from a bird, toss it away. When in doubt, throw it out! It is better to be safe than oh so sorry.

SAFE SMOKING

Review the safe handling and storage information in Chapter 6 before you start preparing poultry. Raw chicken is notorious for food safety issues because of bacterial contamination from microorganisms, like listeria and salmonella. Both of these can be avoided if you take the proper precautions. Wash your hands and all items used with raw foods in hot soapy water before and after preparation. And *never* carve a cooked chicken on the same board you've handled raw chicken on!

As with most things to do with the smoker, thorough preparation ensures success. All poultry will need a bit of work to get ready for the smoker. You want to trim excess fat from the bird but keep a little bit because this is like a built-in baste that will keep the meat moist during smoking. Next you brine the bird and cut it up into pieces, or truss it if keeping it whole. Trussing ensures that the bird is nice and snug and nothing gets overly crispy. Then it's time to add more flavor by either rubbing it with a seasoning mixture or placing it in a marinade.

Make sure whatever recipe you have in mind matches the type and cut of bird you intend to use it with, because you don't want to dry out the meat. If you are using pieces instead of the whole birds, remember leaner cuts (like breasts) will need special attention so that they don't dry out. Indirect heat—that's the trick! Use a smoker that has the wood box off to the side or, if you're smoking in your BBQ, set the pieces over indirect heat. This means only one side is lit and the chicken is on the other side; this will create great smoke and not burn the tips. It's wise to periodically move the chicken pieces around to take advantage of hot spots and cool spots. Moving the chicken also promotes even browning and picture-perfect chicken!

And possibly most importantly, make sure the fire is nice and low. This advice is even more important when it comes to duck, where very low and very slow is what is going to get you success. Duck has a large amount of fat under the skin, which can't be removed without taking off all the skin—and who wants to do that?! If you have the right temperature and the patience to take your time, the fat will render at the perfect rate so it gets absorbed by the meat and doesn't cause flare-ups.

Fatty skin, combined with a sweet sauce and high heat, is a recipe for disastrously crispy (charred) skin, so easy does it in all respects. Don't apply your sauce until the last quarter of smoking/cooking time. The sauce only needs to warm up and to stick to the meat, so no more than 2 to 3 minutes before it is done. When you can gently twist the drumstick and it comes away from the bird easily, it means that bird is done! Congratulations, you have just found what I like to call a bird's "sweet spot." But when it comes to doneness, nothing is as accurate as a thermometer, so always double-check to ensure that the meat is fully cooked.

Air-Chilled vs. Water-Chilled Birds

There are two types of poultry available commercially: air-chilled and water-chilled. Air-chilled poultry is cooled down by blasting them with cold air. Their surfaces are dried out a bit from the fans but the natural flavors are maintained.

The water-chill process is done one of two ways: the natural method is when the birds are tumbled in a water tank filled with crushed ice and cold water. In the other, more broadly used method, the chicken is tumbled in very cold, chlorinated water. The USDA considers both methods safe and in both methods tumbling causes damage to the birds. It also washes away a lot of the natural flavors and the birds pick up 5 to 7 percent of their body weight, making the meat a bit waterlogged. This is why air-chilled is preferred by many; but again, buy the best you can afford.

TASTY TIDBIT

Here are three interesting (even if they are useless) facts to know about chicken: alektorophobia is the fear of chickens. Chickens are cannibals. Chickens lay a variety of colored eggs: white, brown, green, pink, and blue!

Assorted Poultry Cuts

These cuts apply to chicken, turkey, and duck, although the fat-to-meat and meat-to-bone ratios vary for each the bird.

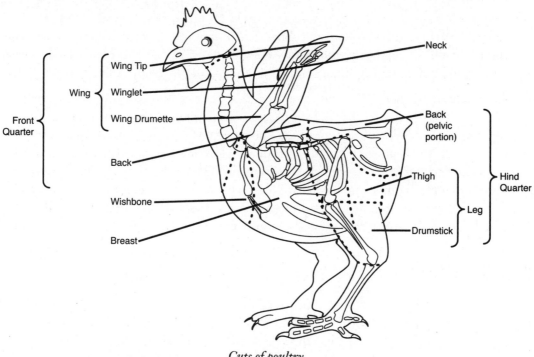

Cuts of poultry.

Here is a list of all the major parts of poultry that are best suited for smoking:

- **Front quarter (breast quarter):** Includes the whole breast and the wing.

- **Hindquarter (leg quarter):** Includes drumstick and thigh, back attached.

- **Wing:** The whole wing is severed at the shoulder joint, so it includes the drumette, winglet, and wing tip.

- **Wing drumette:** The part that resembles a drumstick, it connects at the shoulder joint to the elbow joint where the winglet is separated.

- **Winglet:** The part of the wing between the drumette and the wing tip.

- **Leg:** The portion between the natural seam through the hip to the knee. It includes the thigh and the drumstick.

- **Thigh:** The top section of the leg from the hip to the knee.

- **Drumstick:** The bottom section of the leg between the knee and the shin.

- **Breast:** The meat portion separated from the wing at the shoulder, from the neck by cutting through the twelfth neck bone, and from the back by cutting through the ribs just above the thigh.

- **Breast fillet:** A thin strip of meat, commonly called the tenderloin and generally removed from the breast in retail cuts.

- **Whole back:** Includes the neck, vertebrae, pelvic bones, and tail. May include parts of the vertebral ribs.

- **Neck:** Includes the bones from the top of the shoulder to the last vertebrae under the beak.

Pork, Cheddar, and Apple–Stuffed Bacon-Wrapped Chicken

This is one of my all-time favorite recipes. It has all the best ingredients: meaty skin-on, boneless chicken thighs that are stuffed with ground chicken, smoked pulled pork, white cheddar, and apple! They are so wickedly delicious when glazed with the bourbon-grape-honey sauce that your family and friends will not only want seconds but thirds, too.

Yield:	Prep time:	Cook time:	Serving size:
12 stuffed chicken thighs	45 minutes	35 minutes	1 to 2 stuffed chicken thighs

¼ cup diced dried apple

3 oz. bourbon whiskey

1 lb. ground chicken

½ lb. Smoked BBQ Pulled Pork, unsauced (recipe in Chapter 15) or shredded smoked chicken

1 cup diced white cheddar cheese

½ cup crispy fried onions

2 green onions, chopped

2 tsp. plus 1 TB. Ted's World-Famous Bone Dust BBQ Seasoning Rub (recipe in Chapter 8)

1 tsp. chopped fresh sage leaves

12 meaty, boneless, skin-on chicken thighs

12 slices Maple Smoked Bacon (recipe in Chapter 11), store-bought bacon

½ cup grape jelly

¼ cup honey

¼ cup prepared gourmet-style BBQ sauce

1. Soak a 2-foot-long by 8-inch-wide by ¾-inch-thick oak, maple, hickory, or pecan plank in cold water for 1 hour. Meanwhile, combine diced apple and 2 ounces bourbon whiskey in a microwave-safe bowl. Heat, on medium, for 45 seconds or until steaming; set aside until apple has absorbed almost all the liquid.

2. In a large bowl, combine ground chicken, Smoked BBQ Pulled Pork, white cheddar cheese, fried onions, green onions, 2 teaspoons Ted's World-Famous Bone Dust BBQ Seasoning Rub, sage, and reserved apple-bourbon mixture.

3. Toss chicken thighs with remaining 1 tablespoon Ted's World-Famous Bone Dust BBQ Seasoning Rub until completely coated. Lay thighs, skin side down, on a clean surface. Spread a layer, about ½ inch high, of the pulled pork mixture evenly over each thigh. Roll up the thighs into tight oval bundles. (Reserve any leftover filling to make sliders.) Place chicken thighs in refrigerator for 30 minutes or until set.

4. Lay each slice of Maple Smoked Bacon out on a clean work surface. Firmly run your finger over each slice to stretch by 2 inches. Wrap a piece of bacon around the center of each chicken thigh to look like a bacon "belt." Arrange chicken thighs, in a single line, down the center of the plank. Cover and refrigerate for 1 hour.

5. In a small bowl, whisk grape jelly, honey, gourmet-style BBQ sauce, and remaining 1 ounce bourbon whiskey until smooth; set aside.

6. Preheat the grill to medium heat, about 350°F to 450°F. Place the plank on the grill and close the lid. Smoke, basting every 10 minutes, for 35 to 40 minutes until the internal temperature of chicken thighs register 170°F on an instant read thermometer.

7. Remove from grill and baste with any remaining glaze. Slice each thigh into 5 thin rounds. Serve immediately.

TED'S TIP

Prepare these little bundles the day before and pack in a picnic lunch. They're equally delicious served cold.

Georgia Peach–Dunked Smoked Chicken Thighs with Potato Chip Crust

Tender, moist, and juicy—I'm all about the thighs. These are smoked to perfection and then dunked in a sweet peach sauce and rolled in potato chips. Any leftover peach sauce can be used to glaze smoked pork chops, smoked ribs, and smoked chicken.

Yield:	Prep time:	Cook time:	Serving size:
12 chicken thighs	10 minutes	3 hours	2 chicken thighs

8 ripe but firm peaches	1 tsp. crushed red pepper flakes
1 cup granulated sugar	1 tsp. kosher salt
1 cup peach preserves	½ tsp. ground black pepper
1 orange, zested and juiced	2 tsp. unsalted butter
½ cup white grape juice	12 chicken thighs, skin-on
¼ cup honey	3 TB. Ted's World-Famous Bone Dust BBQ Seasoning Rub (recipe in Chapter 8)
2 oz. spiced rum	
2 tsp. lemon juice	4 cups coarsely crushed potato chips (whatever flavor you like)
1 tsp. white vinegar	

1. Blanch peaches in a large pot of boiling water for 30 to 45 seconds. Immediately plunge peaches into an ice water bath; let stand for 5 minutes. Peel and halve peaches and remove the pits.

2. Coarsely chop peaches and place in a medium saucepan set over medium heat. Add sugar, peach preserves, orange zest and juice, white grape juice, honey, spiced rum, lemon juice, white vinegar, red pepper flakes, kosher salt, and black pepper.

3. Cook, stirring often, until mixture comes to a light simmer; remove from heat. Purée using a blender, adding unsalted butter in two additions, until mostly smooth but still slightly chunky. Sauce can be stored in an airtight container in the refrigerator for up to 2 weeks.

4. Preheat the smoker per manufacturer's instructions to 220°F, using maple, oak, pecan, hickory, orange, or peach wood.

5. Peel back skin from chicken thighs, but make sure to leave it attached on one side. Season meat with 1½ tablespoons Ted's World-Famous Bone Dust BBQ Seasoning Rub. Pull skin tightly around meat and season with remaining 1½ tablespoons Ted's World-Famous Bone Dust BBQ Seasoning Rub.

6. Arrange thighs, evenly spaced, on the smoker rack. Insert thermometer probe into the center of a chicken thigh. Set the internal temperature for 170°F. Close the door and smoke for 2½ to 3 hours or until internal temperature is achieved.

7. Remove thighs from the smoker and dunk, one at a time, into the warm peach mixture. Remove from the sauce and immediately roll in crushed potato chips until evenly coated. Serve immediately.

TED'S TIP

Place potato chips in a zipper-lock plastic bag and pound with a rolling pin or heavy saucepan until coarse crumbs are achieved.

Smoky Chicken-Cheese Dogs

This hot dog is not your conventional store-bought dog. These require a bit of work, but you don't need a meat grinder or a sausage stuffer to make them. The filling is moist and delicious and gets topped with a cheese stick that becomes ooey and gooey in the smoker!

Yield:	Prep time:	Cook time:	Serving size:
6 chicken dogs	2 hours	2 hours	1 chicken dog

6 boneless, skinless chicken breasts (about 4 oz. each)

12 oz. ground chicken

8 oz. boneless, skinless chicken thighs, coarsely chopped

3 TB. crispy fried onions

2 TB. plus 1 tsp. chopped mixed fresh herbs, such as sage, thyme, or parsley

2 green onions, chopped

2 cloves garlic, minced

1 tsp. Dijon mustard

Kosher salt

Freshly ground pepper

6 mozzarella string cheese sticks

Pinch Memphis Rib Rub (recipe in Chapter 8)

2 cups Apple Jack Spritz (see Smoked BBQ Pulled Pork recipe in Chapter 15)

½ cup Apple Butter BBQ Glaze (recipe in Chapter 9)

1. Using a sharp knife, butterfly chicken breasts by slicing through the middle about ¾ of the way to open like a book. Place between two sheets of plastic wrap. Pound out to be a rectangular shape and about ¼ inch thick; set aside.

2. In a large bowl, gently mix ground chicken, chicken thighs, crispy fried onions, 2 tablespoons mixed fresh herbs, green onions, garlic, and Dijon mustard until well combined. Season with kosher salt and black pepper.

3. Lay a 12-inch square of plastic wrap on a flat work surface and top with a flattened chicken breast. Arrange ⅙ of ground chicken mixture in an even layer at the longest end of chicken breast; top with a mozzarella string cheese stick. Using the plastic wrap, tightly roll up chicken breast into a sausage-shaped log to enclose filling securely. Twist the ends of the plastic wrap to compact the chicken dog. The chicken dog should be about 6 inches long by 2 inches around. Repeat with remaining chicken breasts and ground chicken mixture. Refrigerate for 1 hour.

4. Preheat the smoker per manufacturer's instructions to 240°F using a blend of maple, apple, and hickory woods.

5. Season outside of each chicken dog with Memphis Rib Rub. Arrange, evenly spaced, on a smoker rack. Insert thermometer probe into the center of a chicken dog. Set the internal temperature for 165°F. Smoke, spritzing with Apple Jack Spritz occasionally for 2 to 2½ hours or until internal temperature is achieved.

6. Meanwhile, warm Apple Butter BBQ Glaze and brush over chicken dogs just before removing from smoker. Serve immediately on toasted buns with your favorite hot dog condiments.

TED'S TIP

Freeze the mozzarella string cheese sticks for an hour prior to stuffing them in the chicken. This will keep the ground meat cool during the first stages of smoking, as well as keep the cheese from oozing out too early.

Cinnamon Sugar-Smoked Chicken Halves

If you've never smoked a chicken before, this is a great recipe to start with. This dish also has a ton of flavor. The cinnamon sticks create a sweet, pepperlike smoke. It's best served when hot out of the smoker.

Yield:	Prep time:	Cook time:	Serving size:
2 whole chickens	24 hours, 15 minutes	4 hours	½ or ¼ chicken

8 cups Basic Brine (recipe in Chapter 7)

24 (3-in.) cinnamon sticks

2 whole chickens (about 3 to 4 lb. each)

¼ cup granulated sugar

2 tsp. ground cinnamon

1 tsp. ground black pepper

⅓ cup olive oil

3 TB. caramel sauce, room temperature

1 TB. prepared gourmet-style BBQ sauce

1. In a large saucepan or stockpot, prepare Basic Brine recipe; add 4 cinnamon sticks to the mixture as soon as it comes off the heat.

2. Wash chickens in cold water and pat dry. Lay chickens, breast side down, on a clean cutting board. Use kitchen shears to remove backbone by cutting down either side of the spine; discard backbones. Turn chickens over and press firmly on the breastbone to flatten the chicken. Turn chickens over again and remove the breastbone.

3. Cut chickens in half. Arrange chicken halves in a deep pot and cover with brine. Top with a heavy plate to weigh chicken down and keep submerged. Cover and refrigerate for 24 hours.

4. In a medium bowl, stir sugar, ground cinnamon, and black pepper; whisk in olive oil until well combined. (The sugar will settle to the bottom of the bowl, so be sure to stir the mixture each time before basting.) Combine caramel sauce and gourmet-style BBQ sauce in a separate bowl; set aside.

5. Remove chicken from brine and discard excess. Rinse chicken inside and out with cold water and pat dry with paper towel. Arrange chicken on a tray and refrigerate for 1 to 2 hours or until completely dry.

6. Preheat the smoker per manufacturer's instructions to 180°F, using soaked hickory chips or chunks.

7. Remove chickens from refrigerator and brush with oil mixture. Arrange chicken pieces, cut side down and evenly spaced, on a smoker rack. Insert thermometer probe into the thickest part of the thigh, away from the bone. Set the internal temperature for 165°F. Close the door and smoke to dry out the chickens, without any wood chips, for 30 minutes or until skin is slightly sticky to the touch.

8. Add the wood smoke and a few of the remaining 20 cinnamon sticks; smoke for 1 hour. Replenish the wood smoke and cinnamon sticks; baste evenly with sugar mixture. Continue to smoke, replenishing fuel, wood smoke, and cinnamon sticks as needed and basting occasionally for 2 to 3 hours or until internal temperature is achieved.

9. Warm caramel mixture on medium-high in the microwave for 30 to 45 seconds, or until warm but not bubbling. Drizzle over chicken and serve immediately.

TED'S TIP

Shred the smoked chicken meat and use for sandwich fillings, pizza toppings, and taco fillings, and to garnish soups and chowders. I like to toss smoked chicken into my pasta dishes and serve it with a sun-dried tomato cream sauce.

Smoked Buffalo Wings with Blue Cheese and Celery

Nothing says tailgating better than some wickedly delicious hot and spicy smoked wings! These wings are finished in a nontraditional manner. I add the crumbled blue cheese and celery right in with the hot sauce. Give 'em a good toss and get the napkins ready for some fingerlicious good eating!

Yield:	Prep time:	Cook time:	Serving size:
30 wings	30 minutes	2 hours	5 wings

1 (12-oz.) bottle beer

1 cup chipotle-flavored hot sauce

30 whole, jumbo chicken wings (winglet, drumette, and tip attached)

6 TB. Crazy Cajun Rub (recipe in Chapter 8)

¾ cup crumbled blue cheese

¼ cup prepared gourmet-style BBQ sauce

2 TB. butter

2 green onions, finely chopped

1 stalk celery, finely chopped

1. Pour beer into a glass and give it a good stir to remove some of the bubbles. Stir in ½ cup chipotle-flavored hot sauce; set aside.

2. Place chicken wings in a large bowl and sprinkle with Crazy Cajun Rub. Toss until evenly coated.

3. Suck up beer mixture into an injector. Inject each wing with a little squirt. Arrange wings, evenly spaced, on 2 smoker racks.

4. Preheat the smoker per manufacturer's instructions to 220°F, using hickory wood.

5. Insert thermometer probe into the meatiest portion of a large chicken wing without touching bone. Set the internal temperature for 170°F or 180°F for a really crispy exterior. Smoke for 2 to 3 hours or until internal temperature is achieved.

6. Transfer wings to a very large bowl. Top with remaining ½ cup chipotle-flavored hot sauce, blue cheese, gourmet-style BBQ sauce, butter, green onions, and celery. Toss until wings are evenly coated and blue cheese and butter have melted into the mixture. Serve immediately.

Variation: Not a blue cheese fan? Try using crumbled goat cheese, shredded pepper jack, or smoked gouda.

Cozy Corner Smoked Cornish Game Hens

I remember the last time I was at the Cozy Corner in Memphis, Tennessee; it was pouring down rain and the roof was leaking, as a result I was wet, cold, and a little out of sorts. All it took was one bite into that succulent smoked Cornish game hen and I was feeling warm and fuzzy. This is my interpretation of that recipe with just a few twists.

Yield:	Prep time:	Cook time:	Serving size:
6 Cornish game hens	12 hours, 45 minutes	2 to 3 hours	1 Cornish game hen

6 Cornish game hens (about 1½ lb. each)

16 cups Apple-Honey Pig and Bird Brine (recipe in Chapter 7)

½ cup Ted's World-Famous Bone Dust BBQ Seasoning Rub (recipe in Chapter 8)

6 oz. Tennessee whiskey

¼ cup apple butter

2 TB. ketchup

2 TB. honey

1 tsp. lemon juice

2 cups Apple Jack Spritz (recipe in Smoked BBQ Pulled Pork in Chapter 15)

1. Arrange Cornish game hens in a deep pot and cover with Apple-Honey Pig and Bird Brine. Top with heavy plate to weigh hens down and keep them submerged. Cover and refrigerate for 12 to 18 hours. Remove hens from brine, discarding excess. Rinse hens inside and out under cold, running water; pat dry with paper towel.

2. Lay hens, breast side down, on a clean cutting board. Use kitchen shears to remove backbone by cutting down either side of the spine; discard backbone. Firmly press down on the breastbone to flatten the hen.

3. Insert 2 skewers into each hen from the breast to the opposite leg, to create an X pattern. Rub game hens with Ted's World-Famous Bone Dust BBQ Seasoning Rub, pressing spices into meat to adhere. Use an injector to inject 1 ounce Tennessee whiskey into each hen in various places. Chill for 1 hour.

4. Meanwhile, in a large bowl, combine apple butter, ketchup, honey, lemon juice, and a splash of remaining whiskey and stir until smooth; set aside.

5. Preheat the smoker per manufacturer's instructions to 200°F to 230°F, using apple wood or a blend of apple and maple or a blend of apple, maple, and hickory woods.

6. Arrange hens, evenly spaced and cut side down, in the smoker. Insert thermometer probe into the thickest portion of the breast. Set the internal temperature for 165°F. Smoke, spritzing frequently with Apple Jack Spritz and basting with apple butter mixture once internal temperature reaches 130°F, for 2½ to 3 hours or until internal temperature is achieved. Let stand for 5 minutes before serving.

TED'S TIP

For added flavor, lift the skin from the flesh of your Cornish game hen (note you can do this with chicken, duck, and turkey, too) and rub your favorite BBQ seasoning directly onto the meat under the skin. This will ensure the flavor of the rub gets into the meat, not just on the skin.

Dry-Cured Smoked Turkey Breast

The reason for dry curing the turkey breast is to remove excess moisture from the breast meat and to tighten it up so that it becomes firm. This makes it easier to slice thinly. This turkey is best served on a hot or cold sandwich.

Yield:	Prep time:	Cook time:	Serving size:
1 turkey breast	4 days, 30 minutes	12 hours	¼ turkey breast

4 cups fresh parsley, roughly chopped

1 cup fresh sage, roughly chopped

1 large boneless, skin-on turkey breast

1 cup Aromatic Cure (recipe in Chapter 7)

1. In a medium bowl, combine parsley and sage; set aside. Rinse turkey breast under cold water and pat dry with paper towel. Line a baking sheet with plastic wrap. Sprinkle ⅓ cup Aromatic Cure evenly down the center of the baking sheet. Sprinkle about one third of herb mixture evenly over the cure. Lay turkey breast, skin side down, on herbs. Fold the thin end of the turkey breast under so that it is of even thickness throughout.

2. Sprinkle remaining herbs and remaining ⅔ cup cure evenly over turkey breast, making sure none of the meat is exposed; cover with plastic wrap. Set a second baking sheet on top of the turkey breast. Weigh it down with a foil-covered brick or large can of tomatoes.

3. Refrigerate for 3 days. (The general rule of thumb is for every 1 inch of thickness, allow 4 days; so if the turkey breast is 1½ inches thick, allow 6 days.) Remove turkey from cure, rinse under cold water, and pat dry with paper towel. Wrap turkey breast in a paper towel or a kitchen towel and refrigerate for 2 hours to dry out completely.

4. Preheat the smoker per manufacturer's instructions to 85°F for cold smoking using hickory, mesquite, or a blend of pecan and oak or apple and maple woods.

5. Arrange turkey breast in the smoker. Insert thermometer probe into the thickest portion of the breast. Set the internal temperature for 165°F.

6. Smoke for 5 hours. Increase smoker temperature to 150°F and smoke for an additional 3 hours. Increase the smoker temperature to 185°F and add a pan of hot water near the fuel source to add humidity to the smoker. Smoke for an additional 3 to 4 hours or until the internal temperature is achieved.

7. Remove from smoker; cool completely and refrigerate for 24 hours. Slice thinly and use in a sandwich with your favorite garnishes and accompaniments. When vacuum packed, the sliced turkey will last 2 weeks in the refrigerator.

TED'S TIP

Use a meat slicer to shave the smoked turkey breast into nice, thin, deli-style slices.

Cajun-Rubbed and Honey-Dipped Smoked Turkey Drumsticks

I remember the first time I had a smoked turkey drumstick. It was at the Taste of Chicago and Manny's Deli served up these whopping, meaty, smoked turkey drumsticks. In this version, the turkey starts in a citrus brine and gets smoked using fruit wood.

Yield:	Prep time:	Cook time:	Serving size:
6 smoked drumsticks	30 minutes	4 hours	1 smoked drumstick

6 turkey drumsticks

8 cups Juicy Citrus Brine (recipe in Chapter 7)

¾ cup Crazy Cajun Rub (recipe in Chapter 8)

½ cup honey

1. Rinse drumsticks with cold water and pat dry with paper towel. Place drumsticks in a large pan or zipper-lock plastic bag. Pour Juicy Citrus Brine over top and turn to coat. Cover and refrigerate for 24 hours.

2. Preheat the smoker per manufacturer's instructions to 230°F to 250°F, using soaked fruit wood chunks for flavor and hardwood maple, apple, pear, peach, apricot, or citrus wood (orange or grapefruit).

3. Remove drumsticks from brine; discard excess. Pat drumsticks dry with paper towel. Use your fingers to loosen the skin from each drumstick and roll the skin down the leg from the wide end to the knuckle. Sprinkle turkey meat with ¼ cup Crazy Cajun Rub. Pull the skin back over the drumstick and sprinkle with additional ¼ cup Crazy Cajun Rub, pressing the spices into the skin to adhere.

4. Arrange drumsticks, evenly spaced, in the smoker. Insert thermometer probe into the thickest part of drumstick, without touching the bone. Set the internal temperature for 185°F. Close the door and smoke for 3 to 4 hours or until internal temperature is achieved.

5. Remove drumsticks from smoker. Warm honey in the microwave on medium-high for 10 to 15 seconds or until flowing. Brush each drumstick all over with honey and sprinkle with remaining ¼ cup Crazy Cajun Rub. Grab a drumstick and chow down!

TED'S TIP

Shredded smoked turkey meat makes great hot or cold sandwiches. It's also nice as a garnish for soups and chowders.

Maple-Cured Smoked Duck Breasts

Curing duck breasts not only imparts great flavor but also reduces the moisture in the meat, making it much faster to smoke. This allows for a better texture and gives the duck a longer life when refrigerated.

Yield:	Prep time:	Cook time:	Serving size:
4 duck breasts	48 hours, 30 minutes	3 hours	1 duck breast

½ cup chopped fresh parsley leaves

½ cup chopped fresh sage leaves

½ cup chopped fresh thyme leaves

4 cups Maple Whiskey Brine (recipe in Chapter 7)

4 large boneless duck breasts

2 tsp. coarsely ground black pepper

¼ cup maple syrup

1. In a medium bowl, combine parsley, sage, and thyme; set aside.

2. Pour 1 cup Maple Whiskey Brine in the bottom of a nonreactive 3-inch-deep pan. Sprinkle with half of herbs. Arrange duck breasts, skin side down, in a single layer and evenly space over the herbs; press firmly so herbs adhere to meat. Sprinkle remaining herbs evenly over duck breasts and top with remaining 3 cups Maple Whiskey Brine. Cover with plastic wrap and top with a heavy plate to weigh the duck down and keep it submerged. Refrigerate for 2 to 3 days.

3. Remove duck breasts from cure, rinse under cold water, and pat dry with paper towel. Rub black pepper all over duck breasts; set aside.

4. Preheat the smoker per manufacturer's instructions to 125°F for cold smoking, using maple, or a blend of hickory and maple or apple and maple woods.

5. Arrange duck breasts, evenly spaced and skin side up, in the smoker. Insert thermometer probe into the thickest portion of one breast. Set the internal temperature for 135°F. Cold smoke for 3 hours or until internal temperature is reached. Remove duck breasts from smoker and baste with maple syrup. Serve immediately.

6. Store in an airtight container in the refrigerator for up to 2 weeks or up to 6 months if vacuum sealed.

TED'S TIP

Check on the duck breasts daily while in the cure to ensure they're not drying out completely. You still want to maintain some moisture for the succulence factor.

Beer-Brine Smoked Pulled Duck

Most restaurant menus showcase duck with Asian flavors or some kind of fruit (orange or berry, usually). Well I prefer BBQ flavors (in case you hadn't noticed yet). The hot smoke helps render the fat, which bastes the duck while it cooks. Serve this succulent duck on toasted croissants garnished with a little coleslaw. Oh yeah, and try not to nibble too much while you shred the duck meat. Go ahead, try not to nibble. I dare ya!

Yield:	Prep time:	Cook time:	Serving size:
1 duck	24 hours	3 hours	¼ duck

1 whole, meaty and fatty duck (about 4 to 5 lb.)

½ cup plus 3 TB. Ted's World-Famous Bone Dust BBQ Seasoning Rub (recipe in Chapter 8)

4 (12-oz.) bottles pilsner or your favorite beer

¼ to ½ cup gourmet-style BBQ sauce

1. Remove any gizzards from duck cavity and discard. Wash duck in cold water and pat dry.

2. Lay duck, breast side down, on a clean cutting board. Use kitchen shears to remove backbone by cutting down either side of the spine. Remove ribs using kitchen shears, being careful not to cut through the skin. Discard backbone and ribs or reserve for another use.

3. Rub duck inside and out with ½ cup Ted's World-Famous Bone Dust BBQ Seasoning Rub. Lay duck, breast side down, in a deep baking dish or in a large zipper-lock plastic bag. Pour pilsner over duck, ensuring that it's completely covered. Cover tightly, or seal bag, removing as much air as possible, and refrigerate for 24 hours.

4. Preheat the smoker per manufacturer's instructions to 275°F, using hickory, oak, or maple wood.

5. Meanwhile, remove duck from marinade and pat dry with paper towel; discard excess marinade. Rub duck inside and out with remaining 3 tablespoons Ted's World-Famous Bone Dust BBQ Seasoning Rub. Place duck, cut side down,

into the smoker. Insert thermometer probe into the thickest part of the thigh, away from the bone. Set the internal temperature for 180°F. Close the door and smoke for 3 to 4 hours or until internal temperature is achieved. Drizzle with a little beer every once in a while to keep duck moist.

6. Remove duck from smoker; let stand for 10 minutes. Carefully remove skin and thinly slice into julienne strips. Pull the meat off the bones; reserve bones for another use. Use your hands or two forks to shred the meat into little strips. Toss the shredded meat and sliced skin in a large bowl with a splash of beer and just enough gourmet-style BBQ sauce to moisten the mixture. Serve immediately.

TED'S TIP

Use the reserved duck bones to make a full-bodied smoked poultry stock. Stock can be stored in the refrigerator for up to 1 week or in the freezer for up to 6 months. Freeze in ¼-cup portions so you can thaw and use as much or as little as you like.

Succulent Fish and Shellfish

In This Chapter

- How to choose fresh seafood
- Cold smoking versus hot smoking fish
- Using the right fish for the recipe
- Smoking recipes for fish and shellfish

Smoking seafood is probably one of the oldest cooking methods in the world. It's certainly true in North America. It's very likely that one of the first foods the pilgrims received from the natives was some kind of smoked fish. Smoking fish is a great way to get your feet wet in the smoking world, without having to spend a whole bunch of time and money to get set up.

Now you know that you can easily smoke in your grill, so it's a great place to start with fish before making any really big investments. You can smoke just about any kind of fish you like, but denser-fleshed fish like tuna, fatty fish like mackerel, and, of course, salmon are ideal for the smoker. You can also smoke shellfish like shrimp, scallops, lobster tails, oysters—the works! You can even smoke crab cakes using a plank. You'll need to marinate some seafood like octopus and calamari before you smoke them but I promise, once you've tried it, you'll never do it any other way.

Fish and Seafood Basics

When it comes to choosing your fish and seafood it requires just as much thought as if you were choosing any cut of meat. First, buy the freshest fish you can. Right off the boat is always nicest, but that's not always an option, so find a great fish market or grocery store that takes pride in their fish department. You want keep the following in mind when selecting which fish you're going to buy:

- The eyes on a whole fish should be clear; the cloudier the eyes, the older the fish.

- Fish shouldn't smell like fish, it should smell like nothing. If it has a strong fishy odor, it isn't fresh.

- The flesh should be firm to the touch, not mushy.

- Scales should be intact.

Get to know your fishmonger and ask him or her these questions about the fish before buying it:

- When did the fish come in or how old is the fish?

- Where is the fish from?

- Was the fish or shellfish previously frozen? Often what looks fresh actually arrived frozen and was thawed for display.

With all the hard work you are going to do to smoke your fish and shellfish, you should buy the freshest ingredients possible. Your dish can only be as good as your ingredients. This is very important.

Make sure the day you are buying the fish is the same day you will start the recipe process. First-day fresh is always the best! Once you get your fish home, get to a quick cleaning and start the preparations. Cure it, brine it, rub it, or marinate it, and then smoke it as soon as it's ready.

SAFE SMOKING

Seafood can make you very sick if it's abused, so make food safety a habit. Keep everything chilled. Seafood should never sit out of the fridge for longer than a few minutes before it goes in the smoker. The shells on mussels, clams, and oysters need to be tightly closed before cooking; discard any that are not closed. You can try pressing the open shells together, but if they don't snap shut, it means it is dead and no longer safe to eat. Throw it away! Always marinate in the fridge. Never put cooked fish on any surface that previously had raw fish on it.

Cold- and Hot-Smoked Fish

There are two ways to smoke fish. One is cold smoking and the other is hot smoking. Cold smoking is basically smoking below 200°F, with the smoke a long distance from the heat. Those paper-thin slices of translucent smoked salmon that everyone loves, those were cold smoked. A properly cold-smoked fish is considered preserved and it will keep nicely in the refrigerator or freezer for a long time. But then again, it'll probably get eaten up before you need to worry about storing it.

The cold-smoked salmon product you get depends on the species of salmon you are planning on using. Atlantic salmon are fattier than Pacific salmon, sockeye or pink. These fish are much leaner and thus the texture of the smoked salmon will be different than the Atlantic salmon. The Atlantic salmon has a higher fat content, making it a bit moister than the others when cold smoked. The Pacific salmon has a beautiful color and it absorbs the flavor of wood extremely well (try a blend of alder with about 15 percent cedar added in), but it has a slightly dryer texture than the Atlantic. Don't get me wrong, they are both delicious and it's ultimately up to you to choose the type of salmon you want to work with. Personally, I am an Atlantic salmon fan but that's probably because I was raised on it. My dad was a Newfoundlander with a passion for fly-fishing for Atlantic salmon.

Cold smoking requires some fairly specialized equipment and probably shouldn't be embarked upon until you are feeling fairly accomplished in your other smoking techniques. Hot smoking is much easier to master and is suitable for all kinds of fish. With hot smoking, you are, in fact, cooking the fish. The texture will be different than a cold-smoked fish, but they're both delicious. Hot smoking cooks the fish rather than preserving it, so it should be eaten right away. Leftovers will keep for a few days in the fridge and about a month in the freezer if wrapped well.

TASTY TIDBIT

I remember the first salmon I ever caught. I was fly-fishing with my dad in Newfoundland on the river he grew up fishing on. He was a pretty talented fly fisherman. He could cast a fly from either hand. So there we were, having some father and son fun, when I hook into a wild Atlantic salmon. Now it was not a big fish, only about 9 pounds, but I fought it for a good 30 minutes before reeling it in. It was beautiful. That was a good day. Thanks, Dad!

The Right Fish for the Right Recipe

Like all other proteins with various cuts, you need to keep in mind that not all fish is the same and therefore won't cook the same. Smoking something with a firm flesh, like halibut or fatty mackerel, is pretty straightforward because the dense flesh is sturdy enough to stand up to the smoking process.

A more delicate fish like sole, perch, or tilapia is going to require more attention and much less time in the smoker than other fish. These are delicate loose-fleshed fish, so you need to handle them gently. They cook quickly and will have a milder smoke flavor. The same goes for adding flavor; delicate fish need more delicate flavors so that you don't overpower the taste of the fish. If you're not sure what category the fish you want to work with falls into, just ask your fishmonger for advice. At the end of the day, you're just cooking, so relax, be patient, and have fun with it!

Irish Whiskey–Smoked Salmon

The key to making good smoked salmon is to cure it properly, allowing the cure to remove all excess moisture. Next, a long and cold smoke makes sure that all the sweet smoke permeates the salmon.

Yield:	Prep time:	Cook time:	Serving size:
1 side salmon	60 hours, 30 minutes	5 hours	2 to 3 slices

7 oz. Irish whiskey

1 Atlantic side salmon, skin-on (about 1½ to 2 lb.)

2 TB. freshly cracked black pepper

2 cups fresh dill fronds

¾ cup kosher salt

½ cup packed light brown sugar

½ cup granulated sugar

1. Line a large roasting pan with plastic wrap. Pour 6 ounces Irish whiskey in the roasting pan. Arrange salmon, skin side up, in the pan. Refrigerate for 2 hours.

2. Turn salmon over. Gently rub black pepper into salmon flesh. Scatter dill fronds evenly over salmon. Drizzle remaining 1 ounce whiskey over dill.

3. In a medium bowl, combine kosher salt, light brown sugar, and granulated sugar and sprinkle evenly over salmon. Cover with plastic wrap. Place a second baking sheet over top and weigh it down with a foil-wrapped brick or heavy can. Refrigerate for 48 hours.

4. Remove salmon from refrigerator. Remove plastic wrap and scrape away salt, sugar, and dill mixture and rinse under cold water. Pat dry with paper towel. Return to the refrigerator on a clean baking sheet to air dry for 12 hours.

5. Preheat the smoker for cold smoking per manufacturer's instructions to 125°F or less, using whiskey barrel, alder, maple, hickory, or pecan wood.

6. Lay salmon on a rack or insert a meat hook through the tail section of fillet and hang in the smoker. This ensures a more even smoke and allows any excess fat to drip off.

7. Let cured salmon dry in the smoker for 1 to 1½ hours before adding the smoke. This helps remove excess moisture from the fish. Cold smoke for 4 hours or until flesh is firm to the touch.

8. Using a very sharp, flexible slicing knife, thinly slice on a sharp angle, as needed. Serve chilled with your favorite smoked salmon garnishes.

9. Store smoked salmon in an airtight container in the refrigerator for up to 1 week or freeze for up to 2 months.

TED'S TIP

Try using a different liquor to change the flavor of your smoked salmon. You can replace Irish whiskey with a variety of other whiskeys (Tennessee, bourbon, Canadian, rye, or Scotch) as well as dark rum, cognac, Armagnac, brandy, or tequila.

Plank Hot-Smoked Salmon

Plank smoking salmon adds the sweet flavor of cedar to the salmon with no need to cure it beforehand. It's absolutely delicious, and in my opinion, the best way to cook and eat salmon.

Yield:	Prep time:	Cook time:	Serving size:
1 side salmon	1 hour, 15 minutes	30 minutes	⅙ to ⅛ side salmon

¼ cup packed light brown sugar

2 TB. freshly cracked black pepper

1 tsp. plus 1 TB. kosher salt

½ tsp. cracked coriander seeds

½ tsp. cracked mustard seeds

½ tsp. granulated garlic

½ tsp. granulated onion

1 side salmon, skin-on (about 2 to 3 lb.)

½ orange

1. Soak a 2-foot-long, $\frac{1}{2}$-inch-thick western red cedar plank in water for at least 1 hour. Preheat the grill to medium-high heat, about 450°F to 550°F. Remove plank from water and dry with paper towel.

2. In a large bowl, stir light brown sugar, black pepper, 1 teaspoon kosher salt, coriander seeds, mustard seeds, garlic, and onion until well combined. Rub mixture all over the top of salmon fillet; set aside.

3. Place the plank on the grill and season the surface of the plank with remaining 1 tablespoon kosher salt; close the lid. Heat for 3 to 4 minutes or until the plank begins to crackle and smoke.

4. Place fillet, skin side down, on the plank; close the lid. Reduce the heat to medium, about 350°F. Smoke, checking for flames occasionally, for 25 to 30 minutes or until salmon is just cooked through and opaque in the center. Remove from grill and squeeze orange over top. Serve immediately.

TED'S TIP

Use leftover plank-smoked salmon in your favorite salmon salad recipe for an awesome sandwich filling.

Smoked Soy-Sesame Salmon

For this smoking recipe, I lay cinnamon sticks across my smoker rack and lay the salmon on top. The flavor of the cinnamon permeates the salmon with a sweet, smoky flavor. Make sure you don't oversmoke or overcook this dish. It's best when the salmon is served medium, which is a warm coral-colored center.

Yield:	Prep time:	Cook time:	Serving size:
1 side salmon	1 hour, 30 minutes	1 hour	⅙ side salmon

20 (6-in.) cinnamon sticks

1 side salmon, skin-on (about 1½ to 2 lb.)

1 tsp. fresh coarsely ground black pepper

¼ cup soy sauce

2 TB. mirin

2 TB. rice wine vinegar

2 TB. packed light brown sugar

1 tsp. sambal red chile sauce

1 tsp. freshly grated ginger

1 tsp. toasted sesame seeds

1 tsp. black sesame seeds

½ tsp. dried wasabi powder

1 lemon, zested and juiced

¼ cup chopped fresh cilantro leaves

2 green onions, finely chopped

Kosher salt

Freshly ground black pepper

1. Arrange all of the cinnamon sticks on a foil-lined baking sheet. Lay salmon over top of cinnamon sticks and cover loosely with plastic wrap. Refrigerate for 1 hour. Sprinkle about 1 teaspooon black pepper evenly over salmon to season.

2. In a large bowl, stir soy sauce, mirin, rice wine vinegar, light brown sugar, sambal red chile sauce, ginger, toasted sesame seeds, black sesame seeds, wasabi powder, and lemon zest and juice until well combined. Stir in cilantro and green onions; set aside.

3. Preheat the smoker per manufacturer's instructions to 250°F to 260°F, using alder wood.

4. Remove salmon from refrigerator and season with kosher salt and black pepper. Brush some of the soy mixture evenly over salmon.

5. Insert thermometer probe into the thickest part of salmon. Set the internal temperature thermometer for 150°F for medium. Transfer salmon, using the foil as a guide, to a smoker rack and place in the smoker. Smoke for approximately 1 hour or until internal temperature is achieved.

6. Remove from smoker. Liberally spoon remaining soy mixture over salmon. Serve immediately.

TED'S TIP

Always ensure your fish and seafood are icy cold before putting them in the smoker. This helps them to stay firm and hold in the natural juices.

Smoked Mackerel with Maple and Dark Rum

Mackerel is quite an oily fish, which makes it perfect for smoking. The fattier the fish, the less likely it will be to dry out during the smoking process.

Yield:	Prep time:	Cook time:	Serving size:
4 whole fish	3 hours, 30 minutes	4 to 6 hours	½ fish

4 whole fresh mackerel (about 1½ lb. each), cleaned and butter-flied with head, rib bones, and backbone removed

9 TB. maple syrup

2 tsp. coarsely ground black pepper

½ cup sea salt

3 TB. packed light brown sugar

4 oz. good-quality dark rum

1. Arrange mackerel, skin side down, open and evenly spaced, on a parchment-lined baking sheet. Brush 6 tablespoons maple syrup on the cut side of each fish. Sprinkle black pepper evenly over top.

2. In a small bowl, stir flaked sea salt and light brown sugar, and sprinkle evenly over fish. Drizzle with 3 ounces dark rum. Cover with plastic wrap and top with a heavy plate to weigh it down. Refrigerate for 2 hours.

3. Use a pastry brush to remove as much of the salt mixture as possible without damaging the flesh. Rinse under cold water and pat dry with paper towel. Arrange, skin side down, on a baking sheet lined with fresh parchment paper.

Place in the refrigerator, uncovered, to air dry for 2 to 3 hours. Stir remaining 3 tablespoons maple syrup with remaining 1 ounce dark rum; set aside.

4. Preheat the smoker for cold smoking per manufacturer's instructions to 145°F, using maple, oak, apple, or hickory wood, or rum- or whiskey-barrel staves.

5. Brush fish with rum mixture and arrange, skin side down, in the smoker. Smoke for 4 to 6 hours or until flesh is golden brown and flakes easily with a fork. Serve immediately or cool completely to use in recipes for dips, salads, or other recipes.

TED'S TIP

Smoked mackerel makes a great dip when combined with cream cheese, green onions, and fresh dill to serve with crackers and chips. It's also really tasty when flaked into a white wine cream sauce and served over fresh pasta.

Honey-Hoisin Smoked Oysters

Smoking oysters is a bit of a process, so it requires some patience. First you need to choose the right size fresh oysters, which is a bit of a Goldilocks-type experience. They can't be too large (they get too mushy when smoked) and they can't be too small (they get too shriveled when smoked). The next key is to not rush the smoke; it'll all be worth it in the end!

Yield:	Prep time:	Cook time:	Serving size:
36 oysters	20 minutes	1½ to 2 hours	3 oysters

3 dozen medium fresh oysters, your favorite type

1 oz. sake

1 TB. packed light brown sugar

1 TB. honey

2 tsp. hoisin sauce

1½ tsp. low-sodium soy sauce

½ tsp. freshly ground black pepper

2 cups kosher salt

1 tsp. sesame seeds

1 green onion, finely chopped

¼ tsp. sambal red chile sauce

2 TB. peanut oil

1. Steam oysters, 12 at a time, over boiling water for 5 to 8 minutes or until the shells pop open. Discard any unopened shells. Using an oyster knife, carefully shuck oysters; reserve shells.

2. Gently pat oysters dry. In a medium bowl, stir sake, light brown sugar, honey, hoisin sauce, ½ teaspoon soy sauce, and black pepper until well combined. Pour over oysters and refrigerate for 12 hours.

3. Preheat the smoker for cold smoking per manufacturer's instructions to 125°F, using oak, maple, or alder wood.

4. Divide kosher salt evenly between 2 baking sheets. Arrange shell bases so they are all level in the salt. Spray shells with nonstick cooking spray. Drain oysters from marinade and pat dry with paper towel. Place one oyster in each shell.

5. Place oysters in the smoker, with no smoke, to dry for 1½ hours, turning every 30 minutes.

6. Get some smoke going and smoke for 1 hour. Increase smoker temperature to 140°F and continue smoking for an additional hour. Increase smoker temperature again to 160°F and continue to smoke for an additional 1 hour or until gills have begun to shrivel and dry.

7. Remove oysters from smoker; cool completely. Refrigerate for 2 hours or until chilled through. Transfer oysters to a small bowl and add sesame seeds, green onion, and sambal red chile sauce. Gently stir.

8. Heat oil in a small skillet set over medium-high heat for 1 to 2 minutes or just until it starts to smoke. Pour sizzling peanut oil over oysters and drizzle with remaining 1 teaspoon soy sauce. Stir and serve immediately.

TED'S TIP

Chop about 6 smoked oysters and stir them into a cream cheese–based dip for a delicious appetizer or snack.

Smoked Razor Clams

The razor clam is given its name because of its elongated shape that looks similar to a folding straight razor. Look for these clams in Asian supermarkets or order them from your fishmonger. It's a soft-shell clam that is best served steamed, but I have found that smoking them, hot and quick, imparts a nice sweet smoke flavor that really complements the salty flesh.

Yield:	Prep time:	Cook time:	Serving size:
2 lb. clams	15 minutes	1½ hours	⅓ to ½ lb. clams

2 lb. fresh razor clams (about 24 to 36)

½ cup melted butter

2 TB. Ted's World-Famous Bone Dust BBQ Seasoning Rub (recipe in Chapter 8)

Clarified butter

1 lemon, cut into wedges

1. Preheat the smoker per manufacturer's instructions to 235°F, using alder, maple, apple, or pecan wood.

2. Rinse clams under cool water to remove excess sand and grit. Pat dry with paper towel. Brush outside of each clam with melted butter. Sprinkle Ted's World-Famous Bone Dust BBQ Seasoning Rub all over shells and any exposed meat.

3. Arrange clams, hinge side down, in a smoker rack with slots that are just slightly smaller than the shells, so they stand upright. Smoke for 1 to 1½ hours or until all shells are open. Remove from smoker. Serve immediately with warm clarified butter and lemon wedges.

DEFINITION

Clarified butter is what you get when the milk solids have been separated and removed from the fat solids in butter. Simply melt butter in a heavy-bottom saucepan set over low heat. Once melted, it will begin to spatter slightly and create a white foam on the surface. When spattering stops and no more foam is accumulating on the surface, remove the pan from heat. Line a fine-mesh sieve with cheesecloth and pour the butter through, into a heatproof container; discard solids. Butter can be stored in the refrigerator for up to 3 months.

Smoked Halibut with Hot Curry Rub and Lime Butter

This recipe calls for hot and fast smoking so the halibut can be served immediately. The flavors of curry and black mustard seeds mixed with lime and ginger work well with the rich flavor of this meaty white fish.

Yield:	Prep time:	Cook time:	Serving size:
6 halibut fillets	45 minutes	45 minutes	1 halibut fillet

1 TB. hot curry powder

1 tsp. ground cumin

1 tsp. ground cardamom

1 tsp. ground ginger

1 tsp. kosher salt

1 tsp. cracked black pepper

3 tsp. granulated sugar

¼ tsp. ground nutmeg

¼ tsp. ground cinnamon

6 (8-oz.) halibut fillets (about 2 in. thick)

3 TB. melted butter

¼ cup finely diced onion

2 tsp. minced fresh ginger

2 hot green chile peppers, minced

2 fresh limes, juiced

2 tsp. black mustard seeds

½ cup (1 stick) unsalted butter, softened

1 cup chopped fresh cilantro leaves

1 TB. fresh lime juice

½ tsp. freshly ground black pepper

1. In a large bowl, stir hot curry powder, cumin, cardamom, ground ginger, kosher salt, cracked black pepper, 1 teaspoon sugar, nutmeg, and cinnamon until well combined. Sprinkle mixture all over each halibut fillet. Arrange fillets, skin side down, on a parchment-lined baking sheet. Refrigerate for 2 hours.

2. Heat 1 tablespoon melted butter in a small saucepan set over medium heat. Add onion and minced ginger; cook, stirring often, for 3 to 4 minutes or until tender but not browned. Add green chile peppers. Cook, stirring often, for 1 more minute or until fragrant.

3. Add juice of 2 limes and remaining 2 teaspoons sugar; remove from heat. Stir in remaining 2 tablespoons melted butter, 1 tablespoon at a time, until fully incorporated. Keep warm and set aside.

4. Set a deep skillet over high heat. Let stand over the heat until smoking. Add black mustard seeds and top the skillet with a tight-fitting lid. Shake the skillet over the burner until seeds are toasted and pop open. Stir seeds into the warm mixture; set aside.

5. In a medium bowl, blend softened unsalted butter, cilantro, lime juice, and ground black pepper; set aside in the refrigerator.

6. Preheat the smoker per manufacturer's instructions to 275°F, using alder, maple, or citrus wood; coconut; or cinnamon sticks.

7. Arrange fillets, evenly spaced, on a smoker rack. Insert thermometer probe into the thickest part of one fillet. Set the internal temperature thermometer for 145°F to 150°F. Smoke, basting with warm black mustard seed mixture every 15 minutes, for 45 to 60 minutes or until internal temperature is achieved and flesh flakes easily. Serve immediately with a dollop of cilantro-lime butter.

Variation: This recipe works well with a variety of seafood. Try grouper, mahi mahi, salmon, kingfish, or scallops. Leftovers can even be turned into a smoky fish sandwich filling just by adding a little mayonnaise.

Whiskey Butter–Injected Smoked Scallops with Halibut and Crab Topping

The higher-than-normal smoker temperature for this recipe allows the scallops to cook faster and still have great flavor. Your guests will be blown away by the decadent yet fresh flavor of these scallops.

Yield:	Prep time:	Cook time:	Serving size:
12 scallops	15 minutes	45 minutes	1 scallop for an appetizer or 3 scallops for an entrée

½ cup butter

2 oz. Tennessee whiskey

12 fresh, *U10* sea scallops

6 slices bacon

½ cup fresh lump crabmeat

8 oz. fresh halibut

Ted's World-Famous Bone Dust BBQ Seasoning Rub (recipe in Chapter 8)

1. Preheat the smoker per manufacturer's instructions to 240°F to 260°F, using alder, apple, or maple wood.

2. Melt butter in a small saucepan set over medium heat. Add Tennessee whiskey and remove from heat; keep warm. Using an injector, suck up most of melted butter mixture. Plunge the needle into the center of each scallop and inject with butter mixture; chill.

3. Stretch each slice of bacon until it's almost doubled in length; cut in half. Wrap each sea scallop with a piece of bacon and secure with a toothpick. Place sea scallops on the smoker rack. Top each sea scallop with a little bit of crabmeat.

4. Cut halibut into 12 thin slices. Lay the slices flat on a clean work surface. Firmly run fingers over fish to create thinner slices. Cut each slice in half and criss-cross over crab. Sprinkle with Ted's World-Famous Bone Dust BBQ Seasoning Rub.

5. Smoke for 45 minutes or until sea scallops are golden and flesh is just opaque in the center. Remove sea scallops from smoker and baste with remaining butter mixture. Serve immediately.

TASTY TIDBIT

U10 refers to the total weight of the scallops; these guys are so big, you only get about 10 per pound. Be sure to remove the connective muscle found on the side of each scallop. This piece of flesh is tough and it's not meant to be eaten.

The Big 5

In This Chapter

- What it takes to compete
- Smoked brisket
- Smoked BBQ pulled pork
- Rib-tickling succulent ribs
- Mouthwatering chicken and turkey
- Smoked whole hog
- Recipes to make life deliciously smoky

The BBQ community is pretty friendly … at least, before things get started. People will chat and laugh, show off their equipment, and so on. But once things get going everyone is all business. People do their best to hide what they're doing to avoid sharing any of their trade secrets. And then, once the food is handed in for judging, out come the beers and play-by-play descriptions of what they each did (and didn't do) right. It's not easy to win one of these competitions, and if you do, it's not for the money (which isn't much)—it's for the bragging rights.

What to Know Before Entering a BBQ Competition

Once the time comes that you think you have the smoking skills it takes to compete, you should find yourself a little BBQ contest to join. The three big organizations that sanction contests are The Kansas City Barbeque Society (kcbs.us), The Memphis in May World Championship Barbecue Cooking Contest (memphisinmay.org), and The International Barbecue Cookers Association (ibcabbq.org). Each of these organizations puts on hundreds of local events and provides links to other local events through their websites, so you can find one near you and go see what's what.

Each of the three big organizations has their own set of rules and their own judging style. The biggest thing you need to learn is that "The Rules" are the *rules*. There will not be any exceptions made nor will they listen to any arguing, begging, or cajoling. I've seen someone who missed the hand-in by 15 seconds get disqualified for being late. And as important as it is to know what the organization wants to see, you need to know what they don't want to see, too. So make sure you do your homework on the rules before competing. Check out their websites for all the details.

The categories in all three organizations vary slightly, so you want to make sure you know exactly whose rules are being used. For example, in some cases, there are rules that specify that you cannot prepare (i.e., inject, marinate, rub, sauce, or precook) any of your meat before the competition. You will also be inspected before the competition starts. The judges make sure your meat is on ice and has a temperature under 40°F. If not, you're outta there. All entries must be cooked on wood or charcoal; you will never see a propane tank at a barbecue contest. You will be given a Styrofoam tray that has been issued a number and this is what you must put your food in. The judges never know to whom the number belongs. There can be no garnish. Some competitions allow you to include one or two small cups of sauce and some don't. There is a hand-in time with about a 15-minute window, and they won't take it before or after that window.

Here are the contest categories seen in nearly every contest:

- Beef brisket
- Pork (shoulder, picnic, or butt)
- Pork ribs (back or spare)
- Chicken (has to be the whole chicken, backbone in)
- Whole hog (requires a big rig and more patience than even I have most days)

Extra categories that are seen in various contests include the following:

- Sausage
- Lamb
- Barbecue sauce
- Cook's choice—could be anything, it's a wild card

Those who want to win big (and who do so) are not part timers. They smoke something nearly every day. They practice and practice, and then they practice some more. They take notes on what they do and whether it worked, and they track their adjustments. If they get a really good result on something they will record what it was, what it looked like raw, how much fat it had, how many times it got basted, how much charcoal or wood was used, and how long it took. It's an obsessive hobby but when someone hands you a ribbon, you are on top of the world!

Brisket

Let's start with the big daddy of beef, the one, the only beef brisket! It's a pretty tough cut of meat, but when a Texas brisket is cooked perfectly, the meat should ooze juicy goodness. So how do you create a brisket that good? It's all about practice.

TASTY TIDBIT

The oyster of the beef brisket, called the decal, is the most prized piece of meat. This piece of beef is surrounded on all sides by fat and sits on top of the thickest part of the brisket point. When the brisket is perfectly cooked, this decal is moist, juicy, and succulent.

Here are some basics to get you started. First, your raw material is the most important. You and your recipe are only as good as the brisket you buy, so get the best you can—this is a competition, right? A whole full brisket will weigh about 15 to 18 pounds—and that's a mighty big piece of meat. It's traditionally sold three ways: whole, or divided into the flat, and the point. The flat is leaner and more expensive, and the point is more flavorful and fattier.

Here are a few things to look for when shopping for a whole brisket:

- It should be relatively uniform in thickness from one end to the other. This will help with a more even smoke.

- It should have uniform fat coverage of at least ¼ inch across the entire cap and the fat should be white, not yellow.

- The meat should be nicely marbled with fat.

- It's best if it's been aged at least 21 days (it helps with the tenderness).

Now the brisket needs to be seasoned—or not. A Texas pit boss once told me that true Texas brisket needs no seasoning. No salt, no pepper, no nothing, just sweet oak smoke and patience. I think it's great either way, so you can smoke it plain or you can use my recipe later in this chapter.

It's time to get that smoker going! Keep it between 180°F and 220°F, which means 200°F is ideal. Insert a thermometer into the meatiest part of the brisket and set the temperature to 185°F for slicing or 205°F for shredding.

Now, all you have to do is sit back and let that brisket smoke while maintaining the temperature, and spritz if you wish (I personally like to share my beer with the brisket). It's going to be a while, about 1 to 1½ hours per pound. That's it; that's all you need to know to smoke a prize-worthy brisket. So start practicing!

Pulled Pork

Traditional BBQ pulled pork starts with a pork shoulder, also known as a Boston butt. The pork shoulder can be bone-in or boneless. Bone-in weighs about 10 to 13 pounds and boneless about 7 to 9 pounds. Professional competitive smokers feel that bone-in offers the most flavor, which I agree with. I also find that the bone acts as "the tell" as to when the butt is ready; if the bone pulls free from the meat with a slight twist of the wrist, it's perfectly smoked. A bone-in shoulder should have the skin or rind removed and have at least a ¼-inch layer of fat on it. Remember fat is flavor and a fattier piece of meat won't dry out in the smoker as easily as a lean piece.

Smoking low and slow is the key again. You want your smoker to sit at 200°F until the internal temperature of the pork is between 185°F and 205°F. Always pull the pork as soon as it comes off the smoker and be sure to do it in a bowl. This way you don't lose any of the fat or juices.

TED'S TIP

I often serve my pulled pork in ice-cream sugar cones topped with coleslaw. I call this Pork-Cone-Eh —*pork* for the BBQ meat, *cone* for the sugar cone, and *eh* just because I'm Canadian!

Ribs

Next up on the list, ribs! You're lucky; I am the rib master, truly. I have been the corporate development chef for one of America's largest rib-processing facilities and

I'm the flavor behind over 35 million pounds of ribs sold each year. Ribs, ribs, ribs 24/7—we make great ribs!

The key to ribs, as in all BBQ, is the quality of the raw ingredients and the low and slow method. I've already talked about the two types of ribs, back and side, in Chapter 11. Back ribs are considered the premium and are leaner with a nice amount of loin coverage. Whole-side ribs are big (around 5 to 6 pounds each). Side ribs are often trimmed of the breastbone and rib tip to create a St. Louis–cut rib. This rib is easier to smoke than the whole-side rib because it's more uniform in shape and size, so it cooks more evenly.

For most competitors the choice of rib to use will be either a back or a St. Louis cut. Ribs in a smoker at 200°F will take about 4 to 6 hours to smoke. The sign of a competition-worthy rib is when the bone pulls firmly from the flesh and the meat is moist, juicy, and tender. Use my rib recipes in this chapter and in Chapters 10 through 12 as a guide, but find your own style. Competitors make 'em dry (dry-rubbed) or make 'em wet (with sauce) but the real joy is in eating them.

Chicken and Turkey

Smoked chicken and turkey also fall under the popular categories. I know that's two species in one category but they are both birds and the principles of smoking a bird are pretty much the same. Here, more than anywhere, it is crucial that your birds are moist and juicy. Here are a few of my secrets:

- First, I always brine my chicken and turkey. Even a simple 24-hour soak in a brine of water, salt, and sugar will help keep the birds moist and juicy during the smoking process.

- Often I use an injection of melted butter or broth, especially into the white meat, early on and spritz or add more injections during the smoking process.

- I cook it low and slow (that goes without saying), using a sweet-flavored smoke.

- I find my happy place so I can practice the art of patience.

- I cook the bird to an internal temperature of 175°F. This is the perfect temperature and it ensures the bird is fully cooked but still moist.

Follow these tips and you'll produce a succulent smoked chicken or turkey every time!

Whole Hog

Smoking whole hogs is huge at BBQ competitions, but not just anyone can do it. Many very seasoned, experienced smokers don't even bother with whole hogs. They take a really long time and a serious amount of patience. But the end results are pure deliciousness. It is very satisfying to be able to smoke a whole hog and have the meat fall from the bone, moist and tender. You get the pleasure of all the cuts.

We're talking butterflied whole hogs, weighing in at about 150 to 200 pounds, and they take upward of 18 hours. The fire needs to be tended almost constantly to make sure it's always full of white-hot coals that have a nice layer of ash on the outside. And you need to keep the temperature between 220°F and 240°F for a perfectly cooked hog.

SAFE SMOKING

There is zero tolerance for late food in BBQ competitions. The trick is to time your food so it comes out of the smoker with enough time to rest for 5 to 15 minutes so the meat can retain all the natural juices before carving. Then tray it up quickly and get it to the judges with only seconds left to spare. This helps ensure that you are serving hot food. Cold food gets poor marks. So practice your smoking and keep track of the time. This could mean the difference between winning big and being disqualified.

The following recipes can be a starting point as you gear up for competition or just good eating with family and friends. You'll notice that there's no recipe for whole hog in this book because, no offense, it's probably a bit out of your league at this point. If you get to the point where you want to tackle smoking a whole hog, you could probably collaborate with me on my next book instead of buying it. So for now, start with the other recipes I've given you to play with!

Big Beefy Texas-Style Smoked Brisket

The hardest thing you will ever smoke is brisket, and that is a fact. Brisket requires patience. Brisket requires love. And brisket requires a bit of luck. I've provided two methods to smoke a brisket. The first is the all-dry, authentic way to do it that will give you more bragging rights. The second is when the brisket gets wrapped up for the second half of cooking, which will offer some insurance that the brisket is going to be moist and tender when it comes out of the smoker. Either way, you're going to have leftovers because as a newbie, you'll want to smoke a whole brisket. A whole brisket has a nice fat cap, which is what's going to keep your meat juicy. You can also get a flat cut but it's really lean and pretty tricky to smoke, so if you are a beginner, I suggest you go with a whole brisket. It's a lot bigger, but leftover brisket is a wonderful thing.

Yield:	Prep time:	Cook time:	Serving size:
3 cups Brisket Rub and 12 to 15 lb. roast	20 minutes	18 to 24 hours	½ lb. roast

½ cup all-natural, no MSG, dehydrated beef soup–base powder

¼ cup coarsely ground black pepper

¼ cup coarsely ground white pepper

¼ cup mustard seeds, cracked

¼ cup coriander seeds, cracked

¼ cup granulated garlic

¼ cup granulated onion

¼ cup crushed red pepper flakes

2 TB. kosher salt

1 whole beef brisket, untrimmed with decal meat and full fat coverage (about 12 to 15 lb.)

2 cups (4 sticks) unsalted butter, melted

<u>Method One</u>

1. In a large bowl, stir dehydrated beef soup–base powder, black pepper, white pepper, mustard seeds, coriander seeds, garlic, onion, red pepper flakes, and kosher salt until well combined. Measure out half of mixture and store the rest in an airtight container in a cool, dry, and dark place for up to 4 months.

2. Rinse brisket under cold water and pat dry with paper towel. Rub spice mixture all over brisket. Suck up about half of unsalted butter with an injector and inject brisket in several places; set aside.

3. Preheat the smoker per manufacturer's instructions to 200°F, using oak or mesquite wood, or a blend of both.

4. If your smoker isn't large enough to accommodate a cut this large, cut the brisket into two pieces, across the middle of the brisket with the thicker end being the smaller of the two pieces because the butt end is heavier and will take longer to cook. This will ensure both pieces cook evenly.

5. Insert thermometer probe into the center of the brisket. Set the internal temperature for 185°F. Close the door and smoke 16 to 24 hours (depending on the weight of brisket and how many briskets are in the smoker), or until internal temperature is achieved.

6. Remove brisket from smoker and tent loosely with foil; let stand for 15 minutes. Slice the brisket across the grain or shred into thin strips.

Method Two

1. Follow steps 1 to 5 above, but once brisket has reached an internal temperature of 160°F, remove it from the smoker and inject with remaining unsalted butter. Wrap tightly in 6 layers of heavy-duty plastic food wrap. Next, tightly wrap brisket in 2 layers of heavy-duty foil.

2. Return brisket to the smoker. Reinsert thermometer probe into the center of brisket and set the internal thermometer for 205°F. Smoke for an additional 2 to 3 hours or until internal temperature is achieved.

3. Transfer brisket to a large bowl. Carefully unwrap brisket, being cautious of the steam. Discard plastic wrap and foil. Carefully transfer brisket to a cutting board. Tent loosely with foil; let rest for 15 minutes. Slice the brisket across the grain or shred into thin strips.

TED'S TIP

I am a firm believer in smoking foods without wrapping them in plastic wrap or aluminum foil but this is one of the exceptions. Wrapping the brisket holds all of the valuable juices from the meat in place, which almost guarantees full flavor and a shreddable tenderness. You want to save the juices when you unwrap the brisket, so you can toss it with the meat after it's been shredded.

Also, depending on the type of texture you want from your smoked brisket, you can cook it to a variety of internal temperatures. The brisket will be fully cooked at 160°F, but it will still be tough. Once it cooks to an internal temperature of 185°F, it should be tender and moist enough to slice, if you don't want to shred it. At 195°F, the meat is a little more tender, and at 205°F, it is perfect (a little messy, but nice) to slice, chop, or shred.

Smoked BBQ Pulled Pork
with Apple Jack Spritz

Low and slow is the way to go for smoked Boston butt, with the flavor of nutty, sweet hickory smoke. It may take a while to cook, but remember what Mom use to say: good things come to those who wait. I have the same motto, just with a different ending: "… with a cold beer." Enjoy this recipe—it's delicious and easy. Just crack a cold one, grab a lawn chair, and sit back and relax while tending to the smoker. Nothing else matters now but moist, juicy, and succulent BBQ pulled pork.

Yield:	Prep time:	Cook time:	Serving size:
4 cups spritz, 2 cups sauce, and 1 smoked pork butt	25 hours	12 hours	1 sandwich

1 cup Ted's World-Famous Bone Dust BBQ Seasoning Rub (recipe in Chapter 8)

1 Pork Boston butt, bone-in and ¼-in. fat cap (about 12 to 15 lb.)

1½ cups apple juice

1½ cups Tennessee whiskey

½ cup cold water

1¾ cups apple cider vinegar

¼ cup prepared store-bought BBQ sauce

2 tsp. kosher salt

1 tsp. freshly ground black pepper

1 tsp. crushed red pepper flakes

1 tsp. hot sauce

1. Rub Ted's World-Famous Bone Dust BBQ Seasoning Rub all over roast. Place on a parchment-lined baking sheet and refrigerate for 24 hours.

2. Meanwhile, use a funnel to fill a spray bottle with apple juice, Tennessee whiskey, cold water, and ¼ cup apple cider vinegar. Shake to mix well; store in the refrigerator for up to 1 week.

3. Combine remaining 1½ cups apple cider vinegar, BBQ sauce, kosher salt, black pepper, red pepper flakes, and hot sauce in a 1-pint glass canning jar. Screw on lid and give the jar a shake to combine. Can be stored in the refrigerator for up to 2 weeks.

4. Preheat the smoker per manufacturer's instructions to 200°F to 230°F, using hickory or a blend of hickory, maple, and apple woods (hickory for the strength, maple for the smooth, and apple for the sweet).

5. Place roast in the smoker on the middle rack. Insert thermometer probe into the center of the roast but not touching the bone. Set the internal temperature thermometer for 185°F. Smoke, spritzing after the first 4 hours, every 30 to 45 minutes, for 12 to 16 hours or until internal temperature is achieved and bone twists and pulls cleanly from meat.

6. Carefully transfer roast from the smoker and place in a large roasting pan. Loosely tent with foil and let stand for 15 minutes. Using either pulling claws or tongs, remove bones from meat. Shred meat with two wooden spoons into thick or thin strips—whatever you like.

7. Serve immediately on toasted buns drizzled with some of the apple-BBQ sauce.

TED'S TIP

I call this spritz Apple Jack Spritz, and it's one of my favorites. Leftover spritz can be used on other cuts of pork, turkey, chicken, and shellfish, especially scallops. You can also use up the rest of that sauce on grilled chicken or pork chops.

Smoked St. Louis Ribs with BBQ Icing

The St. Louis–cut side ribs in this recipe are meaty with a good amount of fat. And that fat—along with the smoke, of course—is what gives these ribs their delicious flavor. You probably wouldn't think to use vanilla frosting on smoked ribs, but that's what I'm here for, to provide you with new and interesting flavor combinations and hopefully inspire you to come up with some of your own.

Yield:	Prep time:	Cook time:	Serving size:
4 racks ribs	24 hours, 45 minutes	6 hours	½ to 1 rack ribs

4 racks St. Louis–cut side ribs (about 2½ lb. each)

½ cup Memphis Rib Rub (recipe in Chapter 8)

2 cups Apple Jack Spritz (recipe in Smoked BBQ Pulled Pork earlier in this chapter)

1 (2 cups) container prepared vanilla frosting

½ cup apple butter

1 TB. plus 1 oz. Tennessee whiskey

1 tsp. freshly ground black pepper

Pinch kosher salt

½ cup crispy fried onions

½ cup crushed peanuts

½ cup panko breadcrumbs

1. Trim ribs according to instructions in Chapter 11. Rub Memphis Rib Rub all over ribs. Place in a large container, cover, and refrigerate for 24 hours.

2. Preheat the smoker per manufacturer's instructions to 220°F to 235°F, using hickory, oak, maple, mesquite, or a blend of woods.

3. Arrange ribs, evenly spaced and meat side down, on a smoker rack. Insert thermometer probe into the meatiest section without touching bone. Set the internal temperature for 185°F. Smoke ribs, spritzing with Apple Jack Spritz every hour and flipping over halfway through, for 4 to 6 hours or until internal temperature is achieved and bones move freely. Remove ribs from the smoker; cool slightly.

4. Preheat your grill to medium, about 350°F. Meanwhile, in a large bowl, stir vanilla frosting, apple butter, 1 tablespoon Tennessee whiskey, and black pepper until well combined. Season with kosher salt; set aside.

5. In a second bowl, toss crispy fried onions, crushed peanuts, and panko bread-crumbs until well combined; set aside.

6. Place ribs, meat side down, on the grill. Cook for 3 to 5 minutes or until lightly charred. Flip over and make sure the heat below ribs is not scorching hot. Spread frosting mixture evenly over the entire surface of ribs. Sprinkle onion mixture over top so they're evenly coated. Close grill and cook for 4 to 5 minutes or until heated through. Open grill lid, standing back to avoid flare-ups, and drizzle remaining 1 ounce Tennessee whiskey over ribs. Remove from grill and serve immediately.

TED'S TIP

You don't have to smoke and grill your ribs in the same day. Ribs can be smoked, cooled completely, and stored in the refrigerator for up to 1 week, or 2 weeks if vacuum packed.

Smoked Chicken with Buttery Love Injection

There is nothing tastier than a whole, smoked chicken—especially when it's right out of the smoker and the drumsticks twist off with ease and the breasts are oozing buttery goodness. Mastering the art of smoking a chicken isn't difficult, but it requires patience. First you brine it, then dry it and inject it, then smoke it and baste it until it's fully cooked and spectacular!

Yield:	Prep time:	Cook time:	Serving size:
2 whole chickens	24 hours, 45 minutes	3 hours	¼ to ½ chicken

2 roasting chickens (about 3 to 4 lb. each)	6 TB. grapeseed oil
16 cups Apple-Honey Pig and Bird Brine (recipe in Chapter 7)	¼ cup Kansas City Rub (see Smoked BBQ Ribs with Redneck White Sauce recipe in Chapter 11)
1 cup (2 sticks) unsalted butter	3 TB. honey

1. Place the chickens in a large stockpot and cover with Apple-Honey Pig and Bird Brine. Top with a clean, heavy object, such as a plate, to weigh chickens down and keep submerged. Cover and refrigerate for 24 hours.

2. Remove chickens from brine; discard excess. Rinse, inside and out, under cold running water; pat dry with paper towel. Wrap chickens in cheesecloth or a kitchen towel and stand up in a bowl. Refrigerate for 4 to 6 hours to allow the birds to drain and dry completely.

3. Cross drumsticks over each other and tie the ends together with butcher's twine so they are tight to the body. Twist wing tips behind shoulder joints and tie the upper parts of wings together behind the body.

4. Place chickens in the freezer for 30 to 45 minutes or until well chilled but not frozen. Suck up unsalted butter with an injector and inject half of butter into various parts of each chicken. Brush any excess butter on the outside of each chicken. Return chickens to the fridge until ready to smoke.

5. In a small bowl, whisk grapeseed oil, Kansas City Rub, and honey until well combined; set aside.

6. Preheat the smoker per manufacturer's instructions to 200°F to 230°F, using hickory or mesquite; a blend of hickory, apple, and maple; or a blend of mesquite and oak woods.

7. Position each chicken on a roasting cone or beer can chicken holder. Place chickens in the smoker. Insert thermometer probe into the center of a chicken thigh. Set the internal temperature for 165°F. Close the door and smoke, basting occasionally with the honey mixture after the first 2 hours, for 3 hours or until internal temperature is achieved. Remove chickens from smoker; rest for 5 minutes before serving.

TED'S TIP

Trussing elastics are available in grocery stores and are often found near the frozen poultry section. They're food-grade elastic strings that make trussing easy. No tying; just wrap the strings around the wings and legs, and it's ready to go!

Thanksgiving Smoked Turkey

There is nothing more pleasing than a smoked turkey on your Thanksgiving holiday. Brined first in beer and chipotle hot sauce, injected with a little maple butter, and then smoked over hardwood hickory until it is fully cooked but still moist and juicy. Delish!

Yield:	Prep time:	Cook time:	Serving size:
1 turkey	25 hours	4 hours	½2 to ½6 turkey

3 qt. water	1 whole turkey (about 12 to 14 lb.)
6 (12-oz.) bottles pilsner beer	½ cup (1 stick) butter
3 cups apple juice	2 TB. ground chipotle powder
1½ cups maple syrup	1 TB. Ted's World-Famous Bone Dust BBQ Seasoning Rub (recipe in Chapter 8)
1¼ cups chipotle-flavored hot sauce	
1 cup chopped fresh sage leaves	½ cup vegetable oil
1 cup kosher salt	

1. Combine water, pilsner beer, apple juice, 1 cup maple syrup, 1 cup chipotle-flavored hot sauce, and sage in a large saucepan set over medium heat. Bring to a rolling boil. Add kosher salt and stir until fully dissolved; remove from heat and cool completely. Refrigerate for 24 hours.

2. Remove neck and giblets from cavity of turkey. Rinse, inside and out, under cold water and pat dry with paper towel; set aside.

3. Pour chilled brine into a clean 5-gallon bucket or a very large stockpot. Slowly lower turkey into brine, making sure cavity fills with brine; add turkey neck. Refrigerate giblets (I don't brine these, as they get too salty). Top with a heavy plate to weigh turkey down and keep it submerged. Refrigerate for 24 to 36 hours.

4. Remove turkey from brine, rinse under cold water, and pat dry with paper towel; discard brine. Place turkey on a large baking sheet to air-dry in the refrigerator for 6 hours.

5. Preheat the smoker per manufacturer's instructions to 200°F using hickory wood.

6. Combine remaining ½ cup maple syrup, remaining ¼ cup chipotle-flavored hot sauce, and butter in a small saucepan set over low heat. Cook until butter is melted and mixture is well combined. Set aside and keep warm. Stir chipotle powder, Ted's World-Famous Bone Dust BBQ Seasoning Rub, and vegetable oil until well combined; set aside.

7. Remove turkey from the refrigerator and pat dry, inside and out, to remove any excess moisture. Cross drumsticks over each other and tie the ends together with butcher's twine so they are tight to the body to truss turkey. Then twist wing tips behind shoulder joints and tie the upper parts of wings together behind the body.

8. Suck up butter mixture with an injector and inject into multiple areas in the turkey. Place turkey, breast side up, in the smoker. Insert thermometer probe into the center of a thigh without touching bone. Set the internal temperature for 170°F. Close the door and smoke for 2 hours. Smoke, basting every hour with some of oil mixture, for an additional 3 to 4 hours or until internal temperature is achieved.

9. Transfer turkey to a platter. Tent loosely with foil and a few kitchen towels; let stand for 20 minutes before carving.

 TED'S TIP

Add an ounce or two of whiskey to the butter injection and use once or twice during the smoking process to ensure your turkey is going to be moist and delicious. And just like any other Thanksgiving bird, this leftover turkey makes killer sandwiches.

Starters, Sides, and Sweets

When people ask me what they shouldn't smoke, I tell them you can smoke anything—at the very least you should give it a shot. I'll try anything once, and usually I'll keep going until I make it work. I'm always trying to find new ways to push the culinary envelope. I have smoked a lot of foods, even a variety of bubble gums. (How did that turn out? Horrible, but not all things work.)

When it comes to food, you're only limited by your imagination. Think outside the box and smoke something different and unexpected; that's how new recipes are created. Who thought that smoked chocolate could be so mouthwatering? The recipes in these chapters use foods that aren't exactly synonymous with a smoker, but they're fantastic and I hope you give them a go. Have fun and even get a little sticky!

Sides and Accompaniments

In This Chapter

- How to bring it all together
- Let's make a meal of it!
- Fun and creative recipes

So you just spent the better part of 16 to 24 hours smoking a tender, juicy brisket. It's a show-stopper but what are you going to serve with it? Here are a few little tips to keep in mind when planning your menu.

Side dishes shouldn't be an afterthought; they are as important as the protein, so make a plan. You've got your smoker going anyway, so why not smoke up some delicious sides? Your gorgeous smoked brisket should be the centerpiece of your meal but it needs a delicious supporting cast on the table so it can really shine! That said, your side dishes shouldn't fight for center stage, either. Keep the sides flavorful but understated when you are presenting your masterpiece.

For instance, with that yummy brisket, I recommend that you try the Smoked Beet and Pear–Blue Cheese Salad with Walnuts later in this chapter. It will add some light, fresh flavors to the plate. If you're looking to make it a bigger feast, go for it, just keep it balanced. Too many "loud" dishes can be overwhelming for the palate and actually have the opposite effect you're going for. Not everything in the meal needs to be smoked, so mix it up with fresh steamed veggies or only serve smoked sides and grill or roast the meal's protein. Sides are a great way to get to know your smoker without the same time and financial commitment many smoked meats require.

SAFE SMOKING

Don't try a recipe for the first time when you're expecting guests. That's not to say you shouldn't try a new recipe at all, just try it out with the family first. This will give you the opportunity to work out all the kinks without all the pressure of making a good impression.

Don't be afraid to be creative and be brave enough to give your ideas a shot. You can be more adventurous when it is a side dish and not the main event. Look ahead in this chapter—you don't think I thought I was crazy when a few of these ideas popped in my head?! But I try everything, just ask my neighbors. I'll be honest, not everything turns out the way I thought, but more often than not, the results are delicious. So take some of my basic ideas here and go wild!

Smoked Eggplant Dip

This is my version of baba ganoush, a.k.a. "smoky ganoush"! Instead of grilling or roasting the eggplant, I like to—you guessed it—smoke the eggplant! The smokiness really gets absorbed by the flesh, making this classic dip a bit more interesting. Salting eggplant helps to draw out excess moisture and bitterness, allowing the smokiness to really come through and dance all over your taste buds.

Yield:	Prep time:	Cook time:	Serving size:
3 cups	1 hour, 30 minutes	2 hours	¼ cup

1 large dark purple eggplant, halved lengthwise

2 TB. kosher salt

2 TB. olive oil

1 medium sweet onion, diced

4 cloves garlic, minced

1 cup whipped cream cheese

2 TB. mayonnaise

2 TB. crispy fried onions

2 green onions, minced

1 TB. chopped fresh cilantro leaves

1½ tsp. Memphis Rib Rub (recipe in Chapter 8)

Freshly ground black pepper to taste

Pinch cayenne

1. Arrange eggplant, cut side up, on a baking sheet. Sprinkle with kosher salt; let stand for 1 hour.

2. Preheat the smoker per manufacturer's instructions to 275°F, using oak, maple, mesquite, or hickory wood or a blend of maple, pecan, and cinnamon sticks.

3. Rinse eggplant under cold running water and pat dry with paper towel. Place eggplant in smoker, cut side down, on a rack. Smoke eggplant for 2 to 3 hours or until skin is wrinkled and flesh is very tender. Transfer to a heatproof surface; cool for 5 to 10 minutes.

4. Scoop flesh out of skin, using a spoon; discard skin. Set eggplant in a fine mesh sieve to drain; cool completely. Coarsely chop the eggplant; set aside.

5. Meanwhile, heat olive oil in a large skillet set over medium-high heat. Add sweet onion and garlic, and cook for 3 to 4 minutes or until tender but not browned; remove from heat and cool.

6. In a medium bowl, whisk whipped cream cheese and mayonnaise until smooth. Add cooked onion mixture, crispy fried onions, green onions, cilantro, and Memphis Rib Rub. Stir in eggplant until well combined. Season with kosher salt, black pepper, and cayenne to taste.

7. Store in an airtight container in the refrigerator for at least 1 hour before serving. Serve with assorted fresh-cut vegetables, grilled pita, and assorted chips or crackers. Dip can be stored for up to 3 days in the refrigerator.

Variation: Stir in a little chilled BBQ pulled pork or crispy-fried smoked bacon pieces to add an extra-smoky twist to the eggplant dip.

Smoked Vidalia Onion Relish

I had a bunch of onions and thought to myself, "self, you should smoke some of these big juicy sweet onions." So that's what I did. The next thing I knew, I was adding orange juice and sugar to make this sweet and delish garnish. It's great with smoked sausages and burgers.

Yield:	Prep time:	Cook time:	Serving size:
12 pints	1 hour, 2 weeks	6 hours	¼ cup

8 large sweet Vidalia onions or other sweet onions, peeled and cut in quarters

1 cup apple cider vinegar

1 cup rice wine vinegar

¼ cup mirin

¾ cup freshly squeezed orange juice

⅓ cup kosher salt

6 thick-skinned sweet oranges

1 cup granulated sugar

1 cup packed light brown sugar

1 cup honey

¼ cup white grape juice

1 TB. coarsely ground black pepper

1. Preheat the smoker per manufacturer's instructions to 230°F, using pecan, apple, fruit wood, oak, or hickory wood.

2. Arrange Vidalia onions on the rack. Smoke for 6 hours or until onions are smoky brown and slightly tender. Remove onions from the smoker. Slice into ½-inch strips and place in a large nonreactive container. There should be about 8 cups sliced onions.

3. Combine apple cider vinegar, rice wine vinegar, mirin, and ¼ cup orange juice in a small saucepan set over high heat; bring to a boil. Stir in kosher salt until dissolved and remove from heat. Pour mixture over onions; cool completely. Top with a heavy plate, to weigh down onions and keep them submerged. Cover with plastic wrap and refrigerate, stirring well once a day, for 2 weeks.

4. Using a vegetable peeler, remove skin from oranges, avoiding the pith (bitter white stuff), and juice the oranges. Cut orange peel into ¼-inch strips.

5. Transfer onion mixture to a large saucepan set over medium-high heat. Add strips of orange peel, remaining ½ cup orange juice, granulated sugar, light brown sugar, honey, and white grape juice. Bring mixture to a low boil, stirring occasionally, and reduce the heat. Simmer, stirring occasionally, for 30 minutes or until the mixture is thick and slightly syrupy. If the mixture is too thick, add a little orange juice to thin it a little. Stir in black pepper.

6. Transfer to 12 (1-pint) sterile canning jars; top with caps and lids. Process for 45 to 60 minutes. Remove from stove and allow to cool; tighten lids. Store for up to 1 year in a cool, dark place.

> **TED'S TIP**
>
> A good-quality apple cider vinegar is tart and sweet with a bright flavor, rather than just acidic. So it's worth the extra couple of bucks to get the good stuff.

Smoked Beet and Pear-Blue Cheese Salad with Walnuts

This is a salad for all the senses. A smoky aroma combined with sweet, tender pears, vibrant-colored beets, and creamy textured cheese, all topped with crunchy walnuts—it's like a sensory overload! It's as beautiful as it is tasty, and it's a perfect choice to serve alongside smoked brisket or beef tenderloin.

Yield:	Prep time:	Cook time:	Serving size:
6 cups	1 hour	1½ hours	1¼ cups

3 large red beets, scrubbed

1 large golden yellow beet, scrubbed

3 pears, peeled, halved, and cored

2 cups plus 2 TB. apple juice

2 cups water

¼ cup granulated sugar

3 cloves

1 bay leaf

1 (1-in.) cinnamon stick

3 TB. olive oil

½ tsp. freshly ground black pepper

Pinch kosher salt

½ cup chopped toasted walnuts or candied walnuts

½ cup crumbled creamy blue cheese

¼ cup diced sweet onion

4 green onions, thinly sliced

2 TB. white balsamic vinegar

1 TB. honey

1 TB. fresh thyme, chopped

1. Preheat the smoker for cold smoking per manufacturer's instructions to 125°F, using oak, maple, or apple wood.

2. Place red beets and golden yellow beet in a medium saucepan and cover with cold water; set over high heat. Bring to a rolling boil and reduce the heat to medium. Simmer for 20 to 30 minutes or until fork tender. Drain and rinse under cold running water. Peel and leave whole; set aside.

3. Meanwhile, place pears in a medium saucepan with 2 cups apple juice, water, sugar, cloves, bay leaf, and cinnamon stick and set over medium-high heat. Bring to a slow boil and reduce the heat to low. Poach for 20 to 30 minutes or until fork-tender. Remove from heat and allow pears to cool in poaching liquid.

4. Add 1 tablespoon olive oil, black pepper, and kosher salt to beets; toss gently to coat evenly.

5. Arrange beets and pears, evenly spaced, on a smoker. Smoke for 1½ hours. Transfer to a heatproof surface to cool completely.

6. Cut beets into ½-inch cubes and thinly slice pears; combine in a bowl. Add walnuts, blue cheese, sweet onion, and 2 green onions.

7. In a medium bowl, whisk white balsamic vinegar, remaining 2 tablespoons olive oil, remaining 2 tablespoons apple juice, remaining 2 green onions, honey, and thyme until well combined. Drizzle dressing over beet mixture and gently stir to combine. Season with kosher salt and black pepper to taste. Serve immediately.

Variation: This recipe also works well with large carrots or butternut squash instead of beets.

TED'S TIP

It's always a good idea to cook root vegetables until fork-tender before smoking them. It would just take way too long to smoke any dense vegetable without cooking it beforehand.

Smoked Corn and Smoked Cream Corn

Smoke once, eat twice—that's how this recipe rolls! We're going to smoke more corn than we need for tonight's dinner, and then use the leftover to make a smoky side dish for tomorrow's dinner. Night one, you'll have smoked corn on the cob and night two, you'll have smoked creamed corn. Genius and delicious!

<u>Night One:</u>

Yield:	Prep time:	Cook time:	Serving size:
8 cobs of corn	15 minutes	2½ hours	5 cups

8 ears fresh corn on the cob, in the
   husk

1. Peel back husk and remove as much silk as possible. Pull husk back up around corn and soak in cold water for 4 to 6 hours.

2. Preheat the smoker per manufacturer's instructions to 250°F, using oak or hickory woods.

3. Arrange corn, evenly spaced, in the smoker and smoke for 2 hours. Remove husks from corn and return to the smoker. Smoke, spritzing with water, for an additional 30 minutes.

4. Using a sharp knife, cut kernels from 8 cobs. Reserve kernels and stripped cobs for tomorrow's dinner

Night Two:

Yield:	Prep time:	Cook time:	Serving size:
1 casserole	30 minutes	20 minutes	⅛ casserole

2 cups chicken stock

2 stripped, smoked cobs of corn

3 TB. butter

1 medium onion, diced

2 cloves garlic, minced

¼ cup all-purpose flour

½ cup 35 percent whipping cream

5 cups smoked corn kernels (cut from about 8 cobs)

2 cups smoked mozzarella cheese (method in Smoky Baked Macaroni and Cheese, later in this chapter)

1 (14-oz.) can creamed corn

1 TB. chopped fresh sage leaves

Kosher salt

Freshly ground black pepper

1 cup panko breadcrumbs

¼ cup grated Parmesan cheese

1. Preheat the oven to 350°F. Place chicken stock and stripped cobs in a medium saucepan set over high heat. Bring to a boil and simmer for 15 minutes. Remove from heat; strain and discard solids.

2. Melt butter in a large saucepan set over medium heat. Add onion and cook for 3 to 4 minutes or until tender but not browned. Add garlic and continue to cook for 2 to 3 minutes or until fragrant. Stir in all-purpose flour and cook, stirring constantly, for 2 minutes or until browned.

3. Add corncob-infused chicken stock, ½ cup at a time, whisking constantly; bring to a boil. Reduce the heat and simmer, stirring occasionally, for 10 to 15 minutes or until thick. Whisk in whipping cream until well combined. Stir in smoked corn kernels, smoked mozzarella cheese, creamed corn, and sage until well combined. Season with kosher salt and black pepper to taste.

4. Pour the mixture into a greased 9×11-inch casserole dish. Sprinkle panko breadcrumbs and Parmesan cheese over the casserole. Bake for 20 to 25 minutes or until top is crisp and golden brown. Serve immediately.

TED'S TIP

Always buy fresh corn with the husks on. If you're looking for good fresh corn, it's always best straight from the roadside stand. I like to smoke either bicolor or white corn because they balance out the smoke flavor better.

Planked Mashed Potatoes

Plank-smoked mashed potatoes are quite easy to prepare and are a great way to use up leftover mashed potatoes. I like to mix up the flavors depending on what they're being served with and what I have in the fridge. Try a variety of cheeses, herbs, roasted garlic, pesto, or even prepared horseradish. If you like it, throw it in there—odds are it'll taste pretty good with the potatoes.

Yield:	Prep time:	Cook time:	Serving size:
8 cups mashed potatoes	45 minutes	45 minutes	¾ cup

8 large Yukon gold potatoes, peeled and quartered	Kosher salt
2 TB. softened butter	Freshly ground black pepper
½ cup 35 percent whipping cream	½ cup creamy goat cheese
	¼ cup chopped fresh chives

1. Cook Yukon gold potatoes in a large pot of salted water for 15 to 20 minutes or until fork-tender. Drain well and return potatoes to the pot. Set the pot over low heat and cook, shaking constantly, for 2 to 3 minutes or until dry.

2. Mash potatoes with butter and whipping cream until smooth. Season with kosher salt and black pepper to taste; cool completely. Cover and refrigerate for 24 hours.

3. Meanwhile, soak 2 untreated maple hardwood planks in cold water for at least 1 hour. In a large bowl, combine cold mashed potatoes with goat cheese and chives. Mix well to combine.

4. Preheat the grill to medium-high heat, about 450°F to 550°F. Remove plank from water and dry with paper towel. Spray top surface of plank with nonstick cooking spray.

5. Use a 2-ounce ice cream scoop or ¼ cup dry measure to divide mashed potatoes into about 24 portions. Form each portion into a firm disk. Arrange the disks, evenly spaced, on the planks; spray with nonstick cooking spray.

6. Place the planks on the grill and close the lid. Smoke for 5 to 10 minutes or until the plank starts to crackle and smoke. Reduce the heat directly under the plank and continue to smoke for 20 to 30 minutes or until potatoes are heated through and golden and crisp on the outside.

7. Carefully remove the plank from the grill and serve potatoes immediately.

Warm Potato Salad with Bacon, Green Apple, and Molten Brie

This will make your guests scream with delight—I'm not even kidding! Sweet smoky flavor in the fingerling potatoes, onions, and bacon get a fresh kick from the tart Granny Smith apple, making this warm salad awesome. And then, as if it wasn't delicious enough, it gets finished with hot smoked Brie—pure smoky decadence!

Yield:	Prep time:	Cook time:	Serving size:
8 cups	1 hour	1½ hours	1 cup

3 lb. fingerling or new potatoes, washed

1 large sweet onion, quartered

1 TB. olive oil

½ tsp. kosher salt

½ tsp. freshly ground black pepper

1 (4-in.) round Brie cheese (about 150 g)

4 slices double-smoked bacon, sliced into ¼-in. strips

1 Granny Smith apple, cored and diced (skin left on)

2 green onions, thinly sliced on the bias

½ cup mixed chopped fresh herbs, such as parsley, chives, oregano, or thyme

1. Preheat the smoker per manufacturer's instructions to 250°F, using hickory wood.

2. Cut larger fingerling potatoes in half if larger than average. Place potatoes and sweet onion into a medium saucepan and cover with cold water. Set over high heat and bring to a rolling boil. Reduce the heat to medium and simmer for 15 to 20 minutes until fork-tender. Drain and transfer to a large bowl; remove onion and set aside.

3. Toss potatoes with olive oil, kosher salt, and black pepper. Transfer potatoes to the smoker rack. Use a grill basket or line the smoker rack with foil that has been poked to make a few holes. Add cooked onion. Smoke for 1½ hours or until vegetables are a smoky golden brown color.

4. Place Brie cheese on a thin, untreated wooden plank or foil-lined baking sheet. Add Brie to the smoker with potatoes during the last hour. Smoke until golden brown and gooey.

5. Meanwhile, cook double-smoked bacon in a large skillet set over medium heat for 7 to 10 minutes or until crisp. Drain bacon on a paper towel–lined plate. Coarsely chop and toss bacon with Granny Smith apple and green onions.

6. Remove potatoes from the smoker and transfer to a clean work surface. Using the bottom of a clean saucepan or skillet, lightly squish potatoes, just enough to crack the skin and expose the flesh slightly; chop onions. Toss potatoes with onions and apple mixture until well combined. Remove hot smoky Brie from the smoker.

7. Arrange Brie over potato mixture and pierce to allow hot cheese to flow over potatoes. Gently break rind into pieces. Add mixed herbs and season with kosher salt and black pepper to taste. Gently toss until well coated. Serve immediately.

Variation: Try this recipe using Cambozola cheese and stir in 1 or 2 tablespoons of grainy-style Dijon mustard for a bit of tang. I also like to add sautéed mushrooms to the smoky cheese mixture for an added treat.

Smoked Risotto with Spinach, Prosciutto, and Smoked Mozzarella

I've done a lot of experimenting with smoking various types of rice and I've found that arborio rice absorbs smoke flavor best. This rice has a high starch content and is porous enough to allow the smoke to penetrate the grain, adding a nice nutty, smoky flavor to this twist on classic risotto.

Yield:	Prep time:	Cook time:	Serving size:
8 cups	30 minutes	7 hours	1⅓ cups

4 cups arborio rice

8 cups chicken broth

3 TB. butter

1 medium onion, diced

2 cloves garlic, minced

½ cup dry white wine

4 cups baby spinach leaves, packed

1 cup shredded smoked provolone cheese, smoked buffalo mozzarella, or smoked mozzarella (method in Smoky Baked Macaroni and Cheese later in this chapter)

½ cup Parmesan cheese, freshly grated

¼ cup 35 percent whipping cream

Kosher salt

Freshly ground black pepper

12 very thin slices prosciutto or smoked prosciutto

Chopped fresh parsley leaves

1. Preheat the smoker per manufacturer's instructions to 200°F, using vine cuttings, oak wine-barrel staves, whiskey-barrel staves, or apple or olive branches. Keep the humidity level very low. Wrap a smoker rack with foil and puncture with the needle of an injector to make several tiny holes.

2. Scatter arborio rice over the rack and place in the smoker. Smoke, stirring every hour, for 6 hours or until rice is slightly colored. Cool completely. Reserve 2 cups to prepare risotto; vacuum pack remaining rice and store for up to 6 months.

3. Pour chicken broth into a large saucepan and bring to a boil. Reduce the heat to low and keep warm.

4. Melt butter in a large saucepan set over medium heat. Add onion and cook for 5 minutes or until translucent. Add garlic and cook for 2 to 3 minutes or until tender. Add rice and stir until well coated and lightly toasted. Pour in dry white wine and simmer for 1 minute or until wine has almost completely evaporated.

5. Pour in 1 cup chicken broth. Stir, slowly and gently, adding up to 6 cups broth, 1 cup at a time, for 15 to 18 minutes or until rice is tender, creamy, and a bit soupy but not gluey. Add additional broth, ¼ cup at a time, until proper consistency is achieved.

6. Stir in baby spinach, shredded smoked provolone cheese, Parmesan cheese, and whipping cream. Season with kosher salt and black pepper to taste. Spoon risotto into serving bowls and garnish with prosciutto and fresh parsley.

TED'S TIP

When stirring the risotto, stir slowly so the rice releases its starch slowly and doesn't make the risotto overly sticky. Risotto should be creamy and the grains of rice should still be a bit firm in the center.

Smoky Baked Macaroni and Cheese

Mozzarella is a mild, melting cheese that absorbs a lot of smoke, which enhances the simplicity of it. The white cheddar you use shouldn't be any older than 2 years or else the strong aged flavor will compete with the smoke. This is the new twist on a family favorite.

Yield:	Prep time:	Cook time:	Serving size:
1 casserole	24 hours, 45 minutes	4 hours	⅛ casserole

1 lb. part-skim mozzarella cheese balls

1 lb. white cheddar cheese (1 or 2 years old)

1½ lb. double elbow macaroni

2 TB. olive oil

3 TB. butter

¼ cup all-purpose flour

2½ cups milk

1 cup 35 percent whipping cream

1 small onion, diced

1 (8 oz.) pkg. cream cheese

½ tsp. freshly ground black pepper

Kosher salt

2 cups crushed sea salt–flavored, kettle-cooked potato chips

1. Preheat the smoker per manufacturer's instructions for cold smoking to 85°F or less, using apple, maple, or a blend of apple, maple, and hickory woods.

2. Arrange mozzarella cheese and white cheddar cheese on a smoke rack and place in the smoker directly above the ice or ice packs.

3. Smoke for 4 to 6 hours, depending on the amount of smoke flavor you're looking for. (You can go longer if you wish, but I find 4 to 6 hours plenty.) Remove cheese from smoker and wrap loosely in parchment paper. Refrigerate for 24 hours to allow the flavor to penetrate cheese.

4. Meanwhile, cook elbow macaroni in a pot of boiling, salted water until it is barely tender. Drain and toss with olive oil until evenly coated. Spread evenly on a foil-lined smoker rack and place in the smoker with the cheese. Smoke, stirring occasionally, for 1 hour. Note you don't want to smoke the macaroni for more than 1 hour because the smoke flavor could get too strong. Transfer macaroni to a zipper-lock plastic bag and store in the refrigerator.

5. Preheat the oven to 350°F. Grease a 2- or 3-quart casserole dish; set aside. Shred smoked mozzarella and cheddar cheeses; set aside.

6. Melt butter in a large saucepan set over medium-low heat. Stir in all-purpose flour until well combined and cook, stirring constantly, for 1 minute. Slowly pour in milk and whipping cream, whisking constantly until smooth. Add onion and sauté for 2 to 3 minutes, stirring until tender.

7. Simmer, stirring frequently, for 10 to 15 minutes or until thickened. Turn heat to low and whisk in cream cheese and smoked mozzarella and cheddar cheeses until smooth; remove from heat. Stir in black pepper and season with kosher salt to taste.

8. Place cooked macaroni in the casserole dish and stir in cheese until thoroughly combined. Bake for 20 to 30 minutes or until cheese is bubbling and golden brown. Top with crushed potato chips and serve immediately.

TED'S TIP

Serve this as a side dish with your favorite smoked ribs or brisket.

Weird and Wonderful

In This Chapter

- It's weird, it's wonderful, and it's smoked
- You can smoke anything, and I do mean *anything!*
- Out-of-the-ordinary recipes

When it comes to the world of smoking food and barbecue, I will smoke, barbecue, and grill anything. And when I say anything, I mean *anything!* I smoke water to make ice cubes for that perfect martini. My smoked honey is beyond delicious and so versatile that I'm still finding new ways to use it every day. (Don't worry, the recipes for both are later in this chapter.) I've even smoked bubble gum. (Now that one didn't turn out to be as good as I thought it would, but at least I tried.) I smoke salt and all kinds of cheeses as well as nuts, fruits, vegetables, and so much more. There are no limitations, just the desire to create something delicious.

When I was asked to make a really special dessert for an old client, I had to dig deep for a new idea. One of the criteria was that it had to be simple but have a "wow factor." In a moment of inspiration, it came to me—cold-smoked chocolate! So that's what I did. But I didn't stop there; I shaved it and mixed it into a homemade ice cream. It was a huge hit, to say the least! Ever since then I have been playing with desserts and discovering that sweet goes extremely well with smoky. They are two extreme flavors, so they balance each other perfectly.

Before we wrap up, let me tell you the story of how the smoked Twinkie was born—possibly the most weird and wonderful recipe in this book. I was tailgating with a bunch of friends and after a good feed, one of my friends said, "So, what's for dessert?" Loving a challenge as I do, I hit the gas station around the corner from the stadium and got some quick dessert provisions. Twinkies were the first thing I grabbed, then peanut butter, jam, chocolate bars, Oreos, mini marshmallows, a bottle of Tennessee whiskey, and more beer (we were tailgating, after all).

So back to the parking lot I went and fired up my grill. I lined those Twinkies up on a plank, spread the peanut butter over the top, then the jam, crushed the cookies and cut up the chocolate bars to sprinkle over top, and then added the mini marshmallows. Onto the grill they went to smoke. Let me tell ya, once I injected each Twinkie with a little whiskey, we were off to the races! I actually had another tailgater offer me $25 for a single Twinkie. Easiest money I've ever made!

Anyway, the point is, when you get into your groove of smoking food, have fun! And always remember the following:

- Make it the best you can and make it tasty.
- It's about the flavor and the smoke.
- It's about having the patience for low and slow.
- It's about family and good friends.

Good luck, enjoy, and happy smoking!

Pulled Pork and Cheese ABTs

An ABT in the world of smoking and BBQ is called an Atomic Buffalo Turd. I am not sure who came up with this name but that's what it's called. An ABT is a jalapeño stuffed with a mixture of cheese and meat, and if you want, wrapped in bacon. Smoked or even grilled, these spicy treats are sure to get any party off to a great start.

Yield:	Prep time:	Cook time:	Serving size:
18 ABTs	1 hour	1½ hours	1 ABT

18 jalapeños

1 cup unsauced Smoked BBQ Pulled Pork (recipe in Chapter 15)

½ cup shredded mozzarella cheese

¼ cup cream cheese

1¼ cups finely crushed corn tortilla chips

2 green onions, finely chopped

1 TB. chopped fresh cilantro

1 tsp. fresh lime juice

1 cup panko breadcrumbs

9 slices smoked bacon

1 TB. Ted's World-Famous Bone Dust BBQ Seasoning Rub (recipe in Chapter 8)

1. Slice down each jalapeño lengthwise, removing about a quarter of flesh to expose the inside and create a jalapeño "canoe." Remove and discard the seeds and ribs from inside each jalapeño. Finely chop the removed jalapeño flesh.

2. In a large bowl, combine chopped jalapeños, Smoked BBQ Pulled Pork, mozzarella cheese, cream cheese, ¼ cup tortilla chips, green onions, cilantro, and lime juice. Pack the pork mixture tightly into each prepared jalapeño.

3. Toss the remaining 1 cup tortilla chips with panko breadcrumbs. Press each jalapeño, filling side down, firmly into the breadcrumb mixture so it is completely coated.

4. Lay each slice of smoked bacon on a clean work surface. Firmly run your finger over each slice to stretch by 50 percent; cut each piece in half through the center. Tightly wrap a piece of bacon around each jalapeño, leaving no gaps, which would allow the cheese to ooze out during smoking. Arrange on a tray and freeze for 30 to 60 minutes until well chilled but not frozen.

5. Preheat the smoker per manufacturer's instructions to 275°F, using hickory, oak, maple, or apple wood.

6. Season jalapeños with Ted's World-Famous Bone Dust BBQ Seasoning Rub.

7. Place jalapeños in the smoker and smoke for 1½ to 2 hours or until the bacon is slightly crispy and filling is heated through. Remove from smoker and rest for 5 minutes before serving. Serve hot.

Variation: Substitute shredded smoked chicken, brisket, turkey, crab meat, or shrimp for the pork. Just about anything would taste good, so use your imagination and create a whole host of ABT fillings.

TED'S TIP

Try and pick out jalapeños that are uniform in size. This will ensure they freeze and cook at the same rate (and that no one gets more or less than someone else—that's how fistfights start!) I like nice big jalapeños because you can load them with filling.

Plank-Smoked Camembert

This recipe is a winner, a head turner, and a crowd pleaser. I have been plank smoking Brie and Camembert cheese for over 10 years. I'm 99.9 percent sure I'm the one who came up with it—not 100 percent sure, but pretty sure. I developed it for my first cookbook, *Sticks and Stones*, back in 1999. Either way, it's fast, it's easy, and it will get your party started right!

Yield:	Prep time:	Cook time:	Serving size:
2 cheese rounds	30 minutes	20 minutes	8 oz.

6 thick slices double-smoked bacon

1 small Vidalia onion, sliced

2 TB. coarsely crushed cashews

1 TB. panko breadcrumbs

1 tsp. chopped fresh thyme leaves

2 oz. maple syrup

1½ tsp. freshly ground black pepper

1 tsp. kosher salt

2 (4-in.) Camembert rounds (about 150 g. each)

1. Soak a ½-inch maple, oak, pecan, or hickory grilling plank in cold water for 1 hour.

2. Meanwhile, arrange the double-smoked bacon in a large skillet set over medium heat and cook for 7 to 10 minutes or until lightly browned and crisp. Transfer to a paper towel–lined plate and set aside.

3. Increase the heat to medium-high and add Vidalia onion. Cook, stirring occasionally, for 5 minutes or until tender but not browned. Remove from heat and drain. Pat onion with paper towel to remove excess bacon fat.

4. In a large bowl, combine bacon, onion, cashews, panko breadcrumbs, thyme, maple syrup, and ½ teaspoon black pepper; set aside.

5. Preheat the grill to medium heat, about 350°F. Remove plank from water and pat dry with paper towel. Place the plank on the grill and close the lid. Heat the plank for 3 to 5 minutes or until it begins to crackle and lightly smoke. Season the plank with kosher salt and ½ teaspoon black pepper.

6. Arrange cheese rounds, evenly spaced and about 1 inch from the edge, on the plank. Sprinkle Camembert cheese with remaining ½ teaspoon pepper. Evenly divide bacon mixture between cheese rounds, mounding into a tall pile; close the lid.

7. Smoke, checking for flames occasionally, for 15 to 20 minutes or until the topping is heated through and cheese is bulging in the rind and golden brown.

8. Transfer to serving platter or a second, uncharred plank; cool slightly. Serve with a variety of breads and crackers.

TASTY TIDBIT

Small wheels of cheese with a hearty rind are the best for plank smoking because the rind keeps the hot, bubbly cheese nice and safe, instead of it oozing everywhere.

Smoked Bacon–Wrapped Meatballs

Not sure who first created this recipe, but I know when and where I first had it. My friend Danielle of Diva Q BBQ gave me a taste at a BBQ event when I was visiting a while back. She calls them Mo-ink Balls; moo for the beef and oink for the pork. They're beef meatballs wrapped in bacon and smoked to mouthwatering awesomeness. Here is my version with the addition of a dunk and a crunch.

Yield:	Prep time:	Cook time:	Serving size:
32 meatballs	2½ hours	1½ hours	2 meatballs

2 buttery croissants, cut into 1-in. pieces

¼ cup whole milk

3 lb. ground beef

1 lb. ground pork

½ cup finely diced onion

4 cloves garlic, minced

3 TB. Ted's World-Famous Bone Dust BBQ Seasoning Rub (recipe in Chapter 8)

2 tsp. Dijon mustard

1 tsp. Worcestershire sauce

1½ cups diced mozzarella cheese

32 slices hickory-smoked bacon

2 cups prepared gourmet-style BBQ sauce

½ cup apple butter

½ cup chipotle-style hot sauce

¼ cup honey

¼ cup apple juice

1 oz. bourbon (optional)

2 (8-oz.) bags kettle-style potato chips, finely crushed

1. Place croissant pieces and whole milk into a medium bowl; soak for 15 minutes or until softened.

2. Meanwhile, in a large bowl, mix ground beef, ground pork, onion, garlic, 1 tablespoon Ted's World-Famous Bone Dust BBQ Seasoning Rub, Dijon mustard, and Worcestershire sauce. Gently mix in mozzarella cheese.

3. Squeeze excess milk from croissants, discarding excess milk, and add croissants to the meat mixture. Gently mix until meat mixture is moist and sticky but not wet.

4. Divide meat mixture equally into 32 portions, using a 2-ounce ice cream scoop or dry ¼ cup measure. Form into round balls.

5. Place meatballs on a parchment-lined baking sheet; refrigerate for 1 hour or until chilled through.

6. Lay each slice of hickory-smoked bacon on a clean work surface. Firmly run your finger over each slice until almost doubled in length. Season one side of each slice of bacon with remaining 2 tablespoons Ted's World-Famous Bone Dust BBQ Seasoning Rub. Tightly wrap a slice of bacon, seasoned side in, around each meatball, so that it is entirely covered. Refrigerate for 1 hour.

7. Preheat the smoker per manufacturer's instructions to 275°F to 300°F, using hickory wood or a blend of hickory, maple, and apple woods.

8. Arrange meatballs on a smoking rack and place in the smoker. Insert thermometer probe in the center of one meatball. Set the internal temperature for 160°F. Close the door and smoke the meatballs for 1 to 1½ hours or until bacon starts to crisp and meatballs are fully cooked.

9. Meanwhile, stir gourmet-style BBQ sauce, apple butter, chipotle-style hot sauce, honey, and apple juice in a small saucepan set over medium heat. Cook until mixture comes to a boil; stir in bourbon (if using) and remove from heat.

10. Remove meatballs from the smoker. Dip each meatball, one at a time, into the sauce mixture and then into chip crumbs until evenly coated. Serve immediately with lots of napkins!

TED'S TIP

Freeze the diced mozzarella before mixing into the raw meat mixture. This is extra insurance that the cheese won't ooze out of the meatballs while in the smoker.

Smoked Frittata with Grape Tomatoes and Cheese

I was smoking some peameal bacon one morning for a delicious breakfast when I got to thinking: I've smoked hard-cooked eggs and soft-poached eggs, but I've never smoked scrambled eggs. This needed to be remedied, and fast. So here is my smoky take on the classic frittata. The egg mixture takes on the sweet smoke, adding a new dimension to your eggs.

Yield:	Prep time:	Cook time:	Serving size:
1 frittata	15 minutes	3½ hours	¼ to ⅛ frittata

1 cup grape tomatoes

Kosher salt

8 extra-large eggs

3 TB. 35 percent whipping cream

2 cups shredded mozzarella or pepper jack cheese

1 cup crispy fried onion pieces

2 TB. chopped fresh herbs, such as thyme and basil leaves

2 green onions, chopped

1. Preheat the smoker per manufacturer's instructions to 240°F, using hickory wood.

2. Arrange grape tomatoes, evenly spaced, on a foil-lined smoker rack with ventilation holes. Sprinkle with kosher salt to taste.

3. Place the rack in the smoker and close the lid. Smoke tomatoes for 2 to 3 hours or until slightly softened and skin is a little wrinkly. Remove from smoker; cool completely. Chop tomatoes.

4. Spray a foil lasagna pan liberally with nonstick cooking spray; set aside.

5. In a medium bowl, whisk eggs with whipping cream until lightly beaten. Add mozzarella cheese, crispy fried onion pieces, herbs, and green onions. Pour mixture into prepared pan. Scatter tomatoes over top.

6. Place pan in the smoker and smoke for 1½ hours or until frittata is set and hot throughout. Remove from smoker.

TED'S TIP

While you're at it, make extra smoked tomatoes to use in smoky BBQ sauces, as salad garnishes, or to serve on *charcuterie* and antipasto platters.

Smoked *Fois Gras* Terrine

The key to smoking fois gras is a very cold smoke. The colder the smoke the better because duck liver is pure fat, so if the temperature is too high it will cause the liver to melt. And this stuff ain't cheap, so we want to make sure the only place it melts is in your mouth.

Yield:	Prep time:	Cook time:	Serving size:
1 terrine	30 minutes	1½ hours	⅛ terrine

2 to 3 TB. Garlic-Herb Fresh Rub (recipe in Chapter 8)

1 large duck liver, rinsed and dried (about 1 lb.)

1 oz. Armagnac

2 TB. honey

¼ cup pistachios, coarsely chopped

Kosher salt

Cracked black pepper

4 to 6 cups boiling water

1. Preheat the smoker for cold smoking with an ice bath and no humidity per manufacturer's instructions to 85°F, using oak wood.

2. Gently rub Garlic-Herb Fresh Rub all over duck liver. Place liver in the smoker and smoke for 1½ to 2 hours, making sure it isn't melting, or until liver is lightly browned and smoky. Remove liver from smoker and refrigerate for 1 to 2 hours.

3. Preheat the oven to 225°F. Meanwhile, pull the liver apart with your hands into two lobes. Remove valves and sinuous tissue; discard. Break lobes into 2- to 3-inch pieces and place in a bowl. Gently toss liver with Armagnac, honey, pistachios, kosher salt, and black pepper.

4. Line a loaf pan with plastic wrap, with excess hanging over the edges. Place liver mixture in the pan and gently press into an even layer with no air pockets. Fold excess plastic over top of liver mixture to create a sealed little package. Place the loaf pan in the center of a roasting pan. Pour enough boiling water into the roasting pan to come halfway up the sides.

5. Transfer the roasting pan to the oven and bake for 20 minutes or until firm. Remove from water bath and cool slightly. Refrigerate for 4 to 6 hours or overnight to set.

6. Carefully remove the wrapped liver from the terrine mold. Remove plastic wrap. Cut into ½-inch slices and serve with grilled bread or on top of your favorite steak.

> **TED'S TIP**
>
> Fois gras is expensive, but not all fois gras is priced the same. Fois gras, like beef, is graded. Grade A is the most premium (two large uniformly sized lobes with no blood spots or blemishes) and the most expensive. A grade B lobe (smaller uneven lobes, sometimes a blemish or blood spot) is usually sold at a reduced cost and is perfectly acceptable for this application, so buy grade B and save some money.

Smoked Honey

Adding smoke to honey is a real treat. It's a great way to naturally add a little smoky flavor into your BBQ sauces and marinades. It's also fantastic basted on ribs! No need to use liquid smoke … smoke-infused honey (or even maple syrup!) will do the trick.

Yield:	Prep time:	Cook time
4 cups	10 minutes	3 hours

1 (2-cup) tub raw honey, refrigerated to harden

2 pieces honeycomb (about 2 in. square)

1. Preheat the smoker for cold smoking with an ice pack per manufacturer's instructions to 85°F or colder with low humidity, using a blend of maple and apple, oak and pecan, oak and mesquite, or maple and cherry woods.

2. Transfer honey from its tub, in a solid block, into a nonreactive pan, such as a roasting pan. Place the honeycomb in the pan along with any liquid honey. Place the roasting pan in the freezer for 10 minutes.

3. Place the roasting pan in the smoker. Smoke, keeping the smokehouse filled with lots of smoke and the vents open, for 3 to 4 hours or until the honey takes on a smoky flavor.

4. Remove the roasting pan from the smoker. Transfer honey to a medium saucepan set over low heat; reserve the honeycomb. Once honey has melted, add honeycomb and remove from heat; let stand, uncovered, for 2 hours or until cool. Cover and let stand at room temperature for 24 hours to allow the flavors to meld.

5. Rewarm honey until fluid. Cut each honeycomb in half and place in a 1-pint, wide-mouthed canning jar. Pour warm honey over the honeycombs and seal jars. Let stand at room temperature. Store at room temperature for up to 2 weeks.

> **TED'S TIP**
>
> Liquid honey doesn't absorb smoke flavor as well as raw honey, which is a cloudy and thick variety of honey that has all the pollen left in. Honeycomb is great for this purpose because it really attacks smoke flavor, which it will continue to infuse into the honey as they sit in the jar together. To remove raw honey easily from the tub, just warm it for a few seconds in a bowl of hot water and turn it out into a pan to refrigerate.

Smoked Ice Martini

Who needs olives or onions or lemon zest when you can have a smoke-infused martini with a bacon garnish? Read it again if you have to, but it's gonna say the same thing—we're smoking water to make a bacon-garnished martini. How could you not make this recipe?

Yield:	Prep time:	Cook time:	Serving size:
12 cocktails	10 minutes	2 hours	1 cocktail

8 cups cold water

1 bottle of your favorite vodka

12 slices hickory-smoked bacon

3 TB. Smoked Honey (see previous recipe)

Freshly ground black pepper

4 TB. ice wine

1. Pour cold water evenly into 2 zipper-lock plastic bags and place in the freezer for 24 hours or until solid.

2. Preheat the smoker per manufacturer's instructions to 125°F or less, using maple, oak, hickory, or cherry wood.

3. Remove plastic bags and place ice blocks in a nonreactive metal container large enough to hold 8 cups of fluid. Place the pan in the smoker and smoke for 2 to 3 hours or until melted and smoky.

4. Remove the pan from the smoker and transfer water to a large pot. Bring water to a boil; boil for 2 minutes. Remove from heat and strain water through a paper coffee filter to remove any carbon particles. Pour water into ice trays and freeze until solid.

5. Place vodka in the freezer and chill martini or rock glasses.

6. Cook hickory-smoked bacon in a skillet set over medium heat until crisp. Drain on a paper towel–lined plate. Arrange bacon on a parchment-lined baking sheet. Brush the top of each slice with a little Smoked Honey and sprinkle with black pepper to taste; set aside.

7. Swirl 1 teaspoon ice wine in each frosted glass until evenly coated; drain off excess. In each glass, pour 2 to 3 ounces chilled vodka and add 2 smoked iced cubes and a strip of honey peppered bacon. Serve immediately. Repeat!

Variation: Add smoked ice cubes to any liquor you like or in your favorite cocktails to add a nice smoky twist. Try them in a Caesar, a mojito, a sidecar, or even a chocolate martini.

TED'S TIP

The reason I freeze the water into a huge ice block before smoking is because the heat will cause it to melt slowly, which means the water will absorb more of the smoke and create a more rounded smoke flavor. A bowl of water will only get the smoke on the top, resulting in too mild a smoke flavor to really complement a cocktail.

Smoked Chocolate-Banana Ice Cream

Smoke blends nicely with chocolate and brings out a whole new dimension of flavor than what we're used to with regular chocolate. Use any remaining smoked chocolate to make a chocolate sauce to garnish other ice creams and desserts, in *mole* and BBQ sauces, in frosting for cakes and cupcakes, or just to snack on in bed with a handful of toasted nuts.

Yield:	Prep time:	Cook time:	Serving size:
8 cups ice cream	48 hours, 30 minutes	1 hour, 20 minutes	½ cup ice cream

3 lb. milk, dark, or white chocolate slab (about 1 in. thick), well chilled

4 cups 35 percent whipping cream

2 cups 10 percent half-and-half

2 vanilla beans, split lengthwise

1½ cups granulated sugar

12 large egg yolks

1 cup mashed ripe banana

1. Preheat the smoker for cold smoking per manufacturer's instructions to 85°F or less, using almond wood or coconut shells; and cherry, pecan, apple, walnut, or mesquite wood. If using a water smoker, fill the water tray with blocks of ice or bags of ice cubes. If you're not using a water smoker, place frozen ice packs on the shelf below chocolate to keep it cold.

2. Arrange chocolate in the highest position of the smoker and as far away from the heat source as possible. Smoke for 30 minutes, being careful to maintain a cold temperature. Remove chocolate from the smoker and let cool completely. Store wrapped in parchment paper and in an airtight container in a cool, dark place for at least 24 hours.

3. Combine whipping cream and half-and-half in a large, heavy-bottom saucepan set over medium heat. Scrape seeds out of vanilla beans and add to the saucepan, along with pods. Slowly bring mixture to a boil and remove from heat; cool slightly.

4. Meanwhile, in a medium bowl, whisk sugar and egg yolks until thick and smooth. Whisking constantly, slowly pour the heated cream mixture into the egg mixture. Return custard to the saucepan and set over medium heat. Cook, stirring constantly with a wooden spoon, for 8 to 10 minutes or until thickened enough to coat the back of a spoon.

5. Add 12 ounces chopped, smoked chocolate; stir until completely melted. Remove from heat and strain through a fine mesh sieve into a large bowl. Stir in banana until evenly distributed.

6. Cover surface of ice cream with a piece of parchment paper. Store in the refrigerator for at least 8 hours, preferably overnight, until well chilled.

7. Prepare ice cream in an ice cream machine according to manufacturer's instructions. Divide ice cream and pack into two airtight containers (about 4 cups each). Freeze for at least 2 hours before serving.

TED'S TIP

The colder the smoker temperature, the less likely it is that the chocolate will melt. Some people line their rack with foil to catch any melted chocolate or smoke it in a pan. I like the challenge of maintaining the right temperature—it gives me more bragging rights! I have smoked chocolate using a variety of smokers and have found electric smokers produce the best results.

PB&J Plank-Smoked Twinkies with Chocolate-Marshmallow Topping

Even the humble Twinkie can be smoked. The cream-filled confections are lined up like little soldiers on a wooden plank and topped with peanut butter, jam, chocolate, and marshmallows, then smoked until ooey and gooey. This is the best dessert for pleasing a crowd of tailgaters or just about anyone.

Yield:	Prep time:	Cook time:	Serving size:
12 Twinkies	15 minutes	15 minutes	1 Twinkie

12 Twinkies, unwrapped

1 cup smooth peanut butter

½ cup strawberry preserves

2 cups white mini marshmallows

½ cup milk chocolate chips

1 Butterfinger candy bar, broken into small pieces

4 chocolate-chip cookies, crushed

3 oz. Tennessee whiskey (optional)

1. Soak a 12-inch-long, ½-inch-thick, untreated maple, oak, pecan, or hickory hardwood plank in cold water for at least 1 hour. Remove from water and dry with paper towel.

2. Preheat the grill to medium-high heat, about 450°F. Arrange Twinkies, right up against each other, on the plank. Vigorously stir peanut butter to loosen. Spread peanut butter evenly over the Twinkies, filling any gaps. Spread strawberry preserves evenly over peanut butter. In a medium bowl, toss mini marshmallows, milk chocolate chips, Butterfinger, and chocolate-chip cookies until well combined. Scatter evenly over Twinkies.

3. Place the plank on the grill and close the lid. Heat for 3 to 5 minutes or until the plank is very smoky. Turn off the heat source directly under the plank and reduce the remaining burners to medium-low, about 300°F to 350°F. Smoke for an additional 10 to 15 minutes or until the Twinkies are lightly browned and crisp and the marshmallows are gooey.

4. Transfer the plank to a heatproof work surface. Use an injector to suck up the Tennessee whiskey (if using). Insert the needle about halfway into each Twinkie and inject with about ¼ ounce whiskey (if using). Serve immediately.

TED'S TIP

Leave out the Tennessee whiskey if this is a treat for the kiddies. And be sure to make extra—most people can't stop after just one!

andouille sausage   A sausage made with highly seasoned pork chitterlings and tripe; a standard component of many Cajun dishes.

arborio rice   Plump, short-grain Italian rice traditionally used for making risotto.

bacteria   Single-cell micro-organisms that can contaminate food and cause food-borne illness.

balsamic vinegar   Vinegar produced from a specific type of grape and aged in wood barrels. It is heavier, darker, and sweeter than most vinegars.

barbecue (BBQ)   Although the origin of the term is debated, it refers to a method of cooking over either an open fire or hot grill outdoors. It can also be used as a noun to describe the actual grilling appliance or a specific flavor profile in foods, such as sauces or cooked meats.

bark   (1) The outer layer of a long, slow-cooked cut of meat, such as a pork shoulder. This layer will be about ½-inch deep, dark, and somewhat tougher in texture than the meat it protects. A good bark is highly prized by barbecue enthusiasts. (2) The outer protective layer of wood.

baste   A technique used to keep foods moist during cooking by spooning or brushing the meat with a sauce, marinade, or other flavored liquid.

blanch   To place a food in boiling water for about 1 minute (or less) to partially cook the exterior and then submerge in, or rinse with, cool water to halt the cooking.

brine   A highly salted, often seasoned, liquid used to flavor, add moisture, and/or preserve foods. Food is submerged in the brine liquid for a period of time ranging from minutes to days. The salt in the brine penetrates the cells of the meat tissues, causing them to take in more water. The increased salinity then causes the cells to hold on to the water, thereby increasing the overall moisture and tenderness of the finished product.

Cajun cooking A style of cooking that combines French and Southern characteristics and includes many highly seasoned stews and meats. Can also refer to characteristic spice blends that may include spices such as thyme, paprika, mustard, and hot dried peppers.

capers The flavorful buds of a Mediterranean plant, ranging in size from *nonpareil* (about the size of a small pea) to larger, grape-size caper berries.

caramelize To cook sugar over low heat until it develops a sweet caramel flavor. In this book, it could be used to describe how the low-and-slow method of smoking creates sweet caramel flavor and browning in meats.

cardamom An intense, sweet-smelling spice, common to Indian cooking; often used in baking and coffee.

chile or **chiles** Any one of many different hot peppers (or Capsicum), dried or fresh, and ranging in intensity from relatively mild to blisteringly hot.

chili powder A seasoning blend that includes cayenne, cumin, garlic, and oregano. Proportions vary among different versions, but all offer a warm, rich flavor.

chimichurri An Argentinean condiment made of a blend of olive oil, vinegar, garlic, onion, parsley, oregano, cayenne, black pepper, and salt; traditionally served with meats.

Chinese five-spice powder A seasoning blend of cinnamon, anise, ginger, fennel, and pepper.

chipotle A smoked jalapeño that is dark brown with a reddish tinge, wrinkled skin, and a sweet and chocolaty flavor with a kick of heat. Chipotle chiles can be dried or pickled, as well as canned in adobo sauce (Mexican sauce).

chorizo A spiced pork sausage eaten alone or as a component in many recipes.

churrasco A term for a style of barbecue that originated in southern Brazil. Churrasco is a variety of meats that may be cooked on a purpose-built *churrasqueira* (a grill, often with supports for spits or skewers).

chutney A thick condiment often served with Indian curries; made with fruits and/or vegetables, vinegar, sugar, and spices.

cilantro A member of the parsley family, this herb is used in Mexican and Asian cuisines. The dried seed of a cilantro plant is coriander.

cold smoking   The process of applying smoke flavor to foods without necessarily cooking them.

crimini mushrooms   A relative of white button mushrooms but brown in color and with a richer flavor. Larger, more mature mushrooms are portobellos. *See also* portobello mushrooms.

crispy fried onions   Typically found in Asian grocery stores, crispy fried onions are thinly sliced onions or shallots that are lightly dusted with starch and fried until golden brown and crisp. Sold packed in cans, jars, or plastic bags, they are ready to use in a variety of applications as a garnish or ingredient.

cumin   A smoky-tasting spice popular in Middle Eastern and Indian dishes. Cumin is a seed; ground cumin seed is the most common form used in cooking. Its flavor is best known as the predominant flavor of chili powder.

cure or **curing**   A term that refers to food-preservation and flavoring processes, especially of meat or fish, by the addition of a combination of salt, nitrates, and/or sugar.

curry   Rich, spicy sauces and the dishes prepared with them. Curries involve complex seasoning bases often with 30 or more ingredients and long, slow cooking to draw out the flavors. Common to the cuisines of India, Southeast Asia, and the Caribbean.

curry powder   A ground blend of rich and flavorful spices used as a basis for curry and many other Indian-influenced dishes. Common ingredients include cayenne, nutmeg, cumin, cinnamon, pepper, and turmeric. Modern curry powder is a blend invented by the English occupiers of India to mimic the Indian *masala* blends in a less intense fashion.

Dijon mustard   Hearty, spicy mustard made in the style of the Dijon region of France.

drizzle   To lightly sprinkle drops of liquid over food, often as the finishing touch to a dish.

dunk   A seasoned liquid or sauce into which a cut of meat, fish, or vegetable is fully immersed either before cooking or before eating.

emulsion   A combination of liquid ingredients that do not normally mix well, such as fat or oil with water, beaten together to create a thick uniform fluid.

fennel In seed form, a fragrant, licorice-tasting spice. The bulbs have a much milder flavor and celery-like crunch, and are used as a vegetable in salads or cooked recipes.

feta A white, crumbly, sharp, and salty cheese popular in Greek cuisine and on salads. Traditional feta is usually made with sheep milk, but feta-style cheese can be made from the milk of a sheep, cow, goat, or a combination.

frenched To french a bone is to cut the meat away from the end of the bone of a rib or chop so that part of the bone is exposed. Done with racks of lamb, beef, and pork to make meats look more pleasing to the eye.

garnish An embellishment not vital to the dish but added to enhance visual appeal.

ginger Available fresh or dried, ginger adds a pungent, sweet, and spicy quality to a dish.

Gorgonzola A creamy and rich Italian blue cheese.

grilling The act of cooking meat (or other foods) by setting it on a grate over a gas flame or hot coals.

herbes de Provence A seasoning mix including basil, fennel, marjoram, rosemary, sage, and thyme, common in the south of France.

hoisin sauce A sweet Asian condiment similar to ketchup made with soybeans, sesame, chile peppers, and sugar.

hot smoking Smoking in an enclosed atmosphere in the presence of heat and smoke.

infusion A liquid in which flavorful ingredients, such as herbs, have been soaked or steeped to extract that flavor into the liquid.

injection A technique where you push liquid into meat in several areas with an injector to increase the internal moisture of the meat and add flavor.

jicama A crunchy, sweet, large round Central American vegetable.

kalamata olives Traditionally from Greece, these medium-small long black olives have a smoky rich flavor.

kosher salt A coarse-grained salt made without any additives or iodine.

macerate To mix sugar or another sweetener with fruit. The fruit softens and its juice is released to mix with the sweetener.

marinate To soak meat, seafood, or other food in a seasoned liquid, called a marinade, which is often high in acids. Its main purpose is to add flavor, although the acids in the marinade may break down the muscle tissue, helping to make it tender.

meld To allow flavors to blend and develop over time. Melding is often why recipes call for overnight refrigeration and is also why some dishes taste better as leftovers.

mirin A sweet, golden rice wine made from glutinous rice. It is low in alcohol and is often used in sauces and dressings. Typically found in Japanese and Asian cuisines.

mop The action of slopping a seasoned liquid over slow-cooked meat or fish using a tool (of the same name) that resembles a miniature old-fashioned string mop.

nitrates or **nitrites** Compounds that contain a nitrogen atom combined with either two (nitrite) or three (nitrate) oxygen atoms. Nitrates and nitrites are used as food additives in cured meats to preserve color and prevent dangerous foodborne illnesses, like botulism.

olive oil A fragrant liquid produced by crushing or pressing olives. Extra-virgin olive oil—the most flavorful and highest quality—is produced from the first pressing of a batch of olives; oil is also produced from later pressings.

panko breadcrumbs Coarse, airy textured white breadcrumbs traditionally used in Japanese cuisine as a breading for seafood, poultry, and pork. Can be found in grocery and specialty food stores in the Asian ethnic food section.

parboil To partially cook in boiling water or broth, similar to blanching (although blanched foods are quickly cooled with cold water).

paste A thick wet mixture that is made by adding a fluid to a seasoning rub or mixture that is massaged on the surface of meat or, in the case of poultry, under the skin and is left to sit for a period of time before cooking.

peameal bacon A Canadian tradition of curing pork loins with a solution of salt and water (brine). Traditionally injected and then rolled in cornmeal. The bacon can be smoked, grilled, and fried.

portobello mushrooms A mature and larger form of the smaller crimini mushroom, portobellos are brownish, chewy, and flavorful. Often served as whole caps, grilled, or as thin sautéed slices. *See also* crimini mushrooms.

prosciutto Dry, salt-cured ham that originated in Italy.

purée To reduce a food to a thick, creamy texture, usually using a blender or food processor.

reduce To boil or simmer a broth or sauce to remove some of the water content, resulting in more concentrated flavor and color.

render To cook a meat to the point where its fat melts and can be removed.

reserve To hold a specified ingredient for another use later in the recipe.

rice vinegar Vinegar produced from fermented rice or rice wine, popular in Asian-style dishes. Different from rice wine vinegar.

risotto A popular Italian rice dish made by browning arborio rice in butter or oil and slowly adding liquid to cook the rice, resulting in a creamy texture.

rub A blend of seasonings that are massaged on the surface of meat and, in the case of poultry, under the skin that is left to sit for a period of time before cooking.

saffron A spice made from the stamens of crocus flowers, saffron lends a dramatic yellow color and distinctive flavor to a dish. Use only tiny amounts of this expensive herb.

sambal A spicy condiment often used in Malaysian and Indonesian cuisines made from crushed chiles, brown sugar, and salt.

shallot A member of the onion family that grows in a bulb somewhat like garlic and has a milder onion flavor.

shellfish A broad range of seafood, including clams, mussels, oysters, crabs, shrimp, and lobster.

shiitake mushrooms Large, dark brown mushrooms with a hearty, meaty flavor. Can be used fresh, dried, or grilled and as a component in other recipes or as a flavoring source for broth.

shuck To remove the shells from shellfish such as oysters, clams, mussels, and scallops. Also a term used to remove the outer husk of corn on the cob.

slather To generously rub or spread a thick pastelike mixture over the surface of food, usually a cut of meat.

smoking The process of flavoring, cooking, or preserving food by exposing it for a lengthy period of time to smoke from burning or smoldering plant materials (most often wood or a wood derivative like charcoal).

spritz A flavored liquid or simply water placed in a spray bottle to periodically mist over meat in a smoker during the cooking process to keep the surface moist and provide added flavor.

Sriracha A type of Thai hot sauce named after the coastal city of Si Racha in the Chonburi Province of central Thailand. It is a paste of chile peppers, distilled vinegar, garlic, sugar, and salt. Quite spicy and delicious as a condiment or when used in sauces, dressings, and glazes.

suprême A boneless breast of chicken or another poultry bird that still has the first joint of the wing (drumstick) attached.

tamarind A sweet, pungent flavorful fruit used in Indian-style sauces and curries, made into a sweet sauce popular in Indian dishes.

tandoor oven A cylindrical clay oven, usually sunken into the ground. The heat for a tandoor is generated by charcoal or wood fire burning within the tandoor itself and cooking the food by hot air and smoke. Versions of this oven are found throughout India and the Middle East.

tomatillo A small, round fruit with a distinctive spicy flavor, often found in south-of-the-border dishes.

truss To secure meats and poultry with string or butcher's twine.

turmeric A spicy, pungent yellow root used in many dishes, especially Indian cuisine, for color and flavor. Turmeric is the source of the yellow color in many prepared mustards.

wasabi Japanese horseradish, a fiery, pungent condiment (most often sold as a paste) used with many Japanese-style dishes.

zest Small, thin slivers of peel, usually from citrus fruit, such as lemon, lime, or orange.

zester A kitchen tool used to scrape zest off fruit.

Resources

Yes, even a seasoned, professional chef uses the books of other chefs. Following are some books and websites I would recommend to a new smoker. They're great for providing additional information, answering questions, and getting inspiration. Smoking should be fun, and these are the words of some of the folks who prove that every day!

Books

Anderson, Warren R. *Mastering the Craft of Smoking Food.* Shrewsbury, UK: Quiller Press, 2007.

Big Green Egg. *Big Green Egg Cookbook: Celebrating the World's Best Smoker & Grill.* Kansas City: Andrews McMeel Publishing, 2010.

Browne, Rick, and Jack Bettridge. *The Barbecue America Cookbook: America's Best Recipes from Coast to Coast.* Guilford, CT: The Lyons Press, 2002.

Davis, Ardie A., and Paul Kirk. *The Kansas City Barbeque Society Cookbook, 25th Anniversary Edition.* Kansas City: Andrews McMeel Publishing, 2010.

Hasheider, Phillip. *The Complete Book of Butchering, Smoking, Curing, and Sausage Making: How to Harvest Your Livestock & Wild Game.* Minneapolis: Voyageur Press, 2010.

Jamison, Cheryl Alters, and Bill Jamison. *Smoke and Spice: Cooking with Smoke, the Real Way to Barbecue.* Rev. ed. Boston: Harvard Common Press, 2003.

Kirk, Paul. *Paul Kirk's Championship Barbecue: Barbecue Your Way to Greatness with 575 Lip-Smackin' Recipes from the Baron of Barbecue.* Boston: Harvard Common Press, 2004.

Knote, Charlie, and Ruthie Knote. *Barbecuing and Sausage-Making Secrets.* Cape Giradeau, MO: Culinary Institute of Smoke Cooking, 1992.

Lilly, Chris. *Big Bob Gibson's BBQ Book: Recipes and Secrets from a Legendary Barbecue Joint.* New York: Clarkson Potter Publishers, 2009.

Marianski, Stanley, Robert Marianski, and Adam Marianski. *Meat Smoking and Smokehouse Design, 2nd ed.* Seminole, FL: Bookmagic, LLC, 2009.

Mills, Mike, and Amy Mills Tunnicliffe. *Peace, Love, and Barbecue: Recipes, Secrets, Tall Tales, and Outright Lies from the Legends of Barbecue.* New York: Rodale Books, 2005.

Mixon, Myron, and Kelly Alexander. *Smokin' with Myron Mixon: Recipes Made Simple, from the Winningest Man in Barbecue.* New York: Ballantine Books, 2011.

North American Meat Processors. *The Meat Buyers Guide: Meat, Lamb, Veal, Pork, and Poultry.* Hoboken: Wiley, 2006.

Perry Lang, Adam. *Serious Barbecue: Smoke, Char, Baste, and Brush Your Way to Great Outdoor Cooking.* New York: Hyperion, 2009.

Reader, Ted. *Napoleon's Everyday Gourmet Grilling.* Toronto: Key Porter Books, 2008.

———. *Napoleon's Everyday Gourmet Plank Grilling.* Toronto: Key Porter Books, 2009.

———. *The Art of Plank Grilling: Licked by Fire, Kissed by Smoke.* Toronto: Key Porter Books, 2007.

Reed, John Shelton, Dale Volberg Reed, and Will McKinney. *Holy Smoke: The Big Book of North Carolina.* Chapel Hill: University of North Carolina Press, 2008.

Tarantino, Jim. *Marinades, Rubs, Brines, Cures and Glazes.* Berkeley, CA: Ten Speed Press, 2006.

Websites

amazingribs.com

barbecuehut.com

barbecuetricks.com

barbequebible.com

bbq.about.com

bbqs.com

bbqsmokersite.hubpages.com

bigsteelkeg.com

biggreenegg.com

bradleysmoker.com

brinkmann.net

www.fsis.usda.gov

godofthegrill.com

greatlakesgrilling.com

grilling24x7.com

horizonbbqsmokersstore.com

hpba.org

kcbs.us

megabbq.com

nakedwhiz.com/nwindex.htm

nordicware.com

proq.forumotion.com

randyq.addr.com

ribolator.com

seriouseats.com

smokepistol.com

Smokingmeatforums.com

southernpride.com

stateofq.com

traegercanada.com

Index

A

accessories, 65, 68, 72-75, 78
  BBQ Guru, 76
  bellows, 76
  cold-smoke generators, 76
  diffuser plates, 77
  fire starters, 68-70
  kamado-style smokers, 78
  meat grinders, 77
  meat hooks, 77
  meat-tenderizing presses, 77
  rib racks, 77
  Rib-O-Lators, 77
  rotisseries, 77
  sausage stuffers, 77
  smoker boxes, 77
  thermometers, 70-72
  vacuum tumblers, 77
accompaniments. *See* side dishes
adjustable vents, electric smokers, 19
adobo sauce, 130
air-chilled poultry, 205-206
airflow
  homemade smokers, 32
  kamado-style smokers, 26-27
  offset barrel smokers, 23
alder wood, 46, 49
almond, 46
aluminum foil, 72

amperage, electric smokers, 18
appetizers
  Smoked Bacon–Wrapped Meatballs, 271-272
  Smoked Eggplant Dip, 254-255
  Smoked *Fois Gras* Terrine, 274-275
Apple Butter BBQ Glaze, 141, 211
Apple Jack Spritz, 211, 245-246
apple wood, 46, 49
Apple-Honey Pig and Bird Brine, 105, 180, 215, 248
apples
  Apple Butter BBQ Glaze, 141, 211
  Apple Jack Spritz, 211, 245-246
  Apple-Honey Pig and Bird Brine, 105, 180, 215, 248
  Stuffed Bacon-Wrapped Chicken, 208-209
  Warm Potato Salad with Bacon, Green Apple, and Molten Brie, 262-263
apricot wood chips, 46
arborio rice, 264
Aromatic Cure, 116, 217
ash, flavoring hardwoods, 46

B

baby-back ribs, 175
bacon, 7, 11, 173-174
  Maple Smoked Bacon, 182-183
  Smoked Bacon–Wrapped Meatballs, 271-272
  Smoked Ice Martini, 276-277
  Smoked Peameal with Bloody Mary Injection, 184-185
  storing, 183
  Stuffed Bacon-Wrapped Chicken, 208-209
  Warm Potato Salad with Bacon, Green Apple, and Molten Brie, 262-263
bamboo skewers, 72
barbecue, origins, 6
barbecue competitions
  categories, 238
    beef brisket, 239-240
    chicken, 241
    pulled pork, 240
    ribs, 240-241
    turkey, 241
    whole hog, 242
  entering, 237-239
  late food, 242

barbecue rigs, 33-34
barbecue sauces, 136-137
  Apple Butter BBQ Glaze, 141
  Bourbon-Wasabi BBQ Sauce, 139
  Carolina Sweet Mustard Sauce, 143
  Four-Ingredient Cherry Cola BBQ Sauce, 140
  Kansas City BBQ Sauce, 138
  lemon pie filling, 140
  Memphis-Style BBQ Sauce, 142
barbecuing tongs, 74
bark chips, 46, 49
Basic Brine, 104, 213
Basic Cure, 114
bastes
  Chocolate Stout and Horseradish Baste, 161-162
  Garlic-Ginger-Lemon Soy Baste, 197-198
basting, 135-136
basting brushes, 72
basting mops, 72
BBQ Guru, 76
BBQ Icing, 246-247
beech wood chips, 47
beef, 149
  Big Beefy Texas-Style Smoked Brisket, 243-244
  Cherry Whiskey–Smoked Eye-of-Round, 160-161
  Coffee-Porter N.Y. Strip Steaks with Blue Cheese–Pecan Butter, 157-158
  color, 152
  cuts, 150-152

Four-Pepper–Crusted Beef Tenderloin with Armagnac Butter Injection, 156-157
  grades, 152
  Korean Bulgogi Smoked Top Sirloin Roast, 155-156
  marbling, 150
  Prime Rib with Whiskey Mist and Hot Horseradish Mustard, 159-160
  protein, 152
  purchasing, 152-153
  ribs, 175
  Santa Maria Tri-Tip with Cabernet Wine Mop, 165-166
  Shredded Beef Sandwiches with Chimichurri Mayonnaise, 153-154
  sirloin, 156
  Smoked Bacon–Wrapped Meatballs, 271-272
  Smoked Beef Ribs with Chocolate Stout and Horseradish Baste, 161-162
  Smoked Prime Rib Demi-Glace Burgers with Smoked Garlic and Onions, 163-164
  tenderloin, 157
  Texas Cowboy Beef Jerky, 166-167
beef brisket
  barbecue competitions, 239-240
  Big Beefy Texas-Style Smoked Brisket, 243-244
Beer-Brine Smoked Pulled Duck, 221-222
bellows, 76

Big Beefy Brisket Rub, 161
Big Beefy Texas-Style Smoked Brisket, 243-244
big rigs, 33-34
bins, 74
birch wood chips, 47
bison, 193
  ribs, 176
  Smoked Bison Short Ribs, 200-201
Black Currant–BBQ Sauce, 200-201
black walnut, 47
Blackberry Butter, 198-199
blenders, 72
Bloody Mary Injection, 184-185
Blue Cheese–Pecan Butter, 157-158
Bon Appétit, 72
Bourbon-Wasabi BBQ Sauce, 139
box smokers, 19-21
brines, 100-101
  Apple-Honey Pig and Bird Brine, 105, 180, 215, 248
  Basic Brine, 104, 213
  cooling, 104-105
  Juicy Citrus Brine, 106, 218
  Maple Whiskey Brine, 107, 166, 219
  timing guidelines, 102-104
briquette charcoal, 39-42
brisket
  barbecue competitions, 239-240
  beef, 151
  Big Beefy Texas-Style Smoked Brisket, 243-244
  decal, 239
Brisket Lump Charcoal Blend, 42

burping kamado-style smokers, 27
butcher's twine, 72
Buttery Love Injection, 248-249

C

Cajun-Rubbed and Honey-Dipped Smoked Turkey Drumsticks, 218-219
Carolina Sweet Mustard Sauce, 143
casings, sausage, 172, 188
cast-iron grates, 19
cedar wood chips, 47
ceviche, 11
charcoal, 39-43
    briquette, 39-42
    fast-light, 40
    hardwood, 40-41
    lump, 4, 39-42
    purchasing, 42-43
    slowly snuffing, 55
charcoal chimneys, 69
charcoal kettle grills, 14-16
charcoal smoking, 54-56
Charles Vergos' Rendezvous, 125
cherries
    Four-Ingredient Cherry Cola BBQ Sauce, 140
    Hot Curry Rub, 234-235
Cherry Cola BBQ Sauce, 140
Cherry Whiskey–Smoked Eye-of-Round, 160-161
cherry wood, 47-49
Cherry-Pom Spritz, 144-145
chestnut wood chips, 47
chicken, 203-205
    air-chilled, 205-206
    barbecue competitions, 241

Chicken Thighs with Potato Chip Crust, 210-211
Cinnamon Sugar–Smoked Chicken Halves, 213-214
Cozy Corner Smoked Cornish Game Hens, 215-216
cuts, 206-207
handling, 204
odors, 204
Smoked Buffalo Wings with Blue Cheese, 214-215
Smoked Chicken with Buttery Love Injection, 248-249
Smoky Chicken-Cheese Dogs, 211-212
Stuffed Bacon-Wrapped Chicken, 208-209
water-chilled, 205-206
Chimichurri Mayonnaise, 153-154
chimneys, 69
Chive Butter Injection, 133
Chocolate Stout and Horseradish Baste, 161-162
churrasco-style meats, 3
Cinnamon Chipotle Rub, 128, 178
cinnamon sticks
    flavoring hardwoods, 48
    grinding, 128
Cinnamon Sugar–Smoked Chicken Halves, 213-214
citrus, flavoring hardwoods, 47
clarified butter, 233
cleaning
    cast-iron grates, 19
    smokers, 29
coconut hardwood charcoal, 41

Coffee-Porter N.Y. Strip Steaks with Blue Cheese–Pecan Butter, 157-158
cold smoking, 5, 10-11
cold-smoke generators, 76
cold-smoked seafood, 225
collagen casings, sausage, 172
competitions, barbecue categories, 238
    beef brisket, 239-240
    chicken, 241
    pulled pork, 240
    ribs, 240-241
    turkey, 241
    whole hog, 242
    entering, 237-239
    late food, 242
compote, Smoked Strawberry and Rhubarb Compote, 177-178
condiments
    Chimichurri Mayonnaise, 153-154
    Smoked Vidalia Onion Relish, 256-257
    Whiskey Mist and Hot Horseradish Mustard, 159-160
cookbooks, 72
cooling brines, 104-105
cost considerations, smokers, 66-67
country-style ribs, 175
Cozy Corner Smoked Cornish Game Hens, 215-216
crab, Smoked Scallops with Halibut and Crab Topping, 235-236
Cranberry-Orange Honey Glaze, 201-202
Crazy Cajun Rub, 122, 201, 214, 218

cross-contamination of
   foods, preventing, 87-90
Cubano Mojo Marinade, 109
cures, 102
   Aromatic Cure, 116, 217
   Basic Cure, 114
   Fish Cure, 115
   timing guidelines,
      102-104
curing meats, 10-11, 116
cuts
   beef, 150-152
   lamb, 190-192
   pork, 169-171
   poultry, 206-207
cutting boards, 73

D

Dark Ale Marinade, 108
decals, beef brisket, 239
demi-glace, 162
desserts
   PB&J Plank-Smoked
      Twinkies with
      Chocolate-Marshmallow
      Topping, 279-280
   Smoked Chocolate-
      Banana Ice Cream,
      278-279
diffuser plates, 77
digital internal-probe
   thermometers, 70
digital-electric vertical box
   smokers, 18
Dinosaur Bar-B-Que, 9
dips
   Smoked Eggplant Dip,
      254-255
   smoked mackerel, 231
   smoked oysters, 232
Diva Q BBQ, 271
domestic lamb, 190

Dragon Marinade, 110
dried spices, flavoring
   hardwoods, 48
drumsticks, poultry, 207
Dry-Cured Smoked Turkey
   Breast, 217-218
drying herbs, 123
duck
   Beer-Brine Smoked
      Pulled Duck, 221-222
   Maple-Cured Smoked
      Duck Breasts, 219-220
   Smoked *Fois Gras* Terrine,
      274-275

E

eggplant, Smoked Eggplant
   Dip, 254-255
eggs, Smoked Frittata with
   Grape Tomatoes and
   Cheese, 273
electric smokers, 14-19,
   37-39
   adjustable vents, 19
   amperage, 18
   electronic-control units,
      17-18
   water pans, 19
electric-coil starters, 69
electrically fired box
   smokers, 21
entering barbeque
   competitions, 237-239

F

fast-light charcoal, 40
fat, lamb, 192
Fine Cooking, 72
Fire Ball Spritz, 178-179

Fire Ball Spritzed–Extra-
   Meaty Back Ribs with
   Smoked Honey Glaze,
   178-179
fire starters, 68-70
fires, preparing, 81
fish, 223-226
   cold-smoked, 225
   Fish Cure, 115
   halibut, Smoked Halibut,
      234-235
   hot-smoked, 225
   mackerel, Smoked
      Mackerel with Maple
      and Dark Rum, 230-231
   purchasing, 87
   salmon
      Irish Whiskey–Smoked
         Salmon, 226-227
      Plank Hot-Smoked
         Salmon, 227-228
      Smoked Soy-Sesame
         Salmon, 229-230
   storing, 89
Fish Cure, 115
flamethrowers, 69
flank steak, Shredded
   Beef Sandwiches with
   Chimichurri Mayonnaise,
   153-154
flavoring hardwoods, 46-48
fois gras, Smoked *Fois Gras*
   Terrine, 274-275
Food & Wine, 72
food safety, 87-90
   marinades, 101
food service smokers, 34
forequarter (beef), 151
Four-Ingredient Cherry
   Cola BBQ Sauce, 140
Four-Pepper–Crusted Beef
   Tenderloin with Armagnac
   Butter Injection, 156-157
freshly ground spices, 75

frittatas, Smoked Frittata with Grape Tomatoes and Cheese, 273
frostings, BBQ Icing, 246-247
fruitwoods, 47
fuel options, 35
  charcoal, 39-43
  electricity, 37-39
  hardwoods, 43-48
    bark, 46
    flavoring, 46-48
    logs, 44
    pucks, 44
    sawdust, 44
    soaking, 45-46
    versus softwoods, 43
    wood chips, 44
    wood chunks, 44
    wood pellets, 44
  natural gases, 36-37
  plank, 48-52
  propane, 36-37

G

galvanized-metal buckets, 73
game, 193
Garlic-Ginger-Lemon Soy Baste, 197-198
Garlic-Herb Fresh Rub, 123, 274
gas grills, 14-15
Georgia Peach–Dunked Smoked Chicken Thighs with Potato Chip Crust, 210-211
glazes
  Apple Butter BBQ Glaze, 211
  Apple Jack Spritz, 211
  Cranberry-Orange Honey Glaze, 201-202

Smoked Honey Glaze, 178-179
grades, beef, 152
Grandinetti, Tim, 29
grape tomatoes, Smoked Frittata with Grape Tomatoes and Cheese, 273
grapevine, flavoring hardwoods, 47
grates, cast-iron, 19
grill brushes, 73
grilling versus smoking, 9-10
grills
  charcoal kettle, 14-16
  gas, 14-15
  kamado-style, 19, 25-28
grinders, 77
grinding cinnamon sticks, 128
grinding meat, 172
guanciale, 171

H

halibut
  Smoked Halibut, 234-235
  Smoked Scallops with Halibut and Crab Topping, 235-236
ham, 170
ham hocks, 170-171
hand blenders, 72
handling raw meat, 89, 204
hardwood charcoal, 40-41
hardwoods, 43-48
  bark, 46, 49
  flavoring, 46-48
  logs, 44
  pucks, 44
  sawdust, 44
  soaking, 45-46
  versus softwoods, 43
  wood chips, 44

wood chunks, 44
wood pellets, 44
Hasselback, Charlie, 173
heat-tolerant plastic wraps, 73
heatproof gloves, 73
herbs
  drying, 123
  flavoring hardwoods, 48
hickory
  flavoring hardwoods, 47
  plank smoking, 49
hickory charcoal, 41
high-heat thermometers, 70
hindquarter (beef), 151-152
hindquarter, poultry, 207
homemade smokers, 28-33
homemade stock, 203-204
honey
  Honey Riesling Wine Marinade, 112
  Honey-Herb Spritz, 145
  Honey-Hoisin Smoked Oysters, 231-232
  Smoked Honey, 178, 267, 275-276
Honey Riesling Wine Marinade, 112
Honey-Herb Spritz, 145
Honey-Hoisin Smoked Oysters, 231-232
hot coals, transforming, 55
Hot 'n' Spicy BBQ Paste, 130
hot smoking, 11-12
hot-smoked seafood, 225
humidity, 85

I

ice cream, Smoked Chocolate-Banana Ice Cream, 278-279
imported lamb, 190

indoors, smoking, 60-63
industrial smokers, 34
injections, 121
    Bloody Mary Injection,
        184-185
    Buttery Love Injection,
        248-249
    Chive Butter Injection,
        133
    Rum Runner's Maple
        Injection, 134
    Whiskey Butter Injection,
        235-236
injectors, 73
instant-read probe
    thermometers, 71
internal temperature, meats,
    90
International Bar-B-Q
    Festival, 192
International Barbecue
    Cookers Association, 237
Irish Whiskey–Smoked
    Salmon, 226-227

J

Jack Daniel's World
    Championship Invitational
    Barbecue, 8
jalapeño peppers, 141
    choosing, 269
Jamaican Jerk Rub, 124
Java-Java Paste, 132, 157
jerky, Texas Cowboy Beef
    Jerky, 166-167
Juicy Citrus Brine, 106, 218

K

kamado-style smokers, 9, 19,
    25-28
    accessories, 78
    burping, 27
Kansas City Barbeque
    Society, 237
Kansas City BBQ Sauce, 138
Kansas City ribs, 175
Kansas City Rub, 248
kiawe charcoal, 41
kielbasa, Smoked Polish
    Sausage, 187-188
knives, 74
Korean Bulgogi Smoked
    Top Sirloin Roast, 155-156

L

lamb, 189-193
    cuts, 190-192
    domestic, 190
    fat, 192
    imported, 190
    Owensboro Smoked
        Lamb Shoulder, 192-196
    ribs, 176, 198
    Smoked Lamb Ribs,
        197-198
    Smoked Veal Chops,
        198-199
    Smoky Rack o' Lamb with
        Goat Cheese, 194-195
Lampe, Ray, 29
late food, barbeque
    competitions, 242
Lemon-Ginger Wine Spritz,
    144
lemon pie filling, barbeque
    sauces, 140
licorice wood, flavoring
    hardwoods, 48

liquid fire starters, 69
logs, 44
looftlighters, 69
lump charcoal, 4, 39, 42

M

mackerel, Smoked Mackerel
    with Maple and Dark Rum,
    230-231
magazines, resources, 72
Manny's Deli, Chicago,
    Illinois, 218
manufacturer's
    recommendations, smokers,
    13
maple, flavoring hardwoods,
    47
maple hardwood charcoal,
    41
Maple Smoked Bacon, 173,
    182-183
maple syrup, 134
Maple Whiskey Brine, 107,
    166, 219
maple wood chips, 50
Maple-Cured Smoked Duck
    Breasts, 219-220
marbling, beef, 150
Margarita Paste, 131
marinades, 101
    Cubano Mojo Marinade,
        109
    Dark Ale Marinade, 108
    Dragon Marinade, 110
    food safety, 101
    Honey Riesling Wine
        Marinade, 112
    Smoked Garlic Marinade,
        111
    timing guidelines,
        102-104
    Whiskey and Cola
        Marinade, 113

martini, Smoked Ice
   Martini, 276-277
meat grinders, 77, 188
meat hooks, 77
meat-tenderizing presses, 77
Mediterranean Spice Rub,
   127
Memphis in May World
   Championship Barbecue
   Cooking Contest, 8, 237
Memphis Rib Rub, 125, 211,
   246-247, 254
Memphis-Style BBQ Sauce,
   142
mesquite, flavoring
   hardwoods, 47
mesquite hardwood
   charcoal, 41
mesquite wood chips, 50
mozzarella cheese
   Pulled Pork and Cheese
      ABTs, 268-269
   Smoked Risotto with
      Spinach, Prosciutto, and
      Smoked Mozzarella,
      264-265
   Smoky Baked Macaroni
      and Cheese, 265
mutton, 192

N

Naked Whiz, 68
national bacon day, 176
natural casings, sausage, 172
natural gas grills, 56-58
needle-nose pliers, 75
New York strip steak,
   Coffee-Porter N.Y. Strip
   Steaks, 157-158
Newfie steak, 186
nonstick cooking spray, 14,
   75
notes, taking, 92-94

O

oak, flavoring hardwoods, 47
oak hardwood charcoal, 41
offset barrel smokers, 19,
   23-25
olives
   flavoring hardwoods, 47
   Smoked Ice Martini,
      276-277
onions, Smoked Vidalia
   Onion Relish, 256-257
Ontario Gas BBQ, 68
orange hardwood charcoal,
   41
organizations, barbecue, 237
oven roasting pan smokers,
   61
oven thermometers, 71
Owensboro Smoked Lamb
   Shoulder, 192, 195-196
oysters
   beef brisket, 239
   Honey-Hoisin Smoked
      Oysters, 231-232
Ozark sirloin, 186

P–Q

pails, 74
paprika, 122
parchment paper, 75
pasta, Smoky Baked
   Macaroni and Cheese,
   265-266
pastes, 117-120
   contaminating, 119
   Hot 'n' Spicy BBQ Paste,
      130
   Java-Java Paste, 132, 157
   Margarita Paste, 131
patience, 81-83

PB&J Plank-Smoked
   Twinkies with Chocolate-
   Marshmallow Topping,
   279-280
peach, flavoring hardwoods,
   47
peaches, Georgia Peach–
   Dunked Smoked Chicken
   Thighs with Potato Chip
   Crust, 210-211
peanut butter, PB&J Plank-
   Smoked Twinkies with
   Chocolate-Marshmallow
   Topping, 279-280
pear, flavoring hardwoods,
   48
pears, Smoked Beet and
   Pear–Blue Cheese Salad
   with Walnuts, 257-258
pecan wood, 48-50
peeking, avoiding, 83
pellet smokers, 17
Pit Masters, 8
pit smoking, 6
Plank Hot-Smoked Salmon,
   227-228
plank smoking, 48-60
Plank-Smoked Camembert,
   270-271
Planked Mashed Potatoes,
   261-262
plastic bags, 75
Polish sausage, Smoked
   Polish Sausage, 187-188
Popular Plates, 72
pork, 169
   bacon, 173-174
      Cheddar, and
         Apple–Stuffed Bacon-
         Wrapped Chicken,
         208-209
      Maple Smoked Bacon,
         182-183

Smoked Bacon–
Wrapped Meatballs,
271-272
Smoked Ice Martini,
276-277
Smoked Peameal
with Bloody Mary
Injection, 184-185
Warm Potato Salad
with Bacon, Green
Apple, and Molten
Brie, 262-263
cuts, 169-171
Fire Ball Spritzed–Extra-
Meaty Back Ribs with
Smoked Honey Glaze,
178-179
grinding, 172
Maple Smoked Bacon,
182-183
Pork T-Bones, 177-178
pulled
barbecue competitions,
240
Pulled Pork and
Cheese ABTs,
268-269
Smoked BBQ Pulled
Pork with Apple Jack
Spritz, 245-246
ribs, 174-176
Smoked St. Louis Ribs
with BBQ Icing,
246-247
sausage, 171-173
Smoked Polish
Sausage, 187-188
Smoked BBQ Ribs with
Redneck White Sauce,
180-181
Smoked Ozark Sirloin,
185
Smoked Spam, 186
Stuffed Bacon-Wrapped
Chicken, 208-209

whole hogs, barbecue
competitions, 242
Pork T-Bones with Smoked
Strawberry and Rhubarb
Compote, 177-178
Pork-Cone-Eh, 240
portable electric smokers, 17
potatoes
Planked Mashed Potatoes,
261-262
Warm Potato Salad
with Bacon, Green
Apple, and Molten Brie,
262-263
poultry, 203-205
air-chilled, 205-206
barbecue competitions,
241
chicken
Chicken Thighs with
Potato Chip Crust,
210-211
Cinnamon Sugar–
Smoked Chicken
Halves, 213-214
Cozy Corner Smoked
Cornish Game Hens,
215-216
Smoked Buffalo Wings
with Blue Cheese,
214-215
Smoked Chicken
with Buttery Love
Injection, 248-249
Smoky Chicken-
Cheese Dogs, 211-212
Stuffed Bacon-
Wrapped Chicken,
208-209
cuts, 206-207
duck
Beer-Brine Smoked
Pulled Duck, 221-222

Maple-Cured Smoked
Duck Breasts,
219-220
handling, 204
purchasing, 87
storing, 89
turkey
Cajun-Rubbed and
Honey-Dipped
Smoked Turkey
Drumsticks, 218-219
Dry-Cured Smoked
Turkey Breast,
217-218
Thanksgiving Smoked
Turkey, 249-250
water-chilled, 205-206
practicing smoking, 91-92
precision welded offset
barrel smokers, 23
preground spices, 75
preserving meats, 5
Prime Rib with Whiskey
Mist and Hot Horseradish
Mustard, 159-160
propane, 36-37
propane grills, 56-58
propane-fired box smokers,
21
prosciutto, Smoked Risotto
with Spinach, Prosciutto,
and Smoked Mozzarella,
264-265
pucks, 44
pulled pork
barbecue competitions,
240
Pulled Pork and Cheese
ABTs, 268-269
Smoked BBQ Pulled Pork
with Apple Jack Spritz,
245-246
purchasing
beef, 152-153
smokers, 65-68

R

rack of lamb, Smoky Rack o' Lamb with Goat Cheese, 194-195
red herring, smoked, 5
red jalapeño peppers, 141
red oak, 50
Redneck White Sauce, 180-181
relishes, Smoked Vidalia Onion Relish, 256-257
rhubarb, Smoked Strawberry and Rhubarb Compote, 177-178
Rib-O-Lators, 77
Ribber's Secret Recipe, 42
ribs, 247
    barbecue competitions, 240-241
    beef, 175
        Smoked Beef Ribs with Chocolate Stout and Horseradish Baste, 161-162
    bison, 176
        Smoked Bison Short Ribs, 200-201
    lamb, 176, 191, 198
        Smoked Lamb Ribs, 197-198
    pork, 174-176
        Fire Ball Spritzed–Extra-Meaty Back Ribs with Smoked Honey Glaze, 178-179
        Smoked BBQ Ribs with Redneck White Sauce, 180-181
        Smoked St. Louis Ribs with BBQ Icing, 246-247
    venison, 176
        Venison Ribs, 201-202
rigs, 33-34

risotto, Smoked Risotto with Spinach, Prosciutto, and Smoked Mozzarella, 264-265
Road Hawg BBQ, 30
rotisseries, 77
round (beef), 151
rubber gloves, 75
rubs, 117-118
    applying, 118
    Big Beefy Brisket Rub, 161
    Cinnamon Chipotle Rub, 128, 178
    contaminating, 119
    Crazy Cajun Rub, 122, 201, 214, 218
    Garlic-Herb Fresh Rub, 123, 274
    Hot Curry Rub, 234-235
    Jamaican Jerk Rub, 124
    Kansas City Rub, 248
    Mediterranean Spice Rub, 127
    Memphis Rib Rub, 125, 211, 246-247, 254
    Tandoori Rub, 126
    Ted's World-Famous Bone Dust BBQ Seasoning Rub, 121-122, 138, 177, 182-184, 208-210, 215, 221, 233-235, 245, 249
rules, barbecue organizations, 238
Rum Runner's Maple Injection, 134

S

safety
    food, 87-90
    smokers, 86

salad spinners, 123
salads
    Smoked Beet and Pear–Blue Cheese Salad with Walnuts, 257-258
    Warm Potato Salad with Bacon, Green Apple, and Molten Brie, 262-263
salmon
    Irish Whiskey–Smoked Salmon, 226-227
    Plank Hot-Smoked Salmon, 227-228
    Smoked Soy-Sesame Salmon, 229-230
salt, smoking, 129
Santa Maria Tri-Tip with Cabernet Wine Mop, 165-166
sauces
    barbecue
        Apple Butter BBQ Glaze, 141
        barbecue, 136-137
        Black Currant–BBQ Sauce, 200-201
        Bourbon-Wasabi BBQ Sauce, 139
        Carolina Sweet Mustard Sauce, 143
        Four-Ingredient Cherry Cola BBQ Sauce, 140
        Kansas City BBQ Sauce, 138
        lemon pie filling, 140
        Memphis-Style BBQ Sauce, 142
    demi-glace, 162
    Redneck White Sauce, 180-181
sausage, 171-173
    casings, 188
    stuffers, 77

Saveur, 72
sawdust, 44
scallops, Smoked Scallops with Halibut and Crab Topping, 235-236
seafood, 223-226
  cold-smoked, 225
  halibut, Smoked Halibut, 234-235
  hot-smoked, 225
  mackerel, Smoked Mackerel with Maple and Dark Rum, 230-231
  salmon
    Irish Whiskey–Smoked Salmon, 226-227
    Plank Hot-Smoked Salmon, 227-228
    Smoked Soy-Sesame Salmon, 229-230
  shellfish
    Honey-Hoisin Smoked Oysters, 231-232
    Smoked Razor Clams, 233
    Smoked Scallops with Halibut and Crab Topping, 235-236
shellfish
  Honey-Hoisin Smoked Oysters, 231-232
  Smoked Razor Clams, 233
  Smoked Scallops with Halibut and Crab Topping, 235-236
Shiraz wine, 201
Shredded Beef Sandwiches with Chimichurri Mayonnaise, 153-154
side dishes, 253-254
  Planked Mashed Potatoes, 261-262
  Smoked Corn and Smoked Cream Corn, 259-260

Smoked Risotto with Spinach, Prosciutto, and Smoked Mozzarella, 264-265
Smoky Baked Macaroni and Cheese, 265-266
Smoked Bacon–Wrapped Meatballs, 271-272
Smoked BBQ Pulled Pork with Apple Jack Spritz, 245-246
Smoked BBQ Ribs with Redneck White Sauce, 180-181
Smoked Beef Ribs with Chocolate Stout and Horseradish Baste, 161-162
Smoked Beet and Pear–Blue Cheese Salad with Walnuts, 257-258
Smoked Bison Short Ribs with Black Currant–BBQ Sauce, 200-201
Smoked Buffalo Wings with Blue Cheese and Celery, 214-215
Smoked Chicken with Buttery Love Injection, 248-249
Smoked Chocolate-Banana Ice Cream, 278-279
Smoked Corn and Smoked Cream Corn, 259-260
Smoked Eggplant Dip, 254-255
Smoked *Fois Gras* Terrine, 274-275
Smoked Frittata with Grape Tomatoes and Cheese, 273
Smoked Garlic Marinade, 111
Smoked Halibut with Hot Curry Rub and Lime Butter, 234-235

Smoked Honey, 178, 267, 275-276
Smoked Honey Glaze, 178-179
Smoked Ice Martini, 276-277
Smoked Lamb Ribs with Garlic-Ginger-Lemon Soy Baste, 197-198
Smoked Mackerel with Maple and Dark Rum, 230-231
Smoked Ozark Sirloin, 185
smoked paprika, 122
Smoked Peameal with Bloody Mary Injection, 184-185
Smoked Polish Sausage, 187-188
Smoked Prime Rib Demi-Glace Burgers with Smoked Garlic and Onions, 163-164
Smoked Razor Clams, 233
Smoked Risotto with Spinach, Prosciutto, and Smoked Mozzarella, 264-265
smoked salmon, 7, 11
Smoked Sea Salt, 129
Smoked Soy-Sesame Salmon, 229-230
Smoked Spam, 186
Smoked St. Louis Ribs with BBQ Icing, 246-247
smoked Twinkies, 267
Smoked Veal Chops with Blackberry Butter, 198-199
Smoked Vidalia Onion Relish, 256-257
SmokePistol system, 15
smoker boxes, 19-21, 77
smoker thermometers, 71
smokers, 13-14, 19, 28
  box, 19-21, 77
  charcoal kettle grills, 14-16
  cleaning, 29
  digital-electric vertical box, 18

electric, 14-19
fuel options, 35
    charcoal, 39-43
    electricity, 37-39
    hardwoods, 43-48
    natural gases, 36-37
    plank, 48-52
    propane, 36-37
gas grills, 14-15
homemade, 28-33
industrial, 34
kamado-style grills, 19,
    25-28
manufacturer's
    recommendations, 13
natural gas grills, 56-58
offset, 23-25
offset barrel, 19
oven roasting pan, 61
ovens, 63
pellet, 17
preparing, 81
propane, 56-58
purchasing, 65-68
rigs, 33-34
safety, 86
stove-style, 61
stove-top kettle, 62
trash-can, 30-32
vertical box, 19-21
water, 19-22
wood-puck, 17
smoking, 4, 79
    avoiding peeking, 83
    charcoal, 54-56
    cold, 5, 10-11
    constant temperature,
        83-84
    hot, 11-12
    humidity, 85
    increased popularity, 8-9
    indoors, 60-62
    origins, 4-8
    patience, 81-83
    pit, 6

plank, 48-52, 58-60
    alder, 49
    apple, 49
    cherry, 49
    hickory, 49
    maple, 50
    mesquite, 50
    pecan, 50
    purchasing, 51-52
    red oak, 50
    sizes, 51
    treated wood, 52
    western red cedar, 50
practicing, 91-92
preparation, 79-81
smoking bags, 63
versus grilling, 9-10
weather, 17
smoking bags, 63, 75
smoking grates, nonstick
    cooking spray, 14
Smoky Baked Macaroni and
    Cheese, 265-266
Smoky Chicken-Cheese
    Dogs, 211-212
Smoky Rack o' Lamb with
    Goat Cheese, 194-195
snuffing charcoal, 55
soaking hardwoods, 45-46
softwoods versus hardwoods,
    43
Spam, Smoked Spam, 186
spatulas, 75
spices, 120
    freshly ground, 75
    paprika, 122
spinach, Smoked Risotto
    with Spinach, Prosciutto,
    and Smoked Mozzarella,
    264-265
spray nozzle settings,
    spritzes, 144
spritz bottles, 75

spritzes, 137
    Apple Jack Spritz, 245-246
    Cherry-Pom Spritz,
        144-145
    Fire Ball Spritz, 178-179
    Honey-Herb Spritz, 145
    Lemon-Ginger Wine
        Spritz, 144
    spray nozzle settings, 144
St. Louis ribs, 175
Stern, Jane and Michael, 8
stock, 203-204
storing
    bacon, 183
    fish, meat, and poultry, 89
    meat, 100
stove-style smokers, 61
stove-top kettle smokers, 62
strawberries
    PB&J Plank-Smoked
        Twinkies with
        Chocolate-Marshmallow
        Topping, 279-280
    Smoked Strawberry and
        Rhubarb Compote,
        177-178
sugar cane-based fuel gel, 69
Szechuan peppercorns, 156

T

T-bone chops, Pork
    T-Bones, 177-178
taking notes, 92-94
Tandoori Rub, 126
Taste of Chicago, 218
Ted's World-Famous Bone
    Dust BBQ Seasoning Rub,
    121-122, 138, 177, 182-184,
    208-210, 215, 221, 233-235,
    245, 249

temperature
constant, 83-84
food safety, 88-90
temperature gauge kits, 14
Texas Cowboy Beef Jerky,
166-167
Texas hot links, 173
Thanksgiving Smoked
Turkey, 249-250
thermometers, 70-72
BBQ Guru, 76
thighs, poultry, 207
timing guidelines, brines,
cures, and marinades,
102-104
tomatoes, Smoked Frittata
with Grape Tomatoes and
Cheese, 273
tongs, 74
tools, 68, 72-75, 78
BBQ Guru, 76
bellows, 76
cold-smoke generators, 76
diffuser plates, 77
fire starters, 68-70
kamado-style smokers, 78
meat grinders, 77
meat hooks, 77
meat-tenderizing presses,
77
rib racks, 77
Rib-O-Lators, 77
rotisseries, 77
sausage stuffers, 77
smoker boxes, 77
thermometers, 70-72
vacuum tumblers, 77
trash-can smokers, 30-32
treated planks, 52
trussing elastics, 249
turkey, 203-205
air-chilled, 205-206
barbecue competitions,
241
Cajun-Rubbed and
Honey-Dipped Smoked
Turkey Drumsticks,
218-219
cuts, 206-207
Dry-Cured Smoked
Turkey Breast, 217-218
Thanksgiving Smoked
Turkey, 249-250
water-chilled, 205-206
Twinkies
PB&J Plank-Smoked
Twinkies with
Chocolate-Marshmallow
Topping, 279-280
smoked, 267

U-V

USDA Beef and Poultry
Hotline, 90

vacuum tumblers, 77
veal, Smoked Veal Chops,
198-199
venison, 193
ribs, 176
Venison Ribs with
Cranberry-Orange
Honey Glaze, 201-202
Venison Ribs with
Cranberry-Orange Honey
Glaze, 201-202
vents, adjustable, electric
smokers, 19
Vergos, Charles, 125
vertical box smokers, 19-21
vertical water smokers, 22
Vidalia onions, Smoked
Vidalia Onion Relish,
256-257

W-X-Y-Z

walnuts, Smoked Beet and
Pear–Blue Cheese Salad
with Walnuts, 257-258
Warm Potato Salad with
Bacon, Green Apple, and
Molten Brie, 262-263
water pans
electric smokers, 19
offset barrel smokers, 23
water smokers, 19-22
water-chilled poultry,
205-206
weather, smoking, 17
western red cedar, 50
Whiskey and Cola
Marinade, 113
whiskey barrels, 48
Whiskey Butter Injection,
235-236
Whiskey Butter–Injected
Smoked Scallops with
Halibut and Crab Topping,
235-236
Whiskey Mist and Hot
Horseradish Mustard,
159-160
whole back, poultry, 207
whole hogs, barbecue
competitions, 242
wings, chicken, Smoked
Buffalo Wings with Blue
Cheese and Celery, 214-215
wings, poultry, 207
wood chips, chunks, and
pellets, 44
wood-puck smokers, 17
wrapping foods, 154, 244

zipper-lock plastic bags, 75